The Murderers Among Us

The Murderers Among Us

History of Repression and Rebellion
in Haiti under Dr. François Duvalier,
1962–1971

BERNARD DIEDERICH

 Markus Wiener Publishers
Princeton

For information, write to:
Markus Wiener Publishers
231 Nassau Street, Princeton, NJ 08542
www.markuswiener.com

Library of Congress Cataloging-in-Publication Data

Diederich, Bernard.
  [Prix du sang. Part 2. English]
  The Murderers among us : history of repression and rebellion in Haiti under
Dr. François Duvalier, 1962-1971 / Bernard Diederich.
     p. cm.
  ISBN 978-1-55876-541-2 (hardcover : alk. paper)
  ISBN 978-1-55876-542-9 (pbk. : alk. paper)
1. Duvalier, François, 1907-1971. 2. Dictators—Haiti—History—20th century.
3. State-sponsored terrorism—Haiti—History—20th century. 4. Political persecution—
Haiti—History—20th century. 5. Government, Resistance to—Haiti—History—20th
century. 6. Diederich, Bernard. 7. Haiti—History—1934-1986. 8. Haiti—Politics and
government—1934-1971. 9. Haiti—Foreign relations—United States. 10. United
States—Foreign relations--Haiti. I. Title.
  F1928.D86D5513 2011
  972.94'06--dc22
                                2011014914

Markus Wiener Publishers books are printed in the United States of America on
acid-free paper and meet the guidelines for permanence and durability of the Committee
on Production Guidelines for Book Longevity of the Council on Library Resources.

Contents

Author's Note

As with *The Price of Blood*, the first book in this two-part account, I derived little pleasure from writing *The Murderers among Us*, for it is essentially a chronicle of a human tragedy—that of the people of Haiti.

For fourteen years, from 1949 until 1963, when I was jailed and expelled, I enjoyed the hospitality of the Haitian people. I grew to love and admire them, and I learned much about their fortitude, wisdom, and rich culture. I did my best in my weekly newspaper, the *Haiti Sun*, and as a resident correspondent reporting for *Time* magazine, *The New York Times*, the Associated Press, and NBC News, to convey Haitians' achievements and their hopes for a better, more equitable future. At the beginning it was a glorious time, not without its political and social challenges, yet full of optimism.

Then the people fell prey to a Machiavellian charlatan and demagogue—François (Papa Doc) Duvalier—who exploited the country's endemic poverty and class system to impose an atrocity-ridden tyranny. Haitians had suffered many strongman regimes since breaking the chains of French colonialism in 1804, but perhaps none as cold-bloodedly murderous as Papa Doc's. Sadly, his demagogic, authoritarian legacy, like some genetic disease, has been passed on to succeeding generations of wannabe Haitian tyrants.

I wanted to recount the history that I lived during Duvalier's regime, but it took years to unearth the horrifying details. Even after all these years, knowledgeable Haitians were still fearful of talking: some of the killers were—and still are—among us. But some interviewees overcame their fears and unburdened themselves of their traumatic experiences. To them I am indebted. For history is made by brave men and women, and Haiti still has brave men and women. And to them, I dedicate these pages.

INTRODUCTION

It was a country petrified by fear, fear of one man who held their lives in his hands. Smiling, with a flick of those hands, he could condemn a person to death or send him to prison where he would ultimately die of disease and starvation. He was truly like the character in Robert Louis Stevenson's famous novel *Dr. Jekyll and Mr. Hide,* in which the good doctor changes into the most evil of men. Such was Haiti's dictator, Dr. François Duvalier, who played the role of the good doctor even as his evil, megalomaniac side took hold. Early in his reign he had wiped out his opposition, including the media. Dr. Duvalier claimed to be the personification of the Haitian state, and those who dared attack him were attacking Haiti and were nothing but lizards. Heroically, Haitians resisted and continued to resist until the end. Everyone smiled, but behind their masks they cried for Haiti.

I was a reporter for the Associated Press, *The New York Times, Time* magazine, and NBC News, playing a cat-and-mouse game under Papa Doc Duvalier—only in time the cat morphed into an angry tiger. It became necessary for me to violate government censorship. I knew the danger. I could lose my newspaper and print shop . . . or worse. In my weekly newspaper, the *Haiti Sun,* even oblique criticism of the regime was suicidal.

By April 1963, the spread of terror made reporting the news more difficult and riskier. Adhering to the ethics of the journalistic profession, it was only basic reporting. No effort was made to editorialize or to sensationalize and embellish my reporting. In reality, I sought to protect Haiti, a country whose people I loved, and who for many years I had defended from salacious sensationalism in the media. Papa Doc's antics only helped the sensationalists disfigure Haiti.

Many of my friends were "disappeared," a euphemism under Papa Doc's rule for execution. Some had died while others, including Haiti's cadre of professionals, fled to work in newly independent states such as

1

Congo. It was heartbreaking to watch the country I loved spiral down into the depths of a bloody dictatorship.

The first part of this history, *The Price of Blood*, which recounts this story from 1957 to 1961, dealt with Papa Doc's path to absolute power and my own journalistic efforts. I still published my English-language newspaper, and, like a lot of Haitians, I believed I could outlive the dictatorship. Sadly, we were wrong, and I paid the price of being during this time the only resident foreign correspondent. Anyone with a regard for the most basic human rights would have been appalled at the loathsome acts committed against innocent citizens.

So much was expected of the young Catholic president, John Fitzgerald Kennedy, when he came to power. He had pronounced himself against dictators. Even Haitian students regarded him as a possible savior as they sought to rid Haiti of their new dictator. But there was only one strongman in the Caribbean who Kennedy feared: Fidel Castro of Cuba. It was an obsession he had inherited from his predecessor, Gen. Dwight Eisenhower, and it gave solace to right-wing Duvalier.

Papa Doc was tolerated because he was anti-Communist, and being anti-Communist gave Duvalier a license to kill. The fact that he murdered his people with impunity did not make a ripple in Washington. The Haitian people were very much alone. The pretense and the lies we fabricated, and the masks we wore to shield ourselves from the Tonton Macoutes, were dehumanizing. It was just what the dictator sought.

Still, our news judgment was never weighed against the risk of reporting the truth. In the end my vibes—and we listen to our vibes—told me the days of my reporting in Papa Doc's Haiti were over. I was sent to prison and then into exile. I considered Haiti my home, and now I considered myself an exile.

Then a new chapter began. I reported on Haiti from across the border in the Dominican Republic, which was free and democratic under its newly elected president, Juan Bosch, himself a target of Papa Doc.

There I began a new life, which is recounted in this, the second part of the story, encompassing the years 1962 to 1971. I had survived Papa Doc to continue to report on Haiti from across the border, thanks to my friends on both sides of that poorly defined frontier. It was not long after my arrival in Santo Domingo that I started reporting on the Haitian exiles' efforts to oust Papa Doc with little but their faith and a few old *zootis* ("guns"). I soon found myself ferrying food supplies in my small Volkswagen to these near-destitute exiles dressed only in their pride.

The rebels—or "*Kamokens*"—so well described in Graham Greene's 1966 novel *The Comedians,* were small in number but utterly determined to liberate Haiti. Encumbered with rusty ancient arms and lacking in logistics, their attacks were unsuccessful. However, even when they were gone, they retained a mythical stature: the Kamoken, much like the *lougarou* ("werewolf"), patrols the country at night.

CHAPTER 1

Papa Doc Takes on JFK and Juan Bosch

Having gained an aura of invincibility within Haiti, Duvalier set about serving as his own example of how the power of one-man rule in a very small nation can defy a superpower on its very doorstep. It was a dangerous course, but Castro had succeeded; now it was Haiti's turn.

The stage was the island of Hispaniola, which had long appeared too small for both Haiti and the Dominican Republic. In the nineteenth century, Haiti had made war against the Dominicans on several occasions and twice occupied the entire island. Trujillo, for his part, had slaughtered thousands of migrant Haitians in a 1937 pogrom.

By 1963 the two geopolitical volcanoes were rumbling side by side as if both were about to erupt.

In the Dominican Republic, Professor Juan Bosch, the country's first freely elected president in more than 30 years, was outraged by Duvalier's conduct and empathized with the suffering of the Haitian people. He appeared prepared to go to war to alleviate their suffering under this tyrant.

In Washington, the last thing the Kennedy administration wanted, only months after the Cuban missile crisis, was a messy war between the Dominican Republic and Haiti that could undermine the former's infant democracy and further roil the Caribbean. Moreover, the U.S. administration had its own clear-cut contingency plans to remove Papa Doc from power if deemed necessary.

On instructions from President John F. Kennedy, the chief of U.S.naval operations had ordered the Caribbean Ready Amphibious Squadron of the U.S. Atlantic Fleet, accompanied by the 4th Marine Expeditionary

Brigade, to stand off of Port-au-Prince in the Gulf of Gonave. For Haitians, it was a déjà vu all over again, a replay of history. The U.S. had sent its gunboats to Haiti numerous times in the past and in 1915 had landed U.S. Marines who occupied Haiti until 1934.

Attached to the staff of the Marine commander aboard ship was the redoubtable Col. Robert Debs Heinl, who provided valuable insight into the composition and stationing of the Haitian armed forces, gleaned from his four-year assignment as head of the U.S. Naval Mission in Port-au-Prince. The intelligence provided by Heinl and other members of the mission detailed exactly what a Marine landing force would encounter once ashore. There was a feeling that it would be a pushover, with the Haitian army in disarray and the Macoutebullyboys not considered an obstacle that a few rounds of ammunition couldn't neutralize. The Macoutes were used to attacking unarmed civilians, not well-trained and well-armed U.S. Marines.

Helicopters of the U.S. Naval Mission still in Port-au-Prince flew out to the *USS Boxer* with the latest daily intelligence reports until Duvalier, exercising his host-country prerogative, ordered the three helicopters grounded at the Haitian Air Force base at Bowen Field. However, even the anti-Duvalier Haitian officers who had sought asylum in the Brazilian Embassy were upbeat about the possibilities of toppling Papa Doc. Col. Kern Delince recalls how a Marine officer of the U.S. Naval Mission requested that they compile a list of Haitian army men on duty or retired to fill posts in a new civilian-military government that would replace Duvalier. U.S. efforts to rid Haiti of Duvalier were a much larger enterprise than events indicated at the time.

During that period a conspiracy that was never uncovered was code-named "Operation Vulcan" after the god of fire. Among those leading the covert operation was Lt. François Benoit, whose own code name was "Sure-shot." Communications between Benoit in the Dominican Embassy and those on the outside were facilitated by the Dominican Embassy driver, Manuel, who happened to be a boyhood friend of Benoit's. Manuel was fearless, and he carried the messages to the outside written in invisible ink with lime juice so that the letters were revealed when heated over a stove. Those in asylum in the Dominican Embassy believed that both the Defense Intelligence Agency (DIA) and the Central

Intelligence Agency (CIA) were involved. U.S. Embassy military attaché Maj. John W. Warren was their contact, and at one point when the conspirators were considering aiding Clément Barbot, Warren told them that Barbot's fortune had turned and he would not advise any contact with him. A few days later they heard the news that Barbot had been killed.

The plot was a simple one. Fires that would be set at different points in the capital would draw Duvalier's troops into ambushes while the main force of Operation Vulcan would strike at the palace.

It was when Maj. Warren requested the names of the conspirators to learn the extent of the plot and assess its possibilities that the group in the Dominican Embassy broke off contact. They believed that in the final analysis "the Americans" were only interested in gathering intelligence on the conspiracy.

Maj. Warren's activities were noted by Duvalier, and a hand grenade was dropped in his backyard on May 22, 1963, the day of the inauguration of Doc's new "term." The grenade exploded but did little damage. The U.S. Embassy lodged a protest, as it also did when a band of armed militiamen marched noisily across the embassy grounds to their bivouac area.

Years later I sought out economist Pierre Cauvin, leader of the centrist *Parti Union Democratique National* and now in exile in France. Even then Cauvin acted with extreme caution. He arranged to meet near a Paris metro station, and he advised me that he could be recognized by the copy of *Le Monde* that he would be carrying under his arm. Luckily not all of Paris was carrying the newspaper that day. Nor was he forthcoming about the Vulcan conspiracy.

*   *   *

It was one of the strangest foreign confrontations in U.S. history. The Kennedy administration wanted Duvalier out. The Haitian people who saw the U.S. flexing its muscles offshore waited . . . and waited. Haitian exiles were in a fever pitch of excitement. Some were packing their bags to return home.

On Sunday, April 29, 1963, the airwaves between Santo Domingo and Port-au-Prince crackled with charges and counter-charges in Kreyól,

French, and Spanish. "We have been suffering with Christian patience all manner of attacks," declared President Bosch in a speech recounting in detail events leading up to the crisis. Dominican citizens in Haiti had been jailed or mistreated, he stated, calling them in effect "prisoners of the [Haitian] government." Bosch revealed what he charged was an assassination plot perpetrated by Duvalier against him. "In January of this year, when I was only president-elect, the Haitian government began a plot to kill me and designated a former member of the SIM [Trujillo's secret police], Michel Brady, a Haitian, to execute the crime." Bosch said his government rejected Brady as chargé d'affaire of the Haitian embassy in Santo Domingo "because we knew why this gentleman was coming." (A CIA telegram dated February 23, 1963 [Report number tde5], which recently was declassified, stated: "Rumored plot between Trujillo family and Haitian officials to assassinate Juan Bosch.") On February 20, 1963, Luc Desyr, top Macoute in the National Palace, sent two militiamen to the border town of Belladere with a sealed letter to be given to a local commander of Volunteers for National Security (VSN). When the militiamen arrived in Belladere later the same day, they repeated to the local leader the following message from Desyr: "Keep ready—the day is coming shortly." The contents of the letter were unknown. However, the talk among militiamen assigned to the palace was that the Trujillo family had given a great deal of money to Haitian government officials for the purpose of carrying out a plot to assassinate President Juan Bosch on or prior to the day of his inauguration.

Bosch likewise censured the presence of members of the Trujillo clan in Haiti and said they were involved in a conspiracy against his government that included a media campaign in the U.S. to paint Bosch as being soft on Communists or a pawn of the Communists. Three nephews and a niece of the late Dominican tyrant had flown in from Europe and checked into the Excelsior Hotel on Port-au-Prince's Champ de Mars.

Recalling the entire "Vulcan" incident in detail, Bosch described how two rifle-bearing Haitian soldiers had entered the Dominican chancellery and searched it, violating all diplomatic norms. "Only a government of savages, of criminals is capable of violating the sanctity of a foreign embassy and threatening with rifles a lady who is an employee of the embassy," he said at the time. "This action is a slap in the face of the

Dominican Republic, an affront which we do not intend to ignore. Since Thursday armed guards have surrounded the Dominican Embassy residence in which are 22 in asylum, including women and children, who are living through indescribable hours of terror because every minute of the day and night they expect the attack which will cost them their lives. This is unpardonable; we do not intend to pardon it. The situation is grave, we have suffered with great patience the outrage . . . but these outrages must end—now. If they do not end within 24 hours we will end them . . ."

The Bosch government warned that if Duvalier did not heed the ultimatum the Dominicans would bomb him out of his palace. Haitian residents living in the vicinity of the palace were advised by the Dominican broadcasts to evacuate the area.

Haitian Foreign Minister René Chalmers replied with a long cable in French, denying Bosch's charges and announcing the breaking of diplomatic relations with the Dominican Republic.

Dominican Foreign Minister Andres Freites cabled back, repeating Santo Domingo's charges and demanding safe conduct for the 22 persons, including Lt. François Benoit, in asylum in the Dominican ambassador's residence. Chalmers replied with counter-accusations that the Dominicans had violated the rights of asylum by allowing the Haitians to keep their weapons, and by permitting Benoit to leave the embassy to carry out the attack on Duvalier's children. (Haiti had claimed that Benoit's car was used in the attack.) Chalmers asserted that Bosch was using the "whole affair to divert the attention of the noble and unhappy Dominican people from the internal situation." That same afternoon Costa Rica's delegate Gonzalo Facio called for an emergency session of the Organization of American States in Washington at 10 p.m.

During the meeting, the Dominican envoy to the OAS, Arturo Calventi, listed 12 charges against Haiti, repeating the 24-hour ultimatum and warning that gunboats would sail for Port-au-Prince the next day unless Haiti pulled its troops back from the Dominican Embassy in Pétionville. He also charged that Duvalier, unable to get aid elsewhere, had gone to the Communist bloc, establishing secret relations with the then-Soviet satellite states Czechoslovakia and Poland. Calventi cited the fact that missions from the two Iron Curtain countries had recently visited Haiti. (The Polish mission had actually been in Haiti since 1959—

Haiti and Poland having especially close relations because Polish troops under Napoleon had sided with Haiti's revolting slaves in 1803— and the Czechs had only just visited in March 1963.) Calventi charged that Haiti was not only receiving "all forms of political counsel from Poland" but also had signed "a secret economic treaty" with the Czechs under which Haiti would aid "communist infiltration in the Caribbean." Haiti replied that it would defend itself by "all means available if the Dominicans attacked."

The OAS voted overwhelmingly (16 "ayes" and 2 abstentions) to invoke the 1947 Inter-American Treaty of Mutual Assistance to ensure that Haiti would observe its international obligations, and to form an investigating commission to go to Haiti and report back to the body. At the same time, it urged Haiti and the Dominican Republic to keep the peace until the investigating committee completed its work.

Max Frankel, reporting in *The New York Times,* wrote:

> The United States has wished for some time for the downfall of the Duvalier dictatorship, and it may have found encouragement in this weekend's Caribbean crisis. By a variety of diplomatic affronts, it has demonstrated its revulsion against what it regards as a corrupt, brutal and inept regime. There are indications that Washington, in secret, may have done even more. . . . Thus, though Haiti is small and insignificant in the swirl of world and hemisphere diplomacy, the problem she has raised for Washington has been great and fundamental. How the United States could tolerate Duvalier's government while trying to promote freedom, justice and economic development in Latin America is a question that has haunted the Kennedy administration since the start of the Alliance for Progress program two years ago.

The U.S. Embassy in Port-au-Prince, which had earlier advised the 1,031 American citizens living in the Haiti chancellery to "take precautionary measures" to cope with the present situation and "prepare for any further disturbances," now began advising them to leave, anticipating a showdown that could become nasty. Evacuees arriving in the U.S. told dramatic stories of a country living on the edge of terror, with Macoutes and roadblocks making travel almost impossible.

In Washington, Costa Rica's OAS delegate Facio announced that Haiti had agreed to restore diplomatic guarantees to the Dominican Embassy and residence and pull back its troops from the grounds of the residence. The Dominicans responded by extending their war deadline until the investigating commission had completed its work. Colombia agreed to assume responsibility for the Dominican Embassy and residence—and its 22 persons in asylum there—when, as diplomatic relations with Haiti were broken, the Dominican chargé d'affaire returned to Santo Domingo.

However, Bosch was still in a bellicose mood. He ordered troops and mechanized units to the border with Haiti and his nation's warships into readiness. President Rómulo Betancourt of Venezuela, in a personal telephone call to Bosch, a longtime friend, offered his country's military support. In Washington, Adm. George W. Anderson, chief of naval operations, said the U.S. was ready to move "in hours if not minutes" to evacuate Americans from Haiti and to carry out the directions of the OAS.

Describing the situation in Haiti as "very ugly," Bosch declared that "one smart and capable Communist could convert Haiti because social and economic conditions are so bad. It is ripe for revolution." On a more personal plane, Bosch said there could be no peace on Hispaniola as long as Duvalier was president of Haiti. "Duvalier is not only a dictator, he is a madman," the Dominican leader raged. "There is no control over him. I hope the Haitians get the job done as the Dominicans did"—an obvious reference to the 1961 assassination of dictator Trujillo.

*   *   *

The OAS commission arrived in Port-au-Prince early on the morning of April 30. Duvalier had tidied up somewhat, for instance, ordering rotting bodies still lying in the charred ruins of the Benoit house to be buried on the spot.

At the palace, the OAS ambassadors were seated. Duvalier finally entered and treated them to a cool reception, then to a long, embarrassing silence. Sitting there he made no effort to break the silence or ease their embarrassment. Then he began slowly to nod to each of them. They nodded back not knowing that Papa Doc—with a slight nod of his head accompanied by a sotto voce Kreyól expletive—was actually cursing each of their mothers. The curses, followed by a Duvalier speech that compounded the rebuff, were all they got.

The OAS delegation, which confined its visit to Port-au-Prince, saw no preparations for war. Instead, thousands of peasants who had been hauled into the capital and given liberal distributions of *clarin,* the powerful raw rum crowd-booster, materialized in the streets, saluting Papa Doc. Late in the afternoon the crowds were directed to the palace, where they pressed against the iron fence until the gates were opened and they poured over the lawn. Whereupon Duvalier appeared on the balcony of his office, raised his hands victoriously, and smiled his slow, cool smile to a throng intoxicated with rum and excitement. It was an effective contrast. Drums pounded, dancers twisted like corkscrews, and cheer conductors chanted, "Duvalier or death." The crowd had swelled to an estimated 20,000 by the time an official party, including the OAS ambassadors, stepped onto a small platform erected on the palace steps.

Antoine Rodolphe Hérard, the longtime radio announcer and Duvalierist, was first to take the microphone. He called the Dominicans liars and blackmailers and then attacked the U.S. for cutting off aid to Haiti. "We prefer liberty to a crust of bread," he intoned. "If foreigners want to take away our freedom in return for a crust of bread, we have no need for it."

Then the small, bespectacled man in formal black appeared on the steps of the palace. Duvalier was sheathed in a serenity so complete it seemed narcotic. Faithful Macoutes and officials stood by entranced, and foreign newsmen crouched directly in front of him, taking notes. He smiled condescendingly, slowly, revealing one gold tooth, patiently hushing the crowd by patting his hands on the air. When he started speaking, without notes, his hands hung limply at his side, never twitching or clasping. The unnatural sheen of his face gave him an otherworldly look.

Some of his words, partly in French, partly in Kreyól, were vulgar and shocked even his boisterous, carnival-mood audience. Sometimes he became incoherent, but his megalomaniacal message was clear: "Listen carefully, people of Haiti. . . . I am the personification of the Haitian fatherland. Those who wish to destroy Duvalier wish to destroy the fatherland. I am and I symbolize a historic moment in your history as a free and independent people. God and the people are the source of all power. I have twice been given power. I have taken it, and damn it [changed to Kreyól], I will keep it forever." His face never changed expression as he continued:

Those who shot at my children shot at me. They know that bullets and machine guns capable of frightening Duvalier do not exist. They know that they cannot touch me because Duvalier is firm and unshakable. I ask you, Haitian people, to raise your souls to the height of the spirit of your ancestors, and to prove that you are men. . . . I don't take orders or dictates from anybody no matter where they come from. . . . As president of Haiti today, I am here to continue the tradition of Dessalines and of Toussaint L'Ouverture. . . . At that moment when it becomes necessary to go into the streets, I will go with the Presidential Guard and with the popular [Macoute] forces. Those who are uncertain about what to do had better put themselves at my side, because . . . I will write an unforgettable page of history against foreigners and the anti-nationals.

It was a remarkable performance. As he walked back into the palace, a cynical smile of victory lighting his face, the crowd was hoarse from cheering. The patriarch, their absolute master, had spoken. Papa Doc had once more made it abundantly clear—this time before an important foreign audience—that he regarded himself above natural law, as a Solomon of unquestionable wisdom, a messiah responsible only to himself, with absolute powers of life and death over every Haitian, over every human who dared slow his path.

*   *   *

Hot and tired, the OAS team departed on May 2 for Santo Domingo after two days of "investigating." Their assignment had been to look into Bosch's charge that Haiti was threatening peace, yet unsurprisingly the delegation could point to no hard evidence. Moreover, in a move that startled the usually slow-moving hemispheric body, Haiti took its case to the United Nations where the regime believed it could engender sympathy by pleading that Haiti was a victim of racism.

The person who appeared least concerned with any confrontation was Duvalier. While harried aides and cabinet ministers fretted and proffered anxious suggestions, he sat confidently in his palace office. If there was one game at which Duvalier excelled it was the game of bluff. Yet such was the powerful combination that now confronted Duvalier that even some of his closest advisors fretted at what they perceived to be presidential indifference. Reflecting their influence, defense preparations began to appear in the capital. The city was soon a checkerboard of roadblocks. Machine gun emplacements were set up to protect the police, military headquarters, and the Dessalines barracks. Duvalier imposed a dusk-to-dawn curfew.

Duvalier agreed to allow 15 of the 22 in asylum in the Dominican ambassador's residence to be issued Haitian passports and to leave the country, but he insisted on blocking the departure of the other 7—including Lt. François Benoit—classifying them as anti-government "conspirators." Among the 15 permitted to leave the country was Father Jean-Baptiste Georges, who had once hidden Duvalier and who had been Papa Doc's first minister of education. The subsequent change in Father Georges was remarkable. In exile, he became the most rabid of anti-Duvalierists, dedicating the next years of his life to launching futile invasions of Haiti to overthrow Papa Doc.

On the other side of the island, the Dominican Republic's outsized military establishment bequeathed by Trujillo, already suspicious of the democratic leftist president Juan Bosch, was having second thoughts about the practicality or feasibility of any invasion of Haiti. Many high-ranking Dominican officers suspected that Bosch was using the crisis to have a liberal new constitution voted through congress or to decapitate the military. They were persuaded that if Bosch was not a Communist he was soft on Communism, which for them was one and the same thing. Bosch, who had spent long years in exile, was often given to making hyper-explosive statements. He also insisted on legalism even when it came to Communists and sought not to harass them.

Late on Sunday night, May 5, Bosch spoke with foreign newsmen at his residence and sent them rushing to the cable office when he declared, "I am going to ask for a break in relations of all American States with the Haitian tyrant," and warned, "On the next aggression by Haiti we will announce our actions to the OAS, not from the Dominican capital—from the neighboring capital." His words proved to be only verbal warfare.

But when the U.S. Embassy in Santo Domingo was informed about them, Ambassador John Barlow Martin and his staff fretted throughout the night.

Martin was not a career diplomat but rather a former newsman and a campaign speechwriter for both Adlai Stevenson and President Kennedy. Thin, aggressive, and plagued by an ulcer, he was, despite all his efforts, overwhelmed by events. He spoke no Spanish, while Bosch was fluent in English. In his book, forthrightly entitled *Overtaken by Events*, Martin devoted a chapter to "The War" with Haiti and quotes Bosch as admitting, "It is clear to us and to everyone that Duvalier is crazy but we can't go in and get him." The Dominican military, built as an internally repressive machine, had lost whatever offensive capability it might have had.

Stressing that an "abnormal situation in Haiti is equivalent to an abnormal situation in our internal affairs," Bosch proposed that Venezuela and Costa Rica join the Dominicans in establishing a "democratic Latin American force" to oust Duvalier. He said that the OAS should not allow its tradition of nonintervention to prevent it from exercising "its responsibility for observance of democracy and human rights, which cannot be subordinated to any other principle."

*   *   *

Meanwhile, the U.S. Naval Task Force headed by the *USS Boxer* steamed into Haiti's Gulf of Gonave and began to flex its mighty muscle. The ships followed a triangular course, which brought them to within six miles of the Haitian coast. "We're just standing by," said Commander M. B. Jackson. With the aircraft carrier *Boxer* were the carrier *Shangri-La* and the *Taconic*, flagship of the U.S. Atlantic Fleet Amphibious Force. The task force also included an attack cargo ship, a high-speed transport, a dock landing ship, and a tank landing ship. Some 2,000 Marines stood ready aboard ship, prepared to land by helicopters. The British, for their part, sent to the area a Royal Navy frigate, the *Cavalier*, to prepare to evacuate British nationals from Haiti if necessary.

In Washington, a State Department official, declaring that the Duvalier government appeared to be "falling apart," ordered the evacuation of dependents of U.S. government personnel and urged all other American citizens to leave because of the "continued deterioration of the situation in Haiti and the difficulty of ensuring the lives and safety of U.S. citizens." Pan American Airways, then the sole U.S. carrier to Haiti, added special flights to accommodate those who sought to leave. Other residents of Haiti were equally concerned. The Argentine Embassy, for instance, on May 5 received five new asylum seekers: Mrs. Rhea Barbot, wife of Papa Doc's Secret Police chief-turned-anti-Duvalier terrorist; their three daughters; and her sick son, Hervé, 23.

It appeared that, with the OAS providing the pretext, the U.S. was on the verge of moving into Haiti. There were contingency plans for a multinational police force—to come from the U.S., Venezuela, and Costa Rica—to join the intervention. There was a movement to have an armed band of Haitian exiles slip over the Dominican border and ignite an incident before the official end of Duvalier's term of office on May 15. It had become a *High Noon* scenario with an international and domestic showdown seemingly imminent.

CHAPTER 2

They Called Them *Kamokens*

Like wary lizards, Haitian anti-Duvalier activists slithered through valleys and over mountains into the safety of the democratic Dominican Republic. Those fleeing Papa Doc throughout his dictatorship were often as naked as the mountainous Haitian border terrain, bled white by erosion from generations of misuse by poor peasants. They were not the usual border-jumpers, the lean Haitian cane cutters whose strong arms traditionally harvested the Dominican sugar crop under primitive conditions—slave-like travail abhorred by even unemployed Dominicans.

They were the first wave of political refugees from Haiti to cross the border into the Dominican Republic in living memory. These political activists had quickly begun the difficult task of organizing and searching for aid in order to launch the armed struggle against Duvalier. They just as quickly discovered, as they proliferated into small groups, that they had brought not only their political baggage with them but also their personal and regional jealousies, suspicions, and antagonisms.

Among the first refugees in 1962 to establish a political group in the Dominican Republic were a former Army officer and diplomat, Pierre Rigaud, and an ex-Haitian diplomat, Paul Verna. Already in exile abroad, they had applied for and received Dominican visas. Verna had been posted in the past at the Haitian Embassy in Ciudad Trujillo and, along with Rigaud, quickly reestablished friendships in the post-Trujillo era with senior Dominican Army officers. The pair named their group the National Democratic Union (UDN) and began seeking recruits.

Meanwhile, a group of youthful Haitian exiles, who spurned "old politicians" and Army officers, had been formed at the same time in Santo Domingo and had christened their group the Liberation Front of Free Haitiens (FLHL). A young and earnest schoolteacher, Fred Baptiste, from Jacmel, was its organizer and took the position of secretary-general of the FLHL. The Baptiste group soon realized that alone they stood little chance of acquiring aid and arms.

It was not until the night of April 17, 1963, after much coaching and pleading, that the first meeting of the exile groups was convened in a little house on the corner of Calle Altagracia and Calle Félix María Ruiz in Santo Domingo.

The meeting had been called by Raymond Cassagnol, who had made a spectacular flight to freedom through Haiti's Pine Forest, with his wife and six children. During the session, however, unity escaped the exiles as it had in Haiti. Neither Rigaud nor Verna attended. Former presidential candidate Louis Déjoie was not present. His position was well known in exile circles. Déjoie was opposed to any exile activities against Duvalier that were not under his leadership. The outcome of the meeting, nevertheless, was the formation of an umbrella organization to be known as the Haitian Revolutionary Movement (MRH), which adopted a plan of immediate action. And so the Kamokens were born and began their long and tortured path to the battlefield against Papa Doc. (Because they were believed to be mulattos, the rebels were quickly christened "Kamokens," after a bitter-tasting yellow malaria pill.)

One of the MRH leaders was the tough, mustached ambassador Antonio Rodriguez Echazabel, the Cuban butcher-shop operator from Port-au-Prince who had quit Castro's Foreign Service, defecting in Pakistan, and was prepared to help exiles rid Haiti of Duvalier.

Shortly after the umbrella meeting, both Raymond Cassagnol and Rodriguez flew off to secure funding in the U.S. But while they were away Jacques Cassagnol, Raymond's half-brother, opened a training camp near the Dominican border town of Dajabon, declaring himself secretary-general of his hastily founded United Revolutionary Force (FRU). Apprised of his half-brother's competitive coup, upon returning, Raymond Cassagnol had to work out an agreement settling their differences before they could encourage recruits to join.

Some thirty recruits were eventually transported in Rodriguez's white Chevy pickup truck to Dajabon, the little town on the banks of the Massacre River, the natural border in the north. Promptly after arrival, and not far from Dajabon's gray Army fort that stood on a high knoll behind the town, the exiles found themselves lined up in formation on the Dominican Army's rifle range. They learned how to fire Thompson submachine guns and Springfield rifles. In a savannah next to the rifle range these first recruits of an exile army lay down under bushes and slept. Eventually they were issued mattresses, but in those first days their only shelter was lean-tos constructed next to the bushes, which left the men exposed to the summer tropical rains. Despite the primitive conditions, the exiles' morale was high. Their numbers grew to 67 with the arrival of new recruits who, in many instances, volunteered the day after they crossed into exile in the Dominican Republic. There was no ammunition shortage, and they were soon firing bazookas and .30-caliber machine guns until their shoulders ached.

Haiti's ex-President Paul Magloire, rumor in the makeshift camp had it, had provided the Cuban Rodriguez with $60,000. Armed with equipment and ammunition, the exile force was preparing to cross the Massacre River into Haiti on May 13 and strike Cap-Haïtien on May 15, the day Duvalier's legal term of office ended.

One Haitian trainee, Gérard Lafontant, who had operated the Paramount Cinema in Port-au-Prince and had been arrested—and then, upon his release, had fled into exile—recalls, "I couldn't believe my eyes when out stepped the military commander of Dajabon, Colonel Ney Garrido." Appearing on the scene to inspect the ragtag Haitian exile force, Garrido professed to be fiercely anti-Duvalier. He had also served as Dominican military attaché in Port-au-Prince for a brief time in 1958, until Duvalier demanded his recall, accusing him of handing out arms to Papa Doc's opposition.

A Dominican Army captain and lieutenant were detailed by Col. Ney Garrido to train the Haitian exile invasion force in the use of a variety of firearms. The captain gave instructions in heavy weapons and target practice, while the lieutenant proffered some brief courses in guerrilla tactics and street fighting.

To prepare Port-au-Prince psychologically for their invasion, the MRH had hired a small plane and, on April 21, a Sunday, dumped bundles of neatly printed leaflets bearing a message in French announcing "Operation Dry Cleaning."

The message threatened to clean Haiti of "all noxious insects who accompany the gorilla Duvalier" and was also directed at the Haitian armed forces, calling upon them to join the revolution. The leaflets warned foreign residents, as well as diplomats "accredited to the 'tyrant —*Voudouisant,*'" to evacuate the city before May 15. All those living in the vicinity of the National Palace were instructed to evacuate the area before the deadline.

Though most of the leaflets were carried into the hills above the capital, the little plane and its leaflets did have an impact. They generated excitement, showing that Duvalier was not invincible—a small plane could fly over and dump leaflets that all Papa Doc's Macoutes couldn't destroy before they were read.

It was approaching D-Day—Duvalier Day— when close to midnight on May 13 the exile army was awakened and ordered to form ranks and salute a distinguished visitor. It was Brig. Gen. Elby Vinas Roman, minister of the Dominican Armed Forces. The midnight visitor told the exiles that they were not alone in their struggle against Duvalier.

The following day, however, Georges Stevenson, the Haitian mechanic who drove the white Chevy pickup back from Santo Domingo, delivered the bad news: they learned that despite what Gen. Vinas Roman had told them, they were indeed very much alone. The camp was to be immediately broken up. Stevenson, a World War II veteran, suggested they quit the camp and cross the river on their own to launch their attack on Duvalier. It was too late; a Dominican Army captain and two lieutenants arrived and ordered that all of the arms be surrendered (when not being used for training purposes, they had been kept in large boxes under constant guard). The weapons were loaded onto a large Army truck and hauled away.

Two hours later two more trucks appeared, and the first Haitian exile army formed in the Dominican Republic was ordered into the trucks and, after an all-night trip, was unceremoniously discharged, broke, onto fashionable Maximo Gomez Avenue in Santo Domingo, as penniless and bewildered as any city's homeless. (Life in this foreign country, even though it was on the same island, proved to be grueling despite the sympathy of average Dominicans so recently freed from tyranny themselves. Penniless, the Haitian refugees lived from hand to mouth, hungry for days at a time. Some were too proud to admit to their poverty.)

Interestingly, the foreign news stories that were filed from Santo Domingo on May 14 reported that exiles preparing to invade Haiti appear to be "bogged down in bickering." In the *New York Times* Raymond Cassagnol was quoted by Tad Szulc as saying he had disbanded his "2,000-man United Revolutionary Force" because of the threat of a foreign occupation of Haiti. Cassagnol implied that the U.S. was backing a rival exile organization, and that he was "unwilling to have Duvalier toppled by anyone other than Haitians." Raymond's half brother Jacques, dressed in army fatigues and looking battle-ready, said that Dominican police had thwarted his plans to invade Haiti (on May 13) by disarming his 200-man force deployed along the border with Haiti. For foreign newsmen it was a confusing story. Tad Szulc wrote in the *New York Times* that a well-armed anti-Duvalier guerrilla force, Movement Jeune Haiti, was ready to move. His report was slightly premature.

The truth of the matter was that Dominican president Juan Bosch had acted. In his book, *The Unfinished Experiment: Democracy in the Dominican Republic*, Bosch revealed:

> I ran into a Cuban exile who told me that Dominican officers were training Haitians at a military base in the interior. How was such a thing possible without my knowledge? I called the Minister of the Armed Forces, questioned him, learned that the story was true, and immediately ordered the encampment to be disbanded. It was one thing to settle matters with Duvalier under favorable conditions, in the open, as a democracy should always act. It was quite another to prepare Haitian troops to launch an invasion of their country. This would be a violation of the principle of nonintervention, and could make us lose our authority if the current Caribbean turmoil led another power to play the same game.

However, President Bosch didn't realize that this episode was only the beginning of his Haitian headache. The Kennedy administration in Washington, smarting from Papa Doc's manipulations, made no secret of the fact that it was shopping around for an alternative to Papa Doc. The Central Intelligence Agency had a new assignment: aiding in the ouster of François Duvalier. There would be further implications for Bosch's Dominican Republic.

CHAPTER 3

Papa Doc Bluffs Kennedy

The cat-and-mouse game continued. At the end of April 1963, Duvalier ordered the withdrawal of the entire U.S. Naval Mission, some 60 officers and men; the embassy replied (April 29) that half of the Marine unit would be evacuated but that the rest would remain for embassy services and "other duties."

With the saber-rattling continuing, Marines abroad the *Boxer* staged landing drills within sight of the Haitian coastline, the Marines charging down the flight deck in full combat gear, boarding helicopters, and flying toward, but short of, their putative objective, Haitian beaches. The Marines' 106-millimeter recoilless rifles, 4.2-inch and 81-millimeter mortars, flame-throwers, and tanks were checked and rechecked.

Members of the OAS commission, who had spent five days on the island, returned to Washington from Santo Domingo on May 5. The OAS voted 18-0 to give the commission authority to recommend solutions rather than just investigate. With Gonzalo Facio, president of the OAS Council, four members of the committee flew to New York to confer with Haiti's Foreign Minister Chalmers, who had taken his country's charges against the Dominican Republic before the United Nations Security Council. Chalmers, emphasizing to the Security Council that Haiti was a small nation, suggested that it was a victim of racial prejudice. "The very honor and pride of a small black people have been attacked. Accomplices have been given the task of leading the destruction and bringing about the death of the only Negro republic of the American continent. . . . In the name of the black world, Haiti, with glory and honor, has carried high [the torch of Liberty] and which today, together with the brother peoples of Africa and colored peoples in general, it will continue to hold high . . ." (It was a smart move and one that Duvalier would use often—ignoring the OAS regional body and going to the U.N. to plead his case.)

The Dominican ambassador to the U.N., Dr. Guaroa Velasquez, rebutted Chalmers by declaring: "A chaotic situation exists in Haiti. It is a focus and danger spot in the Caribbean. But the reasons . . . lie in the very nature of the political situation in Haiti, and do not result from pressures exercised from the Dominican Republic."

After a talk with Facio and the OAS group, in which they demanded his support, Chalmers [Papa Doc] buckled and agreed to let the OAS handle the situation. The Soviet Union and its chief U.N. delegate, Nicolai T. Fedorenko, had been reluctant to enter the dispute for fear they would appear to be siding with Duvalier. But Fedorenko did get mileage out of the crisis. He said the threat to peace in Hispaniola lay not in the attitude of the Dominican Republic but in that of the United States. "A well-known Japanese proverb says the crab has fun without emerging from the water," Fedorenko pointedly intoned. He accused the U.S. of interfering and cited press reports implying that a U.S. investment of $50 million in Haiti was one reason.

Jean Richardot, head of the U.N. mission in Haiti, found the government slow in issuing exit permits to his U.N. employees and cabled a long protest to U.N. Secretary General U Thant. His protest brought results. Twenty exit permits came through quickly, and Richardot was notified that he was being expelled from Haiti.

Faced with similar problems of foot dragging over exit visas, U.S. Ambassador Thurston told Duvalier bluntly that the U.S. would use force if necessary to get its citizens out of Haiti. The exit visas for U.S. citizens began flowing.

*   *   *

Thurston's performance during the month of May 1963 set a high standard for bluntness on the part of a U.S. diplomat in Haiti, even though overall U.S. performance came off poorly. If Thurston spoke frankly and directly in May, it was only after frustrating months of trying to reason with Papa Doc. In his first week as ambassador in Haiti, Thurston had spoken enthusiastically about developing a working relationship with Haiti. This approach failed. He found, as had his predecessors, that he could not both represent the best interests of the U.S. and please Duvalier. Thurston then got tough. To protect U.S. citizens, he spoke a language Duvalier did not like but understood.

As the month progressed, however, the geopolitical initiative seemed to slip away from Washington. Along the Haitian-Dominican border, army patrols of the two countries maintained habitually convivial relations, exchanging cigarettes. Dominican war fervor also began to ebb, and Dominican military leaders read an appraisal generated by U.S. officers in Port-au-Prince stressing the vulnerability of any enemy force trying to penetrate Haitian territory through *Malpasse*—literally the "Bad Pass"—a rutted, narrow road at the foot of a steep mountain skirting a lake. It was the only route open to Dominican armor for entering Haiti.

Bosch himself observed the Dominican public's war ardor cooling and gradually shifting in favor of letting the OAS handle Haiti.

*   *   *

In Haiti, Duvalierists continued their "Month of Gratitude" speeches but did not always follow the script. Gérard Latortue, head of the highly regarded School of Business Administration, rejected a pro-Duvalier speech he was ordered to deliver at the La Saline slum, and instead sought asylum in the Guatemalan Embassy. Emmanuel Mompoint, professor of Law at the University of Haiti, refused to make a speech outlining the legal arguments for Duvalier's claim on the presidency and escaped into the Chilean Embassy. Leslie Manigat, who also had fled into exile, later was to write that Duvalier was exploiting the Dessalinian doctrine of "necessary involvement." In Haiti's early post-independence period, the doctrine proscribed any sort of neutrality on the part of intellectuals or liberal professionals on the theory that "who is not on my side is against me and who is on my side must get involved." There was no neutral ground.

Papa Doc, who had not left the palace in three weeks, ventured across the street on May 12 to inaugurate the new five-story Tax Offices. A public show of confidence was needed. But even on this abbreviated trip he was accompanied by a heavy guard. It was symbolic that Duvalier's rule had produced two buildings side by side in front of the National Palace: one for taxes and the other for police, the Casernes Dr. François Duvalier.

Notwithstanding Duvalier's bravado, as May 15, 1963, approached— the last day of Papa Doc's initial, constitutional term—something strange happened. Rumors exploded that Doc had done a turnabout, had thrown in the towel, and would leave officially before the May 15 deadline. When Haitians tuned into their radios early on those warm and humid May mornings, suddenly the official threats and rantings had disappeared, and in their place were love songs and classical music. Outside, the roadblocks had vanished overnight. The rumors had begun with an Associated Press report out of Curaçao in the Netherlands Antilles that the Haitian government had asked landing permission for a four-engine plane with six unidentified "military" men on board. The Dutch government conferred with the U.S. Embassy in The Hague. Suspecting that Papa Doc might be one of the six occupants, the Dutch agreed to allow the plane to land if the U.S. government would accept Duvalier as a political exile. Before any decision was taken, the strange request, according to the AP, was cancelled. Had the Haitian government really made such a request, or was the report a ploy by Papa Doc to bring to a halt any plans for U.S. intervention?

Then rumors spread that a well-known Haitian lawyer, Georges Leger Jr., had made several quick trips to the U.S. in early May, and that a friend of the lawyer's had declared that Duvalier had decided to leave. Hosner Appollon, director of the Regie du Tabac (the slush fund through which millions in unbudgeted accounts were available to Duvalier), bought $6,000 worth of tickets on a May 15 Pan American World Airways jet to Paris. The bookings were made in the name of the Duvaliers, with little secrecy. The CIA confirmed that Papa Doc and his family not only had seats on the Paris-bound plane out of New York but also had reservations on Air France from Paris to Algeria, whose leader, Ahmed Ben Bella, was supposedly expecting them.

There was no sleep the night of May 14 at the U.S. Embassies in Port-au-Prince and Santo Domingo. Ambassador Martin, in the Dominican Republic, recalls receiving a long coded cable from Washington past midnight stating that if Duvalier actually left, chaos might ensue, and that the aircraft carrier *Boxer* would move in toward Haiti by morning. In

Port-au-Prince, U.S. Ambassador Thurston was instructed that, as soon as he knew that Duvalier had left, he and Latin American diplomatic colleagues in Port-au-Prince should help set up a temporary governing council of Haitians, resisting any efforts by Duvalier henchmen to seize power. Later, returning exiles could establish a broadly based provisional government. The U.S. would not land any forces unless asked, and then only to protect the lives of Americans and others, including diplomatic asylum seekers.

As Martin recalls in his book, *Overtaken by Events*, he went to see President Bosch in Santo Domingo at 5 a.m. on May 15, and he advised him about the cable. Bosch, according to Martin, smiled slightly, shook his head, and said, "Duvalier will not leave." Nevertheless, a pre-dawn siren at the newspaper *La Nación* in Santo Domingo shattered the stillness, announcing that the next-door nemesis had fled. A few minutes later Dominican radio stations announced that Duvalier had indeed fled. The Voice of America broadcast the report that Duvalier was leaving.

United Press International had filed a story from Port-au-Prince reporting Duvalier had fled. Then UPI filed a "kill" order on its dispatch. Duvalier had not fled.

In Haiti, Ambassador Thurston had invited U.S. news correspondents covering the crisis to his hilltop residence with its splendid panoramic view of the city and the Gulf of Gonave. He served rum punch to 22 foreign reporters on the lawn. The U.S. naval amphibious task force took station under their eyes, and the world waited. The newsmen believed they were there to watch the fleet sail in and perhaps to see the Marines land. However, to everyone's surprise, the fleet paraded around the bay and headed back to the open sea.

Then, a press conference was called for 1:30 p.m. on May 15 at the National Palace. Inside, two guards stood at the foot of the dual red-carpeted stairways. Between the two staircases was a bare desk flanked by more guards, their pistols bulging loosely in their trouser pockets or stuck inside their belts. A sign on the desk warned: "No armed member of the military is authorized to enter the president's office."

Each news correspondent's name was checked against a prepared list. Each was asked whether he were carrying any weapons and then was ushered into the Salon Jaune next to the president's office in the east wing of the palace. A large portrait of Toussaint L'Ouverture looked down from the south wall and toward the open French windows and balcony. Pink roses decorated a center table, their fresh touch contrasting with the cobwebs laced across the chandelier and the dusty yellow drapes.

Outside sirens sounded, as if on cue, and a parade of 38 vehicles, mostly open trucks crowded with peasants and militiamen, drove into the palace grounds. Journalists crowded the Salon's windows to gawk at the spectacle. Precisely at 2:15 p.m., Col. Gracia Jacques, instantly recognizable by his pot belly, emerged from a small door, paused, and dramatically announced, "*Le president de la République.*"

Duvalier came out of the doorway, with his head bowed. He walked slowly to his desk, sat for a moment, then peered up through thick glasses and smiled faintly. It was an entrance both humble and masterfully timed.

An aide quietly read a 252-word statement in English, stressing key points by punching the air with an index finger. Copies of the statement were passed out, and a newsman asked whether the total censorship in place would be lifted to enable correspondents to telephone or cable their stories. "Yes," Duvalier replied without changing expression, "because this is a democracy."

Duvalier didn't answer direct questions, but speaking in French he covered subjects raised by written questions that had been submitted to him in advance. He formally proclaimed himself "Chief of the Revolution." He accused the United States of trying to create panic in Haiti by evacuating U.S. dependents (but added that he believed relations would now improve). He denied the reports that he had requested landing clearance for a plane to carry him and his family to Curaçao.

He likewise denied instituting repression and said that there had been only necessary acts against armed subversion and invasions, asserting, "Unfortunately this situation has been brought about by the shortcomings of certain men of the United States who should have directed their effort toward understanding Haiti and its people by studying, comparing, and then judging." According to an aide, Duvalier was referring to Ambassador Thurston.

Papa Doc droned on: "There is no doubt that the Naval and Air Force missions of the United States have provided valuable technical knowledge to the armed forces of Haiti, as well as to other small countries. However, when some irresponsible officers misuse their knowledge and training, in effect betraying their assigned mission, by meddling in the internal affairs of the host nation, there can be no alternative but to ask for their withdrawal."

Duvalier declared that he would never proclaim Haiti a socialist state, as had been implied in some quarters, and that he knew of no provision in the OAS charter that would allow it to curb a country's internal violence. "If it does exist, why has it not been used in Birmingham [Alabama], where there are not only possible threats of violence but actual acts of violence?"

In concluding, Papa Doc smiled and said, "I would like to stay more time with you but I'm very busy today." He rose slowly and shuffled back out the small door into his adjoining apartment.

In New York at 5:30 p.m. that same day, the Haitian consulate called Pan American World Airways and cancelled the Duvalier reservations on the 8:30 p.m. flight to Paris.

*   *   *

A few minutes after the press conference in Port-au-Prince, 1,200 members of Duvalier's militia staged a goose-stepping parade through the city. They wore a crazy quilt attire of khaki, blue denim, and assorted civilian garb. One platoon leader crossed the rifle resting on his right shoulder with a machete in his left hand. Just before 7 p.m., explosions were heard and there was a rush to see whether the anti-Duvalier putsch had come after all, but they were only the sounds of exuberant Duvalierists celebrating with fireworks.

Papa Doc, crazy like a fox, had evidently outwitted his enemies again. From all indications he had conned them into thinking he was abdicating, thus cleverly defusing the situation and leaving Washington wondering.

Both diplomatically and militarily, the U.S. seemed to be at a loss about what to do next. In Washington the State Department press officer, Joseph W. Reap, issued a statement endeavoring to define the U.S. position. "We are reviewing the whole Haitian situation, including the constitutional position of the present regime. The question of our relations with the Duvalier government is a matter under urgent study and is being discussed with other governments . . ."

In Port-au-Prince Ambassador Thurston cut off all contact with the Duvalier government and announced that the U.S. had "suspended" relations with Haiti. However, the embassy made clear that it was not to be regarded as a "break" in diplomatic relations. And indeed, Uncle Sam would ultimately lift the "suspension" and resume relations with the Duvalier regime.

CHAPTER 4

"Clément, You'll Bring Me Your Head"

No person in the early years of Papa Doc's rule was more feared than Clément Barbot. The sound of his Macoute-packed DKW jeep, the sight of the man in black, with his trademark dark glasses and both hands clasped on his American M-3 submachine gun, would produce a cold shiver in anyone.

While Barbot exuded a Mafia appearance and aura, he was not the average Duvalier henchman. Those whom he had arrested and who survived to tell their story state that Barbot did not himself indulge in torture, that he did not appear to be a sadist. At the same time, however, he exhibited total loyalty in defending the regime against attack and had no hesitation in consigning its enemies to agonizing suffering or gruesome death.

Barbot's longtime friendship with Duvalier imparted to the former special powers and access. Duvalier had decorated Barbot for personally taking an active part in fighting the invaders of 1958 and 1959. And it was public knowledge that Barbot had been instrumental in saving the president's life in 1959 when Doc suffered a heart attack brought on by insulin shock. The Duvalier and Barbot families were so close that Clément Barbot was known to the Duvalier children as "Uncle Clément."

As the regime's "Secret Police chief" (a title he awarded himself), he could also lay claim to having been instrumental in creating Papa Doc's notorious Tonton Macoutes. Even though other, competing Duvalierists had set up their own gangs of bullyboy Macoutes, Barbot became formal leader of the Macoutes.

As did many powerful, once financially strapped Duvalierists, Barbot was quick to take every gangster-like opportunity to improve his own financial standing. Indeed, in the end it was Barbot's business deals with the International Casino, the state gambling monopoly, that ended his celebrated friendship with Doc Duvalier. In orchestrating the sale of the Casino concession, Barbot had somehow overlooked cutting the palace into any commission on the deal. It was a foolish error. When he was arrested by heavily armed palace guard officers on the night of July 14, 1960, an unexplained $28,000 was reportedly discovered at Barbot's home.

There were other factors contributing to the downfall of Papa Doc's loyal domestic spy chief. The fact that he was close to several U.S. Marine officers, including Col. Heinl, didn't bode well. It was common talk in Port-au-Prince business circles that the Macoute chieftain had made a good impression on them as an administrator when running the government while the president was convalescing. Clément had become too powerful. He had evidently forgotten who was boss!

Moreover, Barbot had provided his Duvalierist competitors with an opportunity to dethrone him. A devoted family man in spite of his job responsibilities, Barbot flew to West Germany after receiving news that his son, Hervé, who was studying medicine in Hamburg, had suffered a serious breakdown. Clément well knew the risk he was taking in vacating his position even for a few days. No sooner had his plane departed from Port-au-Prince than Duvalierists set about feeding Papa Doc's paranoia with stories that Barbot had become power-hungry.

Returning from Germany, Barbot discovered that he could hang up his M-3 submachine gun, that he no longer was expected to personally escort the president. His enemies had done an effective job. The back stairs of the palace leading to the president's office had become crowded with a motley crew of Macoute spies reporting directly to the president.

Thus, it didn't take long for Barbot to realize that he no longer occupied the most powerful position in Doc's entourage. Accordingly, he now enjoyed more time for business deals and his family until the night of July 14, when he was seized returning from attending the Bastille Day fête at the French Embassy.

Dreaded Ft. Dimanche was to be Barbot's home for the next eighteen months. Yet he was not thrown into one of the Kafkaesque cells where he had personally dumped so many of the regime's enemies. He was provided special quarters—a large room in the administration building but in which all windows and doors had been sealed shut. He was held absolutely incommunicado even when allowed to take a shower. It was days, weeks, and then months of darkness in enervating heat and humidity in his makeshift cell. A camp cot, not the usual mat, was his only sleeping amenity. Nor did he know what fate awaited him at the end of this long night.

Finally, after 1½ years, Papa Doc released his erstwhile friend from Ft. Dimanche and sent him home to his family under house arrest. Papa Doc, as was sometimes his custom, also sent along an expensive present. In Barbot's case it was a brand new, British-made, dark green Vauxhall automobile.

*   *   *

The only outings that Barbot was allowed to take from his elegant home in the exclusive wooded Lyle Estates in the foothills above the capital were to the Jesuit Villa Manrese retreat house. Rumors circulated in Port-au-Prince that Barbot had undergone a spiritual awakening, that he had found God and could be considered a born-again Christian atoning for the sins he had had to commit in the name of Duvalierism. Instead of his submachine gun, his hands now clasped a lighted votive candle, or so it was said.

Duvalier discovered too late that Barbot was using the Villa Manrese retreat to make contact with his still-loyal lieutenants and organize an escape into the underground with the intention of overthrowing Duvalier. There is no evidence to suggest that the Jesuits knew of Barbot's activities. He also made contact with a U.S. marine he knew and made his intentions known.

Army Lt. Sonny Borges, in charge of the guard detail at Barbot's home, was unsure as to when Barbot finally departed his home for his big move. There was speculation that he had slipped out of his house curled up on the floor of a car driven by his daughter, and that he had disappeared into the city. After eight years, Barbot was back in the *maquis*. This time Duvalier was not a co-conspirator but Clément's target.

By March 1963 Barbot, flitting from hiding place to hiding place, was once more back in business. He had grenades, arms, and ammunition supplied by a friendly U.S. marine from the Naval Mission emergency armory at its headquarters on the Champ de Mars. Officially the Marine commanders deny that they had supplied Barbot with any arms or aided him. Nevertheless, some noncommissioned officer did.

On March 30 a small detail of police was dispatched to apprehend Barbot, whom they discovered was hiding out in a house in the poor, crowded Cour Brea section in Martissant, on the southern edge of the capital. The police were met by a grenade attack and Barbot escaped.

Duvalier never suspected that his old friend Barbot was behind the attack on his two youngest children, even though "Uncle Clément" later took credit for the assault. According to what Barbot later told an American journalist, he and three members of his cohort had followed the palace car as it turned into Rue du Interrment, where another car was awaiting to join the attack. A woman dropping her children at school had inadvertently cut in front of his car, allowing the two Duvalier children time enough when the shooting started to climb out of their car and run into the school.

The tactic of going after Papa Doc's offspring was a strange one. Barbot knew Duvalier well enough to know that Doc would probably never give up power even if his children's lives were at stake. Yet to this day many believe the operation was not really an attempt to kidnap the youngsters and ransom them for Papa Doc's resignation, but rather a simple warning to Papa Doc. That is what Barbot himself, weeks later in hiding, told two American newsmen. He stated that he was responsible for the attack, but that it was only a warning to Duvalier to quit, that he had planned neither to kidnap nor kill the children.

However, that single act on April 26, 1963, resulted in the worst retaliatory bloodbath Haiti had known in many years. It also touched off a five-month war against Papa Doc.

*   *   *

As the May 22, 1963, inauguration of Doc's new term of office approached, Duvalier made frequent public appearances designed to help reestablish an air of normalcy. In one three-day period he appeared publicly seven times. He attended two separate university ceremonies—one at the medical school, the other at the school of economics. Security precautions were extreme. Duvalier was surrounded by a staggering assortment of armed guards, all with fingers on the trigger. Duvalier himself carried a U.S.-made carbine during his limousine ride back and forth to his public appearances. There was good reason for tight security, as Barbot had Papa Doc in his sights.

Several tales about the Barbot-Papa Doc clash quickly entered the realm of legend. One story leaked from the palace reported that Barbot had made a telephone call to Duvalier, saying, "*Allo* François, do you recognize my voice? I am on your tail and one day you will find a cup of coffee on your desk. You had better drink it because it will give you a quick and agreeable death." As working telephones were rare, another call from Barbot was suspected as coming from the Education Department, and Barbot's brother Ernest, who held a high administrative position, and other staff members were arrested. Barbot's psychological telephone war continued. Papa Doc, from all accounts, was unintimidated. During one such call Duvalier finally advised Barbot, "Clément, you'll bring me your head."

Rumors of Barbot's terrorist activities against Duvalier continued to excite the populace. Daily stories made the rounds. The rich imaginations of ordinary Haitians ran wild. Barbot became the invisible man. In a land where the *lougarou*—winged werewolves—still prowl at night, all kinds of powers were attributed to Barbot. A well-planned ambush of militiamen that resulted in heavy loss of life, and which was reportedly orchestrated by Barbot, only strengthened his wraith-like stature.

"To Haitians," *Time* magazine ineffably noted (in its issue of July 26, 1963), "it was a choice between a scorpion and a tarantula: 'What would you do with a killer who delivered the country of a homicidal maniac?'" Yet the military officers refuged in Latin American embassies in Port-au-Prince were prepared to join the devil, in this case the mother of the Macoutes, in ridding the country of Duvalier. Nevertheless, they never received a signal from Barbot.

Mrs. Francesca St. Victor, the president's secretary, was shocked to find a note in Barbot's familiar handwriting on Duvalier's desk containing death threats. It was anyone's guess how it got there, but to most palace aides it meant that Barbot still had men in high places in the National Palace. The situation became a deadly game of hide- and-seek between the two old friends. Duvalier put a $10,000 price on Barbot's head to speed delivery of his new nemesis.

In one government attack on a Barbot hideout, an old wooden shack in the Martissant district, combined Duvalier forces literally perforated the place with bullets to the point where it was about to collapse. However, at the end of their long fusillade the attackers themselves were seized by fear when a lean black dog emerged from the shattered structure and ran away. The house itself was found deserted. Superstitious militiamen knowingly looked at each other. There were those who wondered whether Barbot had the power to change into a dog. But the ensuing story that Duvalier had then ordered all black dogs to be shot on sight was stretching a legend too far.

On the night of May 19, Jeremiah O'Leary, a reporter for *The Washington Star* and relatively new to the Latin American beat, stood with photographer Eddie Adams of the Associated Press outside the Sans Souci Hotel. With the country under martial law and an 8 p.m. to 5 a.m. curfew in effect, the tall, ruddy-faced, fair-haired Irishman, O'Leary, and the shorter photographer, Adams, were a conspicuous sight on the narrow street. When a car pulled up shortly after 9 p.m., O'Leary produced half of a baseball card as the prearranged "password" and was beckoned into the back seat. A reserve major in the U.S. Marine Corps, O'Leary believed he had managed to get his impending interview with Barbot because of a Marine gunner with the U.S. Naval Mission whom O'Leary had known when he was stationed on Guam. However, it was also true that Barbot wanted to "go public" and needed the interview; according to O'Leary, the Marines arranged it. O'Leary described to me what happened:

> Two Haitians picked us up that Sunday night and drove us around and around and we finally headed for the Northern highway where they passed two roadblocks and the soldiers and VSN. They didn't stop us. If you looked like you knew where you were going in Haiti in those days they figured you were some big TTM. I kept thinking how to explain the presence of two white men being driven around after curfew. We turned off the main road near the Cazeau police

post and a mile inland from the highway—there seemed to be a rifle-man behind every bush—must have had twenty to thirty armed men. Barbot's men. We came upon a couple of little thatched huts among sugarcane. Clément Barbot and his brother, Harry, a pediatrician who had come down from Chicago to help Clément fight Duvalier, greet-ed us in one of the huts. They were dressed in white T-shirts and boxer shorts. Everything, including the T-shirts, appeared to be Marine issue and freshly laundered. Two .45 pistols were close at hand in the hut. The interview in the little hut with sugarcane stacked in a corner was mostly about what Barbot intended to do and why, and that he was responsible for the shooting of the bodyguards and driver of the Duvalier children as a warning to Papa Doc.

According to O'Leary, Barbot promised that when he overthrew Duvalier, elections would be held in six months, and that if the people insisted, he, Clément Barbot, would be a candidate for the presidency (which is the way Haitians usually phrase the fact that they aspire to the highest office). Barbot even had a name for his group—the "Comité des Forces Democratiques Haitiennes" (Haitian Democratic Forces Com-mittee). The unlikely "democrat" said he had plenty of men, weapons, and confidence. "I have many friends who say they are with Duvalier now but inside they are with Barbot," he told O'Leary. Barbot promised that if he succeeded in taking power, he would abolish the militia, reor-ganize the army, and restore law and order. Barbot told the two newsmen of repeated conversations with Duvalier in which the president had emphasized that he wanted to kill 300 persons a year, not 150 or 200, but 300. Barbot added that he and his brother Harry had almost been caught a few days before. While they were watching television in a hideout, 60 militiamen surrounded the house. In the shootout that followed, Barbot said, he just missed having a rifle butt slammed against his head only because he tripped. Flat on his back, he shot the militiaman with a pistol. In spite of being outnumbered, the Barbots had managed to escape.

That Barbot was receiving material aid from the U.S. Naval Mission O'Leary had no doubt. The rumor at the time was that the Marines had conveniently left the key to the lock of their armory at their Champ de Mars headquarters. Barbot and his band helped themselves to a generous supply of fragmentation grenades, M-1 rifles, and .45-caliber automatic pistols and ammunition. Eddie Adams photographed the Barbot brothers posing with .45-caliber automatic pistols. O'Leary said that the Barbots, to prove they meant business, showed off their stock of weapons. "They were all Marine issue, M-1 rifles, pistols, and fragmentation grenades," explained O'Leary, who was still a reserve Marine major. (To this day, the Marines deny that they furnished the weapons. Col. Charles Williamson told me that a Marine officer, who he didn't name, suggested that Barbot received help from the Defense Intelligence Agency [DIA] and Army counterintelligence agents in Puerto Rico.) These agencies may have been involved or their names may have been used to provide cover for a CIA covert operation. Clément Barbot produced a map and pointed out to the newsmen his planned objectives for the following evening— schools where militiamen were bivouacked as well as HASCO (Haitian-American Sugar Company) heavy bunker oil storage tanks.

Barbot dismissed Duvalier now as a "madman." It had become a habit with former aides and friends of Duvalier to excuse their earlier alliances with Doc by saying that he had become insane after his 1959 heart attack. Conversely, Papa Doc often referred to his ex-friends who had become his enemies, such as Barbot, as having been made *fou* ("mad") by politics. In effect, Haiti had become a land of madmen made mad by political ambition. (In Haiti, aggression or criminal behavior could traditionally be excused by this one word, *fou*.)

Returning to the Sans Souci Hotel close to midnight in pouring rain, the two newsmen encountered a detachment of mounted, armed Macoutes. Yet, O'Leary said, again he and Eddie Adams were not stopped, even though he could almost touch the horses.

The next night, Monday, May 20, as promised, the final terrorist act was committed by the man who fortified with the gun Duvalier's first term in office and now hoped to prevent Papa Doc's unconstitutional second term due to begin May 22.

O'Leary was invited by his Marine contact to join him and a dozen other Marines to their BOQ—living quarters—which by interesting coincidence happened to be Barbot's old house in the Lyle Estates. According to O'Leary, the Marines carried pistols in their flight bags, even in their jockstraps, and could look down on the city with field glasses.

At precisely 8 p.m., O'Leary said, the shooting started—all hell broke lose and fires flared. Cane fields went up in flames—but the oil tanks did not explode, as Barbot had assured him. (It was later determined that the fragmentation grenades succeeded only in denting the tanks.) Barbot also carried out grenade attacks on St. Pierre College and Lycée Pétion, where some 15,000 peasants and militia brought to the capital for the May 22 ceremony were housed. That afternoon 5,000 members of the rural militia had paraded through the capital led by mounted horsemen. Also that afternoon Papa Doc had made a self-congratulatory visit to the French Institute to hear himself praised by members of his own judiciary. However, Barbot turned the night into a scene of terror. His men, who had hurled grenades into the crowded courtyards of three schools, killed six peasants. The explosion of grenades was mixed with the nightmarish cacophony of celebratory drums, police sirens, screaming people, and gunfire. Yet the night of terror had little effect on Papa Doc. Celebrations continued as if nothing was amiss.

Correspondent O'Leary said his Marine colleagues believed that Barbot was the best hope for Haiti, noting that Barbot had guts and was highly motivated, willing to do anything to rid the country of his former colleague.

In subsequent interviews years later, O'Leary told me that he felt at the time it was either a "cowboy operation" or a special quasi-covert operation. O'Leary speculated that Gen. Victor Krulak—who headed counterinsurgency at the Pentagon—may have sanctioned or endorsed it, or even that Lt. Col. Fred Quint, who was the quartermaster of the Naval Mission at the time, may have facilitated it. But Col. R.J. Batterson, who was appointed chief of the Marine Mission after Col. Heinl was made persona non grata, strongly denied privately and officially a report published by O'Leary in *The Washington Star* 12 years later, in April 1975, that members of the Marine Mission had supplied Barbot with small arms, ammunition, and grenades. "Sure as hell they were involved," countered O'Leary.

U.S. Ambassador Thurston, concerned for O'Leary's safety, suggested that he leave the next day on a Marine mail plane for Guantánamo Naval Base in Cuba. Thirteen men lugged mail sacks aboard the aircraft, but only 12 came off. The 13th—stowaway O'Leary—hid aboard until the plane eventually took off. Meanwhile, the AP's Eddie Adams left Haiti via a commercial flight. His photographs of the gun-toting Barbot broth-

ers were published widely around the world. Haitian police were not
pleased. After carefully examining Adams's published photographs, the
police thoroughly searched the Sans Souci hotel room of Dick Eder of the
New York Times, believing the sugarcane pattern on the walls of his room
matched those in the photographs.

*   *   *

As scheduled on May 22, Duvalier inaugurated his new term of office
before a screaming crowd of thousands, mostly peasants trucked in to
provide the cheers. Standing on the palace steps under a blazing sun,
Papa Doc told Haitians they faced "a difficult and even frightening"
future. The country's problems, he declaimed, were not political but economic, and he announced that a "new order" was about to begin.

In the wake of Barbot's May 20 assault, the "new order" was more like
the old. Though newly anointed, Duvalier huddled in his palace, which
was now more of a bunker guarded by floodlights and tanks, and continued his search for Barbot. Dr. Auguste Denize, a respected specialist who
was director of the Haiti Tuberculosis Sanatorium and Duvalier's second
Minister of Public Health, was arrested and thrown into Ft. Dimanche as
was his wife, Monique, a nurse. Dr. Denize had been best man at Barbot's
wedding, and the government suspected that he had treated the renegade's hand wound.

*   *   *

The U.S. still lacked a happy solution to its Haiti dilemma, and it was
obvious that a new policy toward Port-au-Prince had to be forged.
Duvalier, however, wanted Ambassador Thurston removed and made this
point to Washington.

Sensing that Washington was weakening, Papa Doc then ordered the
removal of the U.S. Naval Mission. Washington complied and followed
up by revealing Thurston's recall at Duvalier's request. Haiti recalled its
ambassador, Dr. Louis Mars, from Washington.

Thurston's departure provided at least some comic relief in a tense and
difficult situation. On the day he was scheduled to leave, the entire diplomatic corps in Port-au-Prince turned up at the tiny, cramped Bowen Field

airport, in a sign of rebuke to Duvalier and sympathy toward Washington's envoy. The day was typically white hot, the sky cloudless. Minutes before the arrival of the Pan American Airways clipper that was to take Thurston out of Haiti to neighboring Santo Domingo, en route to Washington, the skies suddenly clouded over, thunder boomed, and a drenching rain began to fall. Moments later the airline announced with regret that because of the rainstorm the plane, inbound from Kingston, Jamaica, had over flown Port-au-Prince. The announcement was barely over when the storm passed, the skies cleared, and the scorching sun returned. As the diplomats filed out of the airport, one turned to another and, giving a nod to the brilliantly clear sky, remarked, "Do you think Thurston believes in Voudou?"

The following day, Duvalier demonstrated his repudiation of diplomatic norms and his contempt for both Thurston and Washington. The scenario unfolded thus: Ambassador Thurston, instead of waiting two days for the next scheduled Pan Am flight to take him out of Haiti, summoned a U.S. military aircraft, a DC-3, to fly him to Santo Domingo. This time only U.S. embassy staff members turned out early the following morning to see the ambassador off. Solemn goodbyes were said, and Thurston boarded the uncomfortable cargo plane and stood at the open door waving farewell.

But at that precise moment, a Haitian officer emerged from the Haitian Air Force headquarters and dashed toward the plane. He talked with Thurston briefly and then with embassy staff members gathered at the door. The ambassador got off the aircraft. The officer had told Thurston that the plane had not received clearance to depart Haiti. The Haitian major was exceedingly pleasant as he explained that permission was being requested. There was a long wait. The hot tropical sun bore down, and both temperatures and tempers mounted. Angrily, embassy staffers suggested all kinds of alternatives, including an emergency call to U.S. Navy units stationed at nearby Guantánamo Bay, Cuba. Finally it was decided not to wait for permission any longer. Reboarding the plane, Thurston again waved goodbye, and the DC-3's engines—reminiscent of the famous scene in the movie *Casablanca*—lumbered into life. Just then, as if trained for the maneuver, vintage Haitian Air Force P-51 mustangs also spluttered to life. Three of the fighter aircraft rumbled off of a nearby ramp and, in a deft ground maneuver, boxed in the DC-3 so that it couldn't move in any direction. Hopelessly cut off, the pilot of the DC-3 cut its propeller engines.

A visibly furious Thurston emerged once more from the plane and conferred with his aides. The pleasant Haitian Air Force officer, acting almost as if thoroughly sympathetic to the Americans, joined them, then returned to his office, ostensibly to press for permission to let the U.S. aircraft leave. Finally, after some 30 minutes more of the American diplomats cooling their heels waiting, the Haitian officer reemerged from his office and clapped his hands to draw the Americans' attention. Then he signaled them, with a wave of the hand, that it was all right to leave. As if on cue, the three P-51s slowly taxied out of the way of the DC-3, in which Thurston, boarding once more, took off. The whole show was witnessed by the AP's roving correspondent Robert Berrellez, who described the account to me. Army officers attached to the Air Force later told me that the whole show was directed personally via telephone by Papa Doc from the palace. Duvalier on the line wanted related to him even the slightest reaction of the ambassador, a man he was determined to humiliate. Duvalier was a consummate expert at humiliation.

The humiliation of Ambassador Thurston was not over. The following week Washington received an official Haitian note, saying that Thurston no longer was welcome and could return "only" to pick up his personal effects. The initial translation of this note turned out to be flawed. When the State Department advised Haiti that Thurston was returning to retrieve his furniture, the Haitians fired off an angry cable to Washington declaring that Thurston positively could not return. The original note was reviewed, translated again, and ascertained to read that Thurston could not return "even" to pick up his belongings.

Whereupon an even more farcical situation ensued when Thurston explained that his own furniture was mixed with embassy-owned furniture and would need sorting out. Trying to resolve the furniture crisis, the State Department endeavored to arrange for Mrs. Thurston to do the sorting. Haiti responded with an official note declaring that Mrs. Thurston could not return either. Ultimately, the State Department arranged for Thurston's furniture to be shipped to the U.S. In a subsequent speech in San Francisco, Thurston described the Duvalier government as "unconstitutional, ineffective, and unenlightened."

On a broader geopolitical plane, the spring of 1963 proved a sorry chapter for the U.S. vis-à-vis Haiti. Uncle Sam had set a deadline, had deliberately encouraged a crisis, had run a bluff with the Marines and the Navy, and had then backed down.

*   *   *

In June, Duvalier's triumph of "statesmanship" over Washington was celebrated among his followers. Papa Doc, feeling ever more immune from Washington's censure, ordered trials in absentia for Haitian officers who had fled to the Dominican Republic or to asylum in Latin American embassies. He further tightened his fiefdom by imposing a *cordon sanitaire*—a military zone two miles deep along the border with the Dominican Republic. Unauthorized persons caught in the zone could be considered the enemy and killed on sight.

Meanwhile, on July 14, 1963—Bastille Day—Clément Barbot and his physician brother, Harry, were poised to ignite an action that they believed would take out Duvalier once and all. From their hideout near Cazeau, three miles to the north of the capital, they had watched the comings and goings of Information Minister Georges Figaro and other high government officials as they made broadcasts over the government station—formerly known as Radio Commerce—near the Barbots' hideout.

The operatically named Figaro and the other officials all had easy access to the National Palace. Barbot's plot called for seizing Figaro and using him to slip two carloads of Barbot's men, dressed as members of the *Milice Civile,* into the palace that July 14 night at 8:00 p.m. Once inside, Barbot expected to be joined by at least 20 Macoutes whose loyalty he still commanded. He also believed that once inside he could take command of the country, as he had done in 1959 during Papa Doc's illness. Barbot's plan called for the on-the-spot liquidation of his old friend. As long as Duvalier lived, Barbot had often conceded, a takeover was impossible. Duvalier's physical elimination with extreme prejudice was necessary. One of the dictator's key palace aides, Seguin Cantave, assistant chief of the National Palace *Milice* and a corporal in the palace guard, had slipped out of the palace and joined Barbot, ready for the big attack.

However, Barbot never had a chance to launch his grand plan.

There are at least two versions about the discovery of Barbot's hiding place, a short distance from the same Cazeau police post on the highway and not far from the Damien Agricultural College where Barbot once worked. One states that on the morning of the scheduled July 14 plot date, a peasant showed up at the Port-au-Prince General Hospital with a bullet wound. He believed he had been shot by Barbot. He gave no reason why Barbot would shoot him. The other version was furnished by Dr. Gérard A. Boyer, a well-known Duvalierist who served 31 years in the *Service de Santé de l'Armée*. Boyer recounts in his 1999 book, *Memini Album Souvenir*, published by *Imprimerie Le Natal* in Port-au-Prince, that it was Barbot's own driver who gave him away. Boyer writes that Elusma Adolph, Barbot's driver, became frightened by the extent of the plot and went to talk to his friend Dr. Jacques Foucand, who took Adolph to the palace, where the driver revealed Barbot's hiding place.

Barbot was lodged in a little concrete house amid smaller thatched-roofed mud huts, and one side of the cluster fronted a field of sugarcane only a stone's throw from the small Cazeau police post. The house belonged to Dr. Harry Barbot's father-in-law, who worked in nearby Damien Agricultural College.

That fateful morning, warned by barking dogs, Barbot, brother Harry, and six followers attempted to escape what turned out to be a heavily armed superior force. The Barbots suddenly found themselves under withering machine-gun and rifle fire.

Dr. Boyer, a regime insider, reports in his 1999 book that Clément Barbot was finally killed by Lt. Edouard Guilliod of the Police's Criminal Research Division. Writes Doctor Boyer:

> The terrorists [Barbot and his followers] tried to escape by launching grenades. Finding an escape tunnel [sic] Barbot jumped out a window and headed toward the Damien highway. Lieutenant Guilliod saw him and shot Barbot in the buttocks. When the officer was about to kill Barbot he realized that the magazine of his M-1 rifle was empty. Desperately Barbot tried to defend himself by throwing a grenade at his attacker. Because of fatigue or lack of skill the projectile was thrown wrongly and it exploded in the air. Guilliod had taken cover without losing sight of his prey. Like an

arrow Barbot crossed the highway to lose himself in the cane field ahead of him. Guilliod, armed with his Colt, gave pursuit and shot him twice. The wounded animal screamed and weaved and with no pity his hunter emptied his magazine [into Barbot].

The man who had dressed so meticulously and been a fashion trend-setter for Macoutes lay in a bloody heap. Dust and grime mixed with blood covered his bare bullet-ridden torso. Clément Barbot had died with his 45-year-old brother, Harry, the doctor, along with seven followers, three years to the day after Duvalier ordered his arrest. A palace photographer was called in to record his death. Official photos of his corpse were published in the newspapers and posted at Police Headquarters. Two captured Barbot men were found to be Macoutes employed at the Regie du Tabac.

Clément Barbot's corpse and that of his younger brother were placed on a stretcher and taken to the National Palace. As Papa Doc had warned Clément, he had brought Doc his head. In the same vein, Boyer notes in his book that Barbot returned to the palace "offering the hideous spectacle of his cadaver."

During a telephone conversation with Edouard Guilliod, living in obscurity in South Florida, I asked him about Dr. Gérard Boyer's assertions in his book that Guilliod had killed Barbot. The once tough policeman would say only, "Hell, there were 150 hunting him."

CHAPTER 5

Riobé's Lonely War

. . . After the rule of the tyrant, Haiti ought to be given the chance to be ruled by heroes. Heroes are produced by tyranny, and they have not been lacking in her [Haiti's] recent history: the Deputy Seraphin, the Senator Moreau, Alexis the writer, the young man Riobé who kept the army and the Tontons at bay from a cave above Kenscoff and shot himself with the last bullet . . .

—GRAHAM GREENE, IN HIS FOREWORD TO *PAPA DOC* (1968)

The celebration at the National Palace in Port-au-Prince over the corpse of Clément Barbot had barely ended on the night of July 16, 1963, when a strange-looking vehicle was seen lumbering across Ruelle Nazon and up Delmas road. It was tank-like in appearance with slits in the sheets of steel for a window screen.

It was 11:00 p.m. when the truck had departed the newly constructed Riobé residence in Turgeau, across the street from the Sacré-Coeur church. There was no traffic on the streets of the capital. As the vehicle climbed towards Pétionville, the occupants scattered homemade, tire-puncturing devices behind them on the roadway. Half way up the hills, the engine overheated, and the driver, a youth named Damas, dropped down from behind the wheel and begged water from a house close to the road. It was then that Hector Riobé realized he had welded a sheet of protective steel across the front of the truck, which blocked the engine's ventilation system. Nothing could be done about it.

When the makeshift tank reached Pétionville around 11:30 p.m., the strain on the overheated engine proved too much. The engine coughed and died—as ill luck would have it, directly in front of the small police post at the corner of the Pétionville market.

44

The policeman on duty came forward offering to fetch water for the overheated radiator. Another policeman, curious, came out of the post, and as he walked around the vehicle, which had the appearance of a Mardi Gras float, he exclaimed, "*Ala yon machin dwol papa!*" ("What a weird-looking vehicle!") The policeman, unarmed, grabbed the side of the truck to pull himself up to see what was in the back. Shocked, he jumped down. Four men, all with blue shirts, lay there armed with 12-gauge shotguns and a .22 caliber rifle. The four instantly began firing in all directions as they abandoned the vehicle and made their escape. The police, caught by surprise, scattered without responding to the attack. Sleeping beside their produce at the dominant town market, the *marchands* awoke, panicked, and joined the stampede to the four winds.

In answer to my questionnaire, Jean-Claude Turnier, the only one of the group in the vehicle who was still alive, recounted details of the breakdown. He finally managed to return home at 1:00 a.m., believing that their plan to attack the main Pétionville Police Headquarters had been aborted. His brother, Wilhelm, also a member of the group, had hidden in the home of the Cajuste family near the marketplace. He eventually arrived home at 7:00 a.m.

Driver Damas, whose first name no one knew, along with Hector Riobé and Jean-Pierre (a.k.a Jean-Pi) Hudicourt, regrouped, halted motorist Antoine Izmery, and ordered him to drive them up the mountain. The police post in Kenscoff, a vacation village eight miles from Pétionville, now became their alternative target. There were no records of any complaint of a hijacking that night; thus, how the three men reached Kenscoff remained a mystery until Izmery, a well known Syrian-Haitian businessman, revealed his secret one day in the post-Duvalier period to Hudicourt's cousin Fred Pierre-Louis.

En route farther up the mountain they stopped in Laboule. "Jean-Pi" Hudicourt entered the home of his first cousin Elsie Pierre-Louis and her husband, Philippe Faubert. Jean-Pi pressed a note into Philippe's hands, stressing that the lives of ten youths could be in danger if the note was not delivered to Rev. Father Adrien at the Petit Séminaire St. Martial. (Elsie's mother, Therese, who happened to be present at the time, related the meeting to her sister-in-Law, Dr. Edith Hudicourt, emphasizing the urgency with which Jean-Pi had pleaded for the delivery of the note.)

Deciding that the risk of delivering it was too great, Philippe Faubert instead handed over the note to the Pétionville Police Headquarters. The note was received by the duty officer, Lt. Fritz (Fito) Germain. Its contents were not revealed, but it was believed to be a simple note (which could have been a coded message) in the form of a greeting to Father Adrien. What the police did with the innocuous note is not known. Father Adrien did not get into any difficulty over the note addressed to him.

Later that same night the three remaining phantom attackers appeared in Kenscoff. Their attack was described to me by villagers, years later, as swift and deadly. A sergeant, two soldiers, and two militiamen were killed. The attackers made off with the post's guns and munitions. According to witnesses' accounts, the post commander, Army adjutant Appollon, awakened by the gunfire, prudently emerged from the post's back room only after the gunfire had subsided and the moaning of the dying could be heard.

It was not long before the quiet, idyllic mountain resort, a favorite of a few wealthy families who sought refuge from the summer's heat and dangerous politics of Port-au-Prince amid the cool, pine-clad mountains, was in turmoil. The village was blockaded. Market women carting freshly grown produce from mountain farms to Kenscoff en route to Port-au-Prince found the roadway closed.

As no one had heard or seen any car enter or leave Kenscoff, police and the *milice* began a house-to-house search for the culprits. Random arrests of summer residents followed. Finally, like packs of salivating bloodhounds, the *milice*, police, and soldiers began scouring the neighboring mountains. They were soon to return like whimpering poodles.

As one search team neared the summit of Morne Godet, they were greeted by gunfire; amazed survivors later related to villagers of Kenscoff that they had watched in astonishment as fellow members crumbled, cried out, and collapsed. Papa Doc's "Little Ones," as he liked to call his *milice*, either threw themselves to the ground or ran down the mountain in terror. They had never been shot at before.

Government reinforcements arrived in Kenscoff and moved into battle positions, but it seemed that every time a soldier or member of the *milice* got close to the summit and was exposed to view, a shot from a cave sent him reeling, dead or wounded, down the mountain.

It was a strategically situated cave, easily defended, and it completely dominated any attacking force. The authorities, at the time, believed that the cave was defended by a group of well-trained sharpshooters. As the number of casualties grew and ambulances careened up and down the mountain road, the Marine-trained Casernes Dessalines battalion was ordered to join the war with mortars and grenades. It was becoming an embarrassment to the palace. The entire country was alive with exciting rumors of a battle that Papa Doc was actually losing.

The fight continued for three days. Then, during the afternoon of Friday, July 19, the cave fell silent. Fearing it was a trick, the government forces dared not approach the cave. On Saturday, the police arrived with Hector Riobé's mother. They placed her on a horse and made her ride up to the cave calling out, "Hector, Hector." There was no reply. Slowly and carefully the heavily armed government troops advanced behind Mrs. Andre Riobé, their forced human shield.

(Mrs. Riobé's maiden name was Laurette Jourdan and a nephew, Reginald Jourdan, would later take up arms against the dictatorship and perish with the "13." Mrs. Riobé and her sister, with the aid of two priests, finally escaped to exile.)

When Papa Doc's forces finally reached the cave, they were astonished to find not a squad of sharpshooters but a single gunman. And that gunman, Hector Riobé, lay dead, with a self-inflicted bullet to the head. In the end, he had robbed them of the last shot.

*   *   *

Following the attack on the Kenscoff post, and having transported the arms to the cave at the summit of Morne Godet, Riobé had sent the other two members of his group home with the knowledge that they were unknown to the authorities and could thus resume their normal activities. If he were discovered, he intended to fight, knowing that the truck could easily be traced to him. He knew he would soon be a wanted man.

Riobé was an unlikely rebel. He was a quiet introvert who had only one good friend, Wilhelm Turnier, age 26. The Turnier family had for a time been neighbors of the Riobés in Port-au-Prince's Ruelle Nazon neighborhood. The Turniers were a big family with four boys and one girl.

Hector, like his father, Andre, held French citizenship and had com-

pleted his compulsory military service in France. He had learned to handle firearms well and demonstrated that he was a good marksman. Hector
had a workshop where he made iron parts. His specialty was *mechanic
d'ajustage*.

The first of Riobé's group to have been captured was Jean-Pi Hudicourt, also age 26. Moving down the mountain, exhausted and thirsty,
Jean-Pi had stopped at a peasant hut and asked for water. It proved a fatal
stop. The word had gone out in the mountains that the authorities were
searching for the Kamoken. The peasant family had provided Jean-Pi
with food and water, but when they learned he might be a Kamoken—and
fearful of harboring a wanted man—they struck him over the head with
a hardwood pilon (used to mash coffee beans and corn) as he dozed.
Apprehended, Jean-Pi Hudicourt was taken to Pétionville Police
Headquarters where, as Lt. Fritz Germain recalled years later to Gilles
Hudicourt, the dead man's younger brother, contrary to local stories,
Jean-Pi was not in a coma but mobile and able to talk. It was later under
intensive torture intended to reveal the names of his accomplices that
Hudicourt went into a coma. Dr. Jacques Foucand, the Duvalierist neuro-
surgeon, reportedly operated on Hudicourt in an effort to make him talk.
Jean-Claude Turnier confirmed for me what a nurse in the military hos-
pital had said at the time—that Hudicourt had been "severely tortured."
In fact, he was tortured to death without revealing the names of fellow
conspirators.

The second fugitive to be seized was the "tank" driver, Damas, who
had managed to descend the mountain to an area near Carrefour where he
lived. Apprehended by the *milice*, he was beaten and finally executed at
Ft. Dimanche.

Wilhelm (Wilo) Turnier had gotten back home in time to return to
work as accountant for the local Volkswagen distributorship and was not
apprehended until 16 days later. On the evening of August 1, Wilhelm
and his brother Jean-Claude were leaving the movies downtown when
agents of the prefecture arrested Wilhelm. The following day the same
agents came to the Turnier house. A leading Duvalierist of the neighborhood, Windsor Day, supervised the arrest of all the men in the household,
including Jean-Claude, age 25, and his two younger brothers, Weber Jr.,
23, and Leslie, 14, who was taken away over the protests of his mother

pleading, "He is still a child." Friends who happened to be visiting the house at the time, Astrel Lamarque, Frantz Trouillot, and Robert Menage, were also arrested. Leslie was released after 24 hours; the visitors soon afterwards. Weber Jr. was released within a month and Jean-Claude after three months. They had all been incarcerated at Ft. Dimanche. The young men were accused of "destabilizing the system."

Jean-Claude explained that what saved him was that his captors had never got around to interrogating him.

In Ft. Dimanche they had been separated in a line of cells, but they could talk to each other. The last time Jean-Claude saw his elder brother was when they spent 24 hours in the same cell. He doesn't know when Wilhelm was executed.

While incarcerated, Jean-Claude learned that Riobé had asked Clément Barbot to carry out a similar attack in the city against the main Police Headquarters. Barbot had cynically pretended to agree, but he then told a confidante who was present during their conversation, "Don't you see that these are a bunch of young people with nothing to do who are going to get themselves killed?"

Jean-Claude Turnier explained that his own informant was a hand-cuffed prisoner who was kept in a completely dark cell and was never let out to bathe. His prisoner-informant's treatment was particularly harsh because he had been part of Barbot's group who had tried to kidnap Jean-Claude Duvalier and his sister Simone, on July 26, 1963, at College Bird. Turnier didn't know the man's name, only that he was an agronomist and proud of his participation in the attempted kidnapping. "I almost suc-ceeded. I had her, little Simone in my arm," he bragged from his cell to anyone who would listen.

*   *   *

As with so many conspiracies, the complete story died with one man— Hector Riobé. What is known is that he prepared his attack well. Riobé had begun by converting his Ford pickup into the attack vehicle, and he contacted Damas, a welder, to help armor the truck. Seeking oxygen for a flame-thrower he was constructing, Riobé got in touch with Jean-Pi Hudicourt who worked for Shanon Yarborough, an African-American who had an air-conditioning business in the capital. Hudicourt was in charge of purchasing the requisite oxygen for Yarborough's firm. Flame-throwers had been used with deadly success by the U.S Marines in fighting the Japanese during World War II in the Pacific, and Hector had decided to use such a makeshift weapon to capture the Pétionville Police Headquarters.

The truck was transformed into the armored vehicle in the backyard of the Riobés' new Turgeau home. (His mother and aunt remained in their old home next to the Hotel Sans Souci). When Damas and Jean-Pierre Hudicourt decided to join the plot, Hudicourt even furnished his own prized .22 caliber rifle. A week before the group's action, Jean-Pi, on a visit to the home of his aunt, Dr. Edith Hudicourt, gave no hint that he was involved in an anti-Duvalier operation. However, Dr. Hudicourt recalls a statement he made at the time: *"L'acceptation de l'injustice est la negation de toute justice."* ("The acceptance of injustice is the denial of all justice.")

*   *   *

To understand that young Hector Riobé—an otherwise law-abiding citizen—did not have as his original intention in life the launching of a suicidal, kamikaze-like attack on the government, it is necessary to understand the environment in which the event took place. By the summer of 1963 Haiti, under Papa Doc, had become a living hell, ghastly in its all-encompassing atmosphere of fear and retribution, devoid of all human dignity. Desperate situations caused normal people to do desperate things. The cause that sent young men such as Hector rising up against the tyranny was the rage and anger of youth. They were expressing their own and others' suffering. They knew the kind of pain that only those who have experienced dictatorship can understand—pain caused not only by the murder of loved ones but also by the loss of human pride, joy, promise, and hope, all because of one man's obsession with making Haiti into a reflection of his own power.

*   *   *

Completely unaware of the tragic events taking place around him on April 26, 1963—that terrible bloody day on which Papa Doc reacted to the attempted kidnapping of his two youngest children—Hector's father, Andre Riobé, a prosperous planter, had been apprehended as he traveled on the main road south with the payroll for the workers on his extensive property (more than a 1,000 hectares) at Gressier, six miles south of Carrefour.

Years after the end of the Duvalier rule in 1986, a man who identified himself as a former agent of the Department of Interior wanted to tell his story. It weighed heavily on him, he told members of the newly formed Human Rights Ecumenical Center. He had precise information as to what took place on that fateful day at the Carrefour Police post where he was assigned. A summary of his account follows:

Orders had been received that there had been an attempt on the Duvalier children, and that they had to be vigilant and take action, which meant all persons leaving the city should be apprehended. In those days there was no separate police, and regular soldiers manned police posts.

Soldiers from the Carrefour post had arrested four people leaving town and placed them in the small police station by the highway. At 9:15 a.m. Maj. Franck Romain arrived, and when he saw the Mercedes-Benz automobile parked next to the police post he ordered, "Bring me the keys." The car's owner, Andre Riobé, and two Vieux brothers, sons of Max Vieux, and their friend, Wihlo Théodore—all three of whom had also been stopped leaving the city to work on their rice farm—were ordered by Romain into the Mercedes-Benz. He drove them to the Army's nearby boot camp, Ft. Lamartin. Meanwhile, the killing fury of the Duvalierists was underway.

That evening as the soldiers and Macoutes played cards on the barricaded road in front of the Carrefour post, they heard bursts of machine-gun fire coming from Ft. Lamartin. An hour later, the agent recounted, an ambulance emerged from Ft. Lamartin. They halted the ambulance and inspected the inside. There were four bodies, those of Andre Riobé, Didier and Paulo Vieux, and Wihlo Théodore, who had been locked up in the post early that morning. The two Vieux brothers and Théodore had been completely ignorant of the events of the morning.

The following day Romain passed by still driving the Mercedes. [The exiled Jean-Claude Duvalier implored me during a series of interviews in the 1990s in France to emphasize this point: According to Baby Doc, some crimes that were committed under his father's rule were personal vendettas, and the government was not responsible for killing Andre Riobé. Jean-Claude accused Maj. Franck Romain of the murder.] Riobé's large land holdings and, syrup and alcohol factory were seized, along with his tractors and other field equipment. Duvalier ordered the confiscation of Riobé's properties, and one of the first to benefit was his loyal aide, Col. Gracia Jacques, who received a large tract of Riobé land at Gressier on which he launched a dairy farm. Romain kept the Mercedes-Benz.

Like so many grieving families, young Riobé, an only son, tried to find his father. The search was in vain. Macoutes had quickly blackmailed his mother, saying his father was still alive, and they could get him released for five thousand dollars.

In sum, four of Hector Riobé's group paid the ultimate sacrifice, but they bequeathed a testament of valor to Haitian youth. Their brief but deadly actions and the casualties they managed to inflict on Duvalier's forces (the total killed in battle numbered officially ten but could have been much higher) were an inspiration for young Haitians opposed to the tyranny. Though the government described Riobé and his band as a gang of degenerate youth, Riobé, by virtue of his "lonely war," entered the pantheon of heroes. To this day, peasant farmers in the region of Kenscoff tell tales of the incredible young man who fought off Duvalier's entire army.

The tragic tales of what happened to the relatives of other young men involved in the Riobé plot attest to the depths of degradation and humiliation to which proud and dignified Haitian families were reduced by the Duvalier regime. While brutal dictatorships cost innocent lives, they also take their toll on self-respect and dignity.

At the Petit Seminaire St. Martial, the tall, gangly "Jean-Pi" was known as *"bale pou b'lau"* (the name for the long-handled broom that cleans cobwebs from the ceiling). When ex-Ambassador Pierre Hudicourt received the news that his eldest son was involved in a plot, he and his family fled their house in the hills near Pétionville in a neighborhood known as Brise Tout (literally "Break Everything"—genesis of the name unknown). Led by his two youngest sons, Didier and Philippe, who knew the way, the elder Hudicourt made his way to Pétionville on foot up a dry ravine that the boys were accustomed to using to reach the town. The boys and girls of the family were left in the care of relatives and friends while their father and mother sought asylum.

The right to offer refuge for political reasons was a time-honored course of action bound by Latin American tradition and treaty. But in 1963 embassies were ringed with Macoutes; furthermore, some embassies didn't care to have their residences overflowing with political refugees. While May Hudicourt was smuggled into the Chilean embassy, Pierre was at first refused the hospitality of the Mexican Embassy by Ambassador Bernardo Reyes, whose personal relationship with the Duvalier regime was warm. Ambassador Reyes's efforts to deny refuge to Hudicourt ended when the latter appealed to Reyes to reread the treaty on asylum signed in Rio de Janeiro. "I know the rules," said ex-Ambassador Hudicourt, "as I signed it for the Haitian government." He was admitted by the Mexican envoy, who prudently decided not to place his government in violation of the hemispheric protocol. (On October 26, 1964, Ambassador Bernardo Reyes of Mexico was personally decorated by his friend, President-for-Life François Duvalier, with La Grand Croix de l'Ordre National Honneur et Mérite.)

One of Mrs. Riobé's brothers, Leon Jourdan, was not so lucky. Refused refuge in the Chilean Embassy, he remained in its courtyard in a steady rainfall, caught pneumonia, and died.

Two of the Hudicourt girls, in hiding at the Jean Desquiron chicken farm at Freres, decided, with young Lilas and Françoise Desquiron, to climb the adjacent hills to return to their parents' home and retrieve some of their dresses, only to witness their possessions being looted by Macoutes. When they saw the baby crib of their little brother Gilles being carted away on the head of a looter, they broke into tears and fled back to the safety of their hideout at the Desquiron farm.

Mrs. Riobé, left without husband or son and with her property confiscated, escaped abroad to live out her misery.

CHAPTER 6

General Cantave's War

One Sunday in June 1963, Dominican border guards manning the five medieval-looking watchtowers overlooking adjacent Haiti reported columns of smoke rising into the sky across the lonely dirt road that served as an international boundary between the two countries. It appeared as though all of Haiti was on fire.

These were not just the familiar fires set by Haitian peasants to clear land before planting their crop of *petit mil,* but a conflagration that extended along the middle of the border. The arsonist turned out to be none other than Papa Doc. He had ordered his Macoutes to torch crops and peasant dwellings to create a *cordon sanitaire* 3 to 5 miles deep along the entire 156-mile frontier. To complete this "sanitary cordon" in northern Haiti, they felled trees along the Massacre River. In the mountainous south, deforestation and resulting erosion, plus over-farming, had done the job for Papa Doc, as years before the region had been stripped of vegetation making it as naked as a moonscape. There was not even a border fence.

In this inhospitable no-man's land, anyone attempting to escape or enter Haiti or any other unauthorized person could be shot on sight. No longer could local peasants shelter, or act as guides for, fleeing Haitians or infiltrating anti-Duvalier guerrillas. Above all, Papa Doc's *cordon sanitaire* punished not only the uprooted Haitian subsistence farmers, who lost their homes and crops, but also the seasonal sugarcane cutters who habitually slipped back and forth over the border. In spite of the new dangers, however, the exodus from Haiti continued, and couriers from Santo Domingo undauntedly slipped across the frontier to deliver messages to contacts in Port-au-Prince.

Into this surreal scenario stepped a new and wraith-like anti-Duvalier rebel group, which the government and the people quickly named after the anti-malaria pill Kamoken. It was not only because the pill was bitter tasting but also because it turned light-colored people yellow, the color of the first Pasquet invaders. From then on all rebels were known as Kamoken. In no time the Kamoken took on all the mystical attributes of the nocturnal airborne werewolf, the Lougarwu. The Kamoken seemed to be everywhere and nowhere. Fearful of surprise attacks at night by the Kamoken, Haitian soldiers abandoned their small military outposts and slept in hiding with their weapons. Yet, as events were to prove, the Kamokens were more intimidating than potent and won more psychological victories in the imagination of the enemy than on the battlefield.

To help keep watch on the border, Duvalier, as was his want, assigned a cabal of weird and violent characters. They reported directly to Papa Doc, and they included Dodo Nassar, a well-known Syrian-Dominican-Haitian smuggler who had spied for both the Dominicans and Duvalier; the bald-headed Artibonite *milice* chief, Zacharie Delva, who like Nassar considered himself a *houngan*—although neither was known publicly to have been initiated into the Voudou priesthood; and André Simon, the deputy from Jacmel who had made himself the undisputed boss of the southwest region (as was Maj. Vir Lherrison in the North).

Notwithstanding Papa Doc's cast of frontier-guarding characters, there were numerous epic escapes across the border by Haitian Army officers, noncommissioned officers, and soldiers, following Duvalier's crackdown on the ranks. Individual U.S. Marines who, in their capacity as Naval Mission advisors, had established friendships with Haitian Army officers, took extraordinary risks to save the lives of Haitian officers who sought help in making it over the frontier.

One such case was that of Maj. Robert André, who had been in charge of the Haitian Signal Corps. André was a highly professional officer, and his father, Col. P. Jules André, had been assistant commandant and chief of staff of the Garde d'Haiti (Gendarmerie) in 1934 when the "Haitianization" of the country's military force by the U.S. occupation troops was terminated. Maj. André had only recently returned to Haiti from the U.S. Naval Hospital in Bethesda, Maryland, where he had been operated on for cancer. He was tipped off that he was high on Papa Doc's list of pro-American officers to be eliminated.

Since, by then, the Latin American embassy residences were heavily guarded by Duvalier forces, André went to the home of Capt. Donald Q. Layne, USMC, who was his friend and the Naval Mission's communications adviser. Lt. Col. George A. Babe of the Mission and Capt. Layne surveyed all of the possible escape routes for Maj. André, but by then most were closed off.

It so happened that Col. Roy J. Batterton Jr., who had succeeded Col. Heinl as chief of the Naval Mission, and Batterton's petite, New Zealand-born wife, Joan, were horse lovers. (A member of the Marine Raiders during World War II in the Pacific, Batterton had been wounded and married his nurse while recovering from his wounds at a hospital in Auckland, New Zealand.) They kept two horses at their home and often went for night rides. With the Battertons' assistance, a novel escape plan unfolded. Maj. André, impersonating Col. Batterton, mounted his horse at night and along with Joan Batterton rode off across the Delmas neighborhood into the Cul de Sac plain, completely fooling the Macoutes guarding the roadblocks. Far from the city, André dismounted and continued on foot. As he was weak from his recent operation, it took him nearly five days of hiding and skirting *milice* patrols to reach the border area. Climbing into the mountains to cross at an unguarded section of the frontier, he fell asleep amidst rock only to awake to find a scorpion crawling up his leg. There were more dangerous Duvalierist nemeses, and Maj. André's last few steps to freedom were with his revolver drawn. Suffering dehydration and exhaustion, he reached the Dominican Republic where I met up with him again.

Many of Papa Doc's fleeing Army officers, like anti-Duvalier civilians, made similar dramatic crossings. Among the Haitian refugees in the Dominican Republic, and amid the ambience of despair and confusion, arrived the tall, dignified, white-haired Gen. Léon Cantave, former commander of the Haitian Army. The 53-year-old exiled general kept such a low profile that his presence was known only to the former officers he recruited to his little army in exile. There were rumors that a sponsor helping to finance his campaign was the Central Intelligence Agency, which had recently taken a hands-on interest in the Haitian exiles.

Cantave arrived in Santo Domingo from New York after having served with the U.N. in Lebanon and the Congo during five years in exile. A 20-

year Army veteran, he had opposed Gen. Paul Magloire's attempt to install himself as Haiti's dictator following one term as elected president. Cantave was jailed but, after Magloire's ousting in December 1956, was promoted to command the Army. Cantave surrendered his command to Col. Antonio Kébreau following a daylong battle on May 25, 1957, between factions of the Army and political groups. The exiled Cantave was supremely confident of getting rid of "the monster," as he publicly branded Duvalier. "Duvalier knows," Cantave declared, "that I am an Army man and that the Army will side with me." He was soon to learn, however, that there was very little left of the Haitian Army he once commanded.

The contempt for, and loathing of, Duvalier was universal among the Haitian refugees, both military and civilian, in the Dominican Republic, who shared a common sense that unless their country was rescued from the hands of this tyrant, they would never go home. Nevertheless, sometimes Duvalier appeared to be a secondary target, so much did the exiles fight among themselves for leadership. Youthful refugees resented the exiled Army officers who had so recently served Duvalier. The crab syndrome, as it was known in Haiti, where crabs stop others from reaching the top of the basket, was at work. With a proliferation of liberation movements, the Haitian exiled leaders became petty and resentful of their competitors—all the while seeming to overlook the fact that they were shockingly unprepared to do battle with Papa Doc. It didn't matter. This was "guerrilla time," when Haitian youth believed they could somehow duplicate Fidel Castro's success against the Batista dictatorship in Cuba. A dozen men had survived Castro's disastrous landing from Mexico to climb into the rugged Sierra Maestra and launch their ultimately victorious rebellion.

When General Cantave arrived on the Dominican scene prepared to take command of the Haitian exiles, among the advisers who met him in Santo Domingo was well-known former Haitian Army officer and diplomat Pierre Rigaud. Another advisor, Paul Verna, had served at the Haitian Embassy in then Ciudad Trujillo and lived in exile in Venezuela. Verna had spent two years touring Latin America seeking to build support for exiles. The two former Haitian diplomats had reestablished their old contacts in the Dominican Army, who had agreed to help the exiles; but they warned that President Juan Bosch was opposed to any anti-Duvalier rebel operations on Dominican soil. Training and the plan to invade Haiti must be completely clandestine, kept secret even from the Dominican president. Bosch, as the country's first democratically elected president, was determined to stick to the letter of international law and not get embroiled in "dirty tricks," which was a hallmark of his predecessor, dictator Rafael Trujillo. Asked about the Haiti situation, Bosch would stress that it was up to the Organization of American States, saying, "The OAS must find a solution."

Early in July 1963, officers of the Dominican Army high command, in an action again unknown to Bosch, gave the green light to begin training Haitian exiles at the Dominican military camp of Sierra Prieta, eight miles northwest of Santo Domingo. Former Haitian officers, young civilian exiles, and illiterates recruited from the cane fields, known as *Congos,* made up the new force. Though the recruits wore Dominican uniforms and steel helmets, most of their training consisted of learning how to shoot straight. The camp was also kept secret from Haitian exiles opposed to Cantave. However, it wasn't long before dissension arose in this camp as well. Civilians didn't like taking orders from Haitian officers, who they saw as responsible for the rise of the Duvalier dictatorship in the first place.

(Ironically, a Roman Catholic priest, Father Gerard Bissainthe, a member of the Holy Ghost teaching order at Petit Séminaire St. Martial, who had fled into exile and become head of Jeune Haiti—a New York–based youthful exile group that had managed to find some CIA funding—was pleading with Bosch to allow his group to open up an educational training center for Haitian exiles. The cleric's pleas were to no avail.)

Not long after the training began Bosch received word that Haitians were being trained by his army. He summoned his Army chief, Gen. Renato Hungria Morel, and angrily demanded to know, "What the hell is going on training Haitians?"

I was at that time based in Santo Domingo and reporting for *The New York Times*, *Time* magazine, and NBC News. That particular day I happened to be interviewing Sacha Volman, an aide to Bosch, when the president telephoned, asking Volman whether he knew that the army was training Haitians. Volman didn't know and asked me. I shrugged. It was news to me. In fact, knowing the trouble Jeune Haiti was having in trying to get the official go-ahead to establish a Haitian exile educational center, I was surprised at the news. Volman said he suspected that "the white-haired man" at the American Embassy (without mentioning the man's name) had something to do with the Dominican Army's training Haitians. Volman speculated that it was the work of the CIA station chief, the white-haired man, but added that it was only a guess.

Gen. Cantave was out of the country when President Bosch ordered his Army commander to cease the training of Haitians immediately. Cantave hurried back, and within a week the Haitians were back in the camp training, this time without the troublesome civilian activists, who were returned Santo Domingo. The majority of Cantave's Congos were more expert with machetes than with machine guns.

On a steamy Friday evening, August 2, 1963, the civilian Haitian activists received the word-of-mouth order to report to Sierra Prieta. The exile invasion of Haiti at last appeared imminent. Many refugees quietly disappeared from Santo Domingo. Mid-morning of August 5, 1963, I received a call from Haitian ex-diplomat Paul Verna who said he had important news to report and would I come quickly to the Hotel Jaragua.

Verna, an old friend, introduced himself as spokesman for the exile force led by Gen. Cantave. Fortified with a tumbler full of Scotch, Verna dramatically announced his "news." It was a theatrical moment, and I didn't know just how theatrical it was at the time.

Taking a deep breath, Verna, bleary-eyed from lack of sleep, described how Gen. Cantave had indeed landed that morning in Haiti at the head of a solid army, and that they were, at that moment, advancing on Cap-Haïtien, the country's second city. It was indeed exciting news.

"Would you like to go to Cap-Haïtien tonight or tomorrow morning to report the story?" the spokesman asked. "The city is expected to fall by early evening." "Yes, of course," I replied. "I certainly would like to cover the war from the front lines." I then asked for more details. For security reasons, Verna said, his information had to be limited. The invasion force, he continued, numbered 250 and had landed in Haiti from "an island in the Caribbean." (He said he could not disclose the name of that island.) They had, he went on, used the element of surprise and had met "little to no resistance in taking the coastal towns of Fort Liberté, Derac, and Phaeton in Haiti's northeastern corner." The exiles were advancing in two columns in a sort of pincer movement. Glancing at his watch, Verna concluded, "It is now only a matter of hours before Cap-Haïtien falls."

Diplomatic sources in Port-au-Prince confirmed that some kind of invasion was underway in the northeast. Filing the story, I made sure that the claims were attributed to spokesman Verna. No independent source could confirm or deny his detailed assertions. The following morning, *The New York Times* played the story at the top of page one, accompanied by a war map showing the purported advance of the rebel force in a pincer movement toward Cap-Haïtien.

Having set off toward the Dominican border area closest to the fighting, and not wishing to be a victim of managed information, I had decided that if need be I would cross the frontier to learn precisely what was happening. While in a boat reconnoitering the Massacre River, which separates the two countries, I observed a Haitian Air force DC-3, which I mistook for a military spotter plane doing what I was doing, searching for the invasion force. Shortly afterwards I learned that that plane was carrying a Haitian government press party that was being treated to an aerial view of terrain the government declared totally rebel-free. Sources on the Dominican side confirmed that the Haitian exiles had returned to Dominican soil and then disappeared. Thus, I returned to Santo Domingo and filed my backtracking dispatches, convinced that the invasion force not only had not taken Cap-Haïtien but also, after a rapid incursion, had all but vanished. Adding insult to injury was a cable I received from *New York Times* correspondent Richard Eder in Haiti jokingly stating the obvious: "Diederich's two columns marched into *The New York Times* and then into the sea." I sent back a message to Haiti, stating that they were "marching to Eder's drums." (The Haitian Army officers escorting the foreign newsmen were quoted in a story by Eder as saying that the drums had told them that there were no rebels in Haitian territory.) The "invasion" in fact proved to be short-lived and a comedy of errors. Finally, I managed to piece the facts together:

At 11 p.m., August 2, the Congos and other exiles had been packed aboard a huge Dominican Army truck at the Sierra Prieta camp. They lumbered across the island to a rendezvous with Cantave and his officers in a little clearing off a side road north of Dajabon, still in the Dominican

Republic but away from any inquisitive eyes. There they were issued khaki uniforms and new boots. For the broad-footed Haitian peasants most of the boots were too small.

This strange-looking army promptly shed their new boots, competed among themselves for shade, and rested the following day. That night they were ordered back onto the large truck and transported farther north to a point where the Massacre River spills into Manzanillo Bay. Only when they were about to plunge into the river up to their necks and wade across into Haitian territory were they issued their weapons, mostly U.S. Springfield rifles, with 150 bullets each.

These worse-for-wear weapons had made the rounds of more than one Caribbean revolutionary enterprise. Seized by Fidel Castro from the Cuban Army when he came to power, the guns had been reissued to the Cuba-based Dominican revolutionary group that invaded the Dominican Republic on June 14, 1959, only to be captured by Trujillo forces. Now Dominican soldiers had reissued the hand-me-down rifles to a new, ill-trained, confused band bent on invading Haiti.

At daybreak on August 5, the invaders moved along the Haitian coast to the little rope-making town of Derac across the bay from Ft. Liberté, part of the American-operated Plantation Dauphin. Derac fell without a shot's being fired, but several undisciplined invaders disobeyed orders and shot two militiamen and a soldier at one outpost. As *Time* recorded, this attempt "made more headlines than it did progress."

Among the force were several ex-Haitian Army officers who had joined Cantave. One of them, former Port-au-Prince Police Chief Col. Pierre Paret, wore his colonel's uniform into battle. Lt. Col. Rene Léon, second-in-command of Cantave's army, who had worked on the Dauphin plantation before fleeing with his pregnant wife, commandeered several of Derac's cordage and sisal factory jeeps and trucks for the assault on Ft. Liberté.

Subsequently, Cantave sent a captured soldier to advise the commander of the little Ft. Liberté garrison to surrender or else. The commander, a Lt. Thomas, sent back a very Haitian reply: "If you feel *garçon* [man] enough, come and try." The lieutenant then ordered his men to slip out of the garrison and take cover in old colonial ruins near the seashore. The defenders fired a few stray shots at the invaders, but there was no battle per se.

As for the invaders, their bazooka jammed, as did their .30-caliber machine gun after firing a single round. One rebel inexpertly tossed a grenade, and the shrapnel tore a piece out of Lt. Col. Léon's behind. With a lack of firepower and concerned that the troops at the nearby garrison at Ouanaminthe had not joined him to oust Duvalier, Cantave—instead of advancing on Cap-Haïtien—ordered a retreat back to the Dominican Republic.

The retreating invaders split into two groups. Lt. Col. Léon and his men bore through the fields of green sisal plants in the commandeered vehicles and then plunged into the Massacre River, losing their weapons and ammunition in the crossing at the deepest point, near the U.S. Granada Fruit Plantation at Manzanillo.

Meanwhile, General Cantave's force headed back on a more direct route and almost collided with a company of soldiers sent out to engage them. The two groups avoided contact. The troops from the Ouanaminthe garrison pretended not to notice the rebels and continued their march. Several of Cantave's officers wanted to speak with the soldiers and encourage them to join the anti-Duvalier fight, but Cantave said they should attack them. Cantave and his officers compromised and let the soldiers go by without challenging them to a fight.

*　　　*　　　*

President Bosch, understandably upset by the news of Cantave's invasion, however amateurish, called the OAS to investigate. The Dominican Army brass was unhappy with Cantave, who had promised them he would take Cap-Haïtien by sundown that first day. In turn, Cantave was unhappy with the Dominican military. He complained that they had provided firearms that belonged in a museum, not on the field of battle.

The OAS called an emergency meeting in Washington on August 6 to hear Haiti's charges of the "new aggression" by the Dominican Republic. Duvalier accused Bosch of allowing the invasion to be launched from Dominican territory. The Dominican ambassador denied the charges, and once more the OAS investigating commission headed for Hispaniola.

The official communiqué out of Port-au-Prince was accurate about some of the facts, even naming former Haitian officers who participated in the invasion, but then, getting carried away, the palace version stated that several of the rebels "fled, throwing themselves into the sea."

Ex-Haitian diplomat Verna provided more vaudeville, this time for the OAS investigating commission as well as for foreign and Dominican newsmen. The fact that the entire Cantave force had returned to the Dominican Republic was concealed from the commission. Instead, the OAS members were taken to a palm-thatched lean-to at the Haitian-Dominican border near Dajabon, where eighteen Haitians relaxed in the shade. One introduced himself as a Haitian soldier who had defected and joined the rebels. He spoke just enough English to be understood and was interviewed by the OAS delegation and reporters for the major U.S. television networks and other media. Asked where Cantave was, the Haitian answered by tossing his head backward in the direction of the distant blue mountains of Haiti. Cantave, he said, was in Haiti.

The Dajabon garrison commander, Col. Garrido, gruffly told the OAS representatives and newsmen that they could ask the Haitians all the questions they wished, that there was nothing to hide. The Haitian defector, who gave his name as Marc Sylvain, told stories of the stirring courage of the invaders armed with only a few tommy guns and grenades, and how the populace had joined them armed with only machetes. As in his case, Sylvain stressed, the poor people were desperate for freedom.

The only thing wrong with this picture was that Sylvain was not his name, and his nom-de-guerre was Timothe; moreover, he was not a defector, but an exile. The only "army" Timothe knew was Cantave's force. As he talked convincingly to the OAS, the Haitian exile force was resting peacefully not far away at Loma de Cabrera on Dominican territory. Timothe could well have had an acting career, but he was later killed in another Cantave invasion, an attack on Ouanaminthe.

Following the collapse of the first incursion, *The New York Times* commented in an editorial, "Haiti remains Haiti." Duvalier interpreted this as an insult. He called in his new aide, a chameleon newsman named Gerard de Catalogne, who had been advisor to several Haitian presidents. De Catalogne had just returned from Europe on a mission for Papa Doc that included decorating every French newsman who would accept the distinction. De Catalogne quickly cranked out a reply to the *Times* that rankled the U.S. In part it said, "The United States thinks they can treat the

Negroes of Haiti as they treat the people of color in America. We are Africans by race, French by language, and American only by geography."

Meanwhile, Cantave pleaded with his Dominican military friends for another chance, saying that one battle had been lost but the war should continue. Again without Bosch's knowledge, Cantave's little army remained in business and moved to a border camp at Don Miguel almost a stone's throw from the frontier. The general lived in a little tobacco shed, and his soldiers slept on the ground under palm fonds.

The second incursion was led by Lt. Col. Rene Léon. With a column of 72 men, this attack had been carefully timed to take place on August 16, during the celebration of "Restoration Day," the anniversary of the Dominican Republic's liberation from Spanish rule. President Bosch was to be visiting the border town of Capotillo, where the insurrection against the Spanish rulers had begun on August 16, 1863. There he received a 21-gun salute from the Dominican Army, and the Air Force flew overhead in review. In preparations for the festivities, the Dominican Army broadcast advisories to the border residents over national radio, in French and Kreyól as well as Spanish, that the border celebrations would include cannon fire and they should not to be alarmed. It was to be a cover for more serious gunfire.

At dusk the night before the celebration, August 15, Léon's force crossed into Haiti and, guided by a peasant, climbed up a mountain to the pleasant little coffee town of Mont-Organisé. Unknown to the invaders, only a medical corpsman—a corporal—and two Army privates defended the town's small garrison. The town's regular 18-man Army garrison had been transferred to Cap-Haïtien the day before, and replacements had not arrived. Lt. Col. Léon took the town by surprise, and the privates fled in their underwear. The corporal-medic switched sides and informed the invaders that the new troops coming to garrison the town were on their way.

Once again indiscipline and lack of training proved the rebels undoing. Although the winding mountain road was perfect for an ambush of the government forces, as the Kamokens lay in wait for the soldiers to fall into the ambush, one trigger-happy invader fired too soon. With the element of surprise gone, and fearing themselves being surrounded and attacked by a superior force with superior firepower, the exile force once again retreated. Lt. Col. Léon himself gave the order to withdraw. Some of Léon's men remained in the town celebrating with confiscated rum the liberation of the town. Two local Macoutes were killed; five of their homes were burned to the ground. When the rebel stragglers finally crossed back into the Dominican Republic, they had with them some 50 villagers who feared retribution by the Duvalier forces. Ironically, as the invaders withdrew, they came upon more than two dozen armed exiles prepared to cross into Haiti and reinforce them at Mont-Organisé, but it was too late.

Haitian Foreign Minister René Chalmers protested to the OAS, threatening again to take Haiti's case to the U.N. At an emergency meeting of the OAS Council, Chalmers called on the OAS to appoint a committee to supervise the border area and prevent further such incursions. The Dominican representative, Dr. Arturo Calventi, again denied the charges of aggression, declaring that they had been made "by a dictatorship that has violated every basic Inter-American principle and which is hardly in a position to accuse others." The Council adjourned without taking immediate action but suggested that the investigating committee appointed to look into the August 5 invasion should also handle the August 16 incident.

*   *   *

On August 22, 1963, after two weeks in Haiti covering the invasion story for the *Sunday Telegraph* of London, British author Graham Greene arrived in Santo Domingo. (Greene's report, "Nightmare Republic," appeared on September 18, and his vivid account of life in Haiti during this period prompted a bitter verbal attack on the author by Papa Doc.) I picked up Greene, whom I had known from his two earlier trips to Haiti, at the Santo Domingo airport.

When Greene left for England three days later, there was just the slightest glint in his pale blue eyes that told me, "Yes I am interested in pursuing the story." The story became his devastating book *The Comedians*.

In Haiti, on August 23, a special session of Papa Doc's rubberstamp legislature officially suspended "constitutional guarantees" of individual rights and awarded Duvalier "extraordinary powers" for six months. Since there had been no guarantees of individual rights anyway, and since Duvalier already possessed complete power, these measures were hardly earthshaking news. More substantive was a decree officially stripping 54 Haitians classified as enemies of the regime of their citizenship and property. Among the 54 were Cantave and his officers and former president Paul Magloire, as well as the heads of the known non-military exile organizations. The Macoutes had already been busy looting houses of the "enemies of the state." After each exile raid, more property turned up in Macoute hands and more people who were suspected as sympathizers were jailed or had disappeared.

The legislative session had also been staged for the benefit of the OAS committee, which returned to investigate Haiti's charges. A crowd of government employees was assembled to cheer each speaker in the legislative chambers calling for action against the exiles.

To demonstrate his capability of keeping his offensive going, Cantave sent a third group across the border and into Haiti. An inexperienced force of 18 men who had missed the Mont-Organisé expedition executed a quick daytime raid. They raced into the village of Ferrier, killed the mayor, and raced back to the safety of Dominican soil. Following the attack on Ferrier, Duvalier ordered more Macoutes and troops into the north, but he was careful not to weaken his defenses in the capital, regarding the frontier attacks as a possible diversion for a major assault on Port-au-Prince.

Meanwhile, Cantave's force had grown to more than 200 men who had undergone stepped-up training. At midnight on August 26, a promise of arms and munitions from the CIA materialized literally out of the sky. Col. Garrido, accompanied by two of Cantave's officers, went to a clearing not far from the military airfield some two miles from Dajabon, lit flares, and waited. Exactly at midnight the drone of a large aircraft grew louder, and then the plane flew in low from the coast. It made two passes, parachuting crates of arms and ammunition; these were loaded onto a truck and transported to Col. Garrido's house, where they were stored. The arms were brand new.

No sooner had the arms landed than an argument developed between Garrido and Cantave. The Haitian general wanted his men to familiarize themselves and train with the new arms immediately, while Garrido, for his own reasons, initially refused, saying that the exiles would get the arms only when they launched their next attack. Cantave won the dispute, threatening to cut off Garrido's $400 weekly compensation that the Haitians were paying him for camp expenses. The Haitians began training with weapons they had only dreamed about: mortars, bazookas, M-1 rifles, M-3 submachine guns, and .30-caliber machineguns.

The OAS committee ultimately submitted its investigative report on the incidents on Hispaniola. It offered a peace plan that called on Haiti to be more careful in observing the rights of diplomatic asylum and to speed up the granting of safe-conduct passes out of the country for asylum seekers. (The total population of asylum seekers was reduced at least somewhat in September when Duvalier released a dozen from the embassies of Brazil, Chile, Ecuador, and Guatemala. They included three officers—Lt. Col. Yves Cham, Maj. Fritz Hodgson, and Lt. Claude Edeline.) The OAS also urged the Dominicans to prevent subversive activities by Haitian exiles on their territory and to take special measures to prevent exile border raids.

Duvalier was not impressed with the OAS report because it did not specifically condemn the Dominicans, and thus he rejected it out of hand. Early in September, Foreign Minister Chalmers submitted a letter to the U.N. Security Council requesting that it consider Haitian charges against the Dominican Republic. He warned that the dispute could "threaten hemisphere security and international peace." Haiti called for a U.N. investigation, contending that "The regional system [OAS] having failed, it is now appropriate for Haiti to bring her case to the United Nations."

While the Dominican-Haitian frontier situation simmered, a quieter crisis flared on another front. For some time there had been an upswing in the number of Haitian refugees trying to flee by boat to the islands of the Bahamas. Bahamian officials regarded their arrival as illegal entry and when possible shipped the refugees back to Haiti. It became a profitable business for certain boat owners who charged $30 per head for the trip. Clément Benoit, former Haitian consul in Nassau and a schoolteacher by profession, unilaterally declared himself the leader of the thousands of Haitians who did manage to remain in the Bahamas. He declared he had a plan of action against Duvalier, but Benoit precipitated his own expulsion from the Bahamas by announcing that he had organized a 3,000 member anti-Duvalier invasion force. Clément Benoit's invasion force caused a flurry of concern in Port-au-Prince, but the Bahamian authorities concluded that it was all "a figment of Benoit's imagination."

Cantave continually worried that President Bosch would learn of his camp and dismantle it once again. But the cooperation of members of the Dominican Army high command managed to keep a tight lid on the Cantave operation. How was it possible that Bosch didn't learn of Cantave's continued presence? Bosch was preoccupied by multiple problems, which included a threat to his presidency. A well-orchestrated campaign was underway to portray the democratic President as soft on Communists and even "pro-Communist" because he refused to get tough with leftists. Trujillo's powerful right-wing military machine was still in place. Like the Mafia, it knew how to keep its secrets.

CHAPTER 7

The Battle of Ouanaminthe

It was the Dominican Army that chose Gen. Cantave's next target and even set the date: Ouanaminthe, September 22, 1963.

News of an impending exile attack spread through Haiti, prompting Duvalier to reinforce his garrison in the border town. When Cantave hedged on the September 22 date, the Dominican officers said he had no choice: attack or disband. Some of Cantave's officers pleaded with him to ignore Ouanaminthe and instead move south and initiate a guerrilla-style action in the hills above Port-au-Prince. They believed it was foolish to undertake such a frontal attack on a dug-in foe in the well-defended Haitian fort across the river. But Cantave was not prepared physically to lead a guerrilla campaign even if he had been free to do so, and the Dominican military restricted the Haitian exile activities to this northern theater. It proved to be more theater for the Haitians than they had bargained for.

Col. Garrido was described as effusive and held out the promise of air and even artillery support to Cantave if needed. A Dominican plane would be painted with exile markings, he said, and the Haitian fort was well within Garrido's artillery range. He could lob a few shells in to help, if necessary. These assurances proved to be false promises.

At 4 p.m. on September 22, Cantave's army was ordered to assemble and was issued khaki uniforms. Except for 15 porters, all 210 men were armed. Some members of the force had flown to the Dominican Republic from exile in Puerto Rico, and several had traveled from New York.

Cantave's officers carried M-3 "grease guns," as the submachine guns were called, and .45 automatic pistols as side arms. There were 13 .30 caliber machine guns, mortar squads, and bazooka teams, plus all the ammunition the force could carry.

Cantave's troops were transported in four trucks downriver, and at 10 p.m., on a moonlit night, they waded across the Massacre River into Haiti. A Dominican sergeant assigned as guide led the first platoon across; upon reaching the Haitian side, he raised his rifle and fired a single shot. The rebels hit the ground, thinking they were already under attack. Equipped this time with walkie-talkies, Cantave contacted the lead platoon and angrily demanded to know what had happened. When a lieutenant explained, Cantave's voice crackled back, "*En avant* [keep moving] even if we have been betrayed." The shot, according to the battle veterans, was no accident. There was a general feeling in the ranks that the Dominican sergeant had tipped their hand, that the shot was a signal to the Haitian troops warning them that Cantave's force was back in Haiti. The Dominican sergeant insisted that it was only a signal to the rest of Cantave's troops that the first platoon had made it across the river to Haiti.

Worse still was that the force faced a long march across a savannah to Ouanaminthe. It was rough going, even with the benefit of moonlight, and became rougher still when clouds began to obscure the moon. Col. Léon, second in command, collapsed from what was believed to be a heart attack and was left behind with a former Haitian medical student.

The night march tramping through thick, thorny bayahonde was exhausting. As they closed in on Ouanaminthe at daybreak, they met peasants off to tend their gardens. The peasants warned the Kamokens that Ouanaminthe was expecting them and reported that a large number of soldiers—much greater than the rebels had expected—were manning the fort.

Half of Cantave's force had the two-story, buff-colored army barracks in their sights by 6:00 a.m., but the first shot in the attack, a bazooka round, fell well short of its target and government troops answered with a barrage of .50 caliber machine-gun fire. The defending soldiers used the same tactics the Army had used at Ft. Liberté. They had moved out of the barracks to easily defend dug-in positions—the cemetery, a school—and had even placed one light machine gun in a huge tree dominating the field of fire.

The following descriptive account of the battle was provided by Fred Baptiste and several other participants:

As the bullets began to fly the attackers again seemed to have no coordinated plan. Cantave himself made what appeared to be a suicidal attack on the fort, firing his carbine as he ran until a self-appointed bodyguard knocked the general to the ground to save him. The defenders had prepared their field of fire well, cutting down all the vegetation and making it difficult for the exiles to find safety. One rebel lieutenant who reached a trench found it was not empty but bobbing with steel helmets like some long green beetle. He managed to retreat amidst a volley of bullets. One platoon made it to within a few yards of the fort and was met by a group of *milice* who yelled and beckoned them to enter the fort to be killed. They also retreated. Cantave received word that the platoon assigned to seize the little military airstrip had failed. The mortar platoon had difficulty finding the range, and their shells sailed over the defenders and into the town of Ounanaminthe.

At 10 a.m., a Dominican Air Force P-51 made two passes over the battlefield. It was not an exile-support plane, however, and it took no hostile action against the Haitian defenders, who fired at it on both passes. Obviously reconnoitering, the vintage World War II fighter craft banked and flew away. Though the battle was one of the fiercest the Haitians had mounted after five hours of fighting, and with the expected aid from Col. Garrido still not having materialized, Cantave ordered the retreat. Dehydrated and parched with thirst from a night and day without water, many of his retreating men threw themselves into the Massacre River and drank its muddy contents.

One platoon attacking the fort, and led by Fred Baptiste, had skirted the cemetery and did not hear the order to quit. Baptiste was in a platoon commanded by Bernard Sansaricq who Baptiste admired, mistakenly, as a "graduate from West Point." Sansaricq had earlier become separated from his platoon and disappeared, and Baptiste took over command. Baptiste and his platoon fought on through the day. Some pockets of defenders were eliminated, but most were too well dug in to rout. Deftly firing a .30 caliber machine gun, Jean Sejour slew a group of militiamen who had taken shelter under an army truck. (The young exile was to become one of the casualties of the Dominican Civil War in 1965, fighting the Inter-American Peace Force from the San Anton commando in Santo Domingo.)

Baptiste and practically every member of his platoon suffered wounds, but carried the battle on into the late afternoon when they realized they were alone. At 2:00 p.m., a Haitian Air Force plane had flown over the battlefield and landed at the military airstrip—sign enough for Baptiste and his men that this first objective had not been taken. Fighting a rear-guard action to remove the wounded who had been left behind by the main rebel force, Baptiste gradually disengaged Duvalier's troops.

Early in the battle a Haitian Army .50 caliber machine gun placed on top of the Haitian custom house across the river from Dajabon had opened fire on a group of invaders who had gotten scared and retreated back across the river. The Haitian machine gunner's bullets had hit the façade of the Dominican customs building at the other end of the bridge as well as a schoolhouse in Dajabon, and many in the Dominican border town mistakenly believed they were under attack by Duvalier. Reports from Dajabon that the area was under Haitian "bombardment" quickly spread to Santo Domingo.

President Bosch was advised that Dajabon was under a Haitian attack. Foreign Minister Hector Garcia Godoy called in the diplomatic corps to acquaint them with what was supposedly taking place. He described the situation between Haiti and his country as "very grave," declaring that Dajabon's 8,000 inhabitants had fled in panic. Official Dominican radio echoed reports of a Haitian attack and announced that President Bosch was once again giving an ultimatum to Duvalier. This time Haiti had three hours in which to cease the aggression and punish the guilty parties, beginning with Duvalier. The ultimatum was broadcast repeatedly in Kreyòl for Haitians, with the added warning that Haitians living in the vicinity of the National Palace in Port-au-Prince should vacate the area because it might be bombed. The Dominican Air Force reported that it was in full readiness.

As the misinformed Bosch government dealt with what it thought was an urgent matter of Haitian aggression, the remnants of Cantave's inva-sion force were straggling back across the Massacre River to the safety of the Dominican Republic. Dominican soldiers, aware of the resale value of firearms, stripped the Cantave soldiers of weapons as they clam-bered up the river's bank. (Weapons too large to conceal, such as bazookas and .30 caliber machine guns, were confiscated by the

Dominican military and stacked in neat rows in the archway of the Customs house on the Dominican side of the international bridge, in full view of the Haitian border.) Gen. Cantave was described as a lost soul, his shoulders slumped, a picture of defeat in his blood-soaked uniform.

Fifteen of his men did not return. Thirteen were killed in the fighting, and two who were wounded were reported by witnesses as having been taken prisoners and, despite the gravity of their wounds, made to load the dead on a truck. These witnesses said the wounded men were then piled onto the corpses and taken to Cap-Haîtien where reportedly the pair was later executed.

One of the first raiders to die was a brash and tough Haitian Army veteran with an unforgettable name—Capt. Blucher Philogenes—who had often bragged that he was immune to bullets. His putative charm ran out before Ounanaminthe, where he was cut almost in two by machine-gun fire. On Duvalier's personal orders, according to reports reaching the Dominicans, an officer cut off Philogenes head, placed it in a bucket of ice, and dispatched the head by special plane to Port-au-Prince. At least in superstition-prone Haiti, where the dispensing of gossip is one of the few free pleasures of life, only Duvalier knew the truth, and he was a master at exploiting this phenomenon.

Fear generated by such terrifying tales acted as a psychological curfew, keeping frightened peasants indoors at night. Whether true or false, the stories were effective in pulling down a Voudou curtain of fear over much of rural Haiti, where magic is real and there is little protection against the supernatural.

When a plane carrying high-ranking Dominican Army investigators finally arrived from Santo Domingo, along with newsmen, to investigate Haiti's "aggression," the investigators encountered a cool Gen. Cantave, nattily attired in a light business suit and carrying an overnight bag stuffed with Kent cigarettes. He was placed under arrest.

The high-ranking officers of the Dominican Army commission were greeted by a jovial, expansive Col. Garrido, a picture of innocence, who explained that the shooting was really nothing more than Haitians firing at Haitian rebels fleeing into the Dominican Republic. However, back in Santo Domingo, Bosch had already fired off a request to the OAS in Washington to investigate the reported Haitian machine gun attack on the

Dominican Republic. Bosch's move threatened to reveal before this legal hemispheric body the embarrassing history of the four Cantave-led rebel attacks from Dominican territory against Haiti—and the involvement of members of the Dominican Army high command.

Yet the Dominican military brass was not perturbed. They had other plans. And unknowingly, Gen. Cantave and his little Haitian rebel army had played their part.

Their incursions into Haiti had set the stage and provided a pseudo-rationale for the Dominican military machine that Trujillo had left behind to carry out its payback against Juan Bosch. It was obvious that Cantave had been duped by his Dominican brothers-in-arms. The Dominican public was not wise to the army's intrigue, nor were all of the high-ranking military, many of whom—including the coup leader, Col. Elias Wessin y Wessin—believed it was Bosch, not a segment of the army, that collaborated with Cantave in his war against Duvalier and placed the country in a dangerous international crisis.

Two days after Cantave's failed attack across the Haitian border on Ouanaminthe, the Dominican generals overthrew President Bosch in a coup d'état.

While the ouster of Bosch by the military quickly obscured the Ouanaminthe episode, and there was little public realization of the role played by the Dominican military in it, the "collaboration" was all part of its coup. The day after Cantave's attack, as Dominicans observed the feast of their patron saint, the Virgin of the Mercedes, there were rumors of an impending coup led by the Air Force. Bosch had stated the month before that a coup would last "less time than a cockroach in a chicken pen."

At 7:00 a.m. on September 25, the Dominican military announced that Bosch had been deposed and later in the day proclaimed the installation of a civilian junta to replace him. In its communiqué, the military endeavored to justify its coup, stating that there was "a chaotic situation," explaining that the country was saddled with "incapacity," and complaining of "dangerous improvisation of international incidents which, in addition to endangering the prestige of the Republic, could have led to a serious and unnecessary international conflict." The Haitian rebels had been used.

Cantave had to sweat it out incommunicado in detention in the February 27 Army Headquarters in Santo Domingo until he was placed on a plane to New York on October 18. He left as he had arrived, in a mood of despair for his army and his country.

The Dominican military had always feared Bosch, the democratic leftist, and above all had sought to retain its privileges. Antagonism toward Bosch had likewise built up among segments of the Roman Catholic Church and business sectors. Loud accusations of Communist infiltration in his government bordered on a campaign of disinformation that was taken up by elements of the conservative U.S. press. The embarrassing Haitian intrigues, of which Bosch was innocent, made him an easy target and provided one of the pretexts for the coup.

Bosch was shunted off to exile aboard a Dominican Navy frigate to the French Caribbean island of Guadeloupe where I interviewed him seated under a sea grape tree. He said that in the final analysis there was little he could have done to prevent the coup, arguing that the root cause was not the military's "fear of communism but their fear of losing their privileges."

Still in exile a year later, Bosch wrote a book about his seven months as the Dominican Republic's first freely elected president in 32 years, calling it *The Unfinished Experiment.* In his book, Bosch attempted to analyze Papa Doc:

> Psychologically . . . Duvalier is the type of man found in primitive societies. The more power he acquires, the more he is filled with haughtiness that day by day transforms him physically, numbing him. So that he resembles nothing so much as a puppet that keeps swelling and swelling until it must either flop over on its back or explode. His eyelids droop, his gaze becomes cold, and his face takes on
> a sheen as if a spell has been cast over him. His face gradually becomes frozen and his voice takes on an increasingly commanding tone that becomes lower and lower and more and more terrifying. In such creatures, the effects of power are more than physical; there are also corresponding changes in the soul, which gradually desensitize them to all human feeling, until they become only receptacles of uncontrolled passions. These men are dangerous. They create an aura of sorcery. They deny being simple human beings, mortal and

fallible, and consider themselves living representatives of the dark forces that govern the world.

"Anyone who doubts my description or analysis," wrote Bosch, "has only to glance at a photograph of Duvalier taken in, say, 1955, and then another made in 1965. They will show two different men, the Haitian version of Oscar Wilde's Dorian Gray." It is doubtful that Duvalier did not read Bosch's appraisal of himself, but nor would he have cared. Bosch was talented with the pen, but Duvalier excelled at politics and understood the military. Through this period, it was Duvalier who commanded the military, not his heavy-set, slow-moving titular commander, Gen. Constant.

As for Papa Doc himself, delighted at the overthrow of Bosch, Duvalier decided against pressing his own international protests, preferring not to stir anger within the new Dominican leadership. The remnants of Cantave's little army, except the wounded who remained in the Dajabon infirmary, were loaded onto two large sugarcane trucks from the Esperanza sugar mill and once again taken back to Santo Domingo, where they were left penniless and without a new patron to fight yet another day. The old soldiers and their orthodox invasion attempts had failed; now it was the turn of Haiti's youth to try new tactics against Duvalier.

CHAPTER 8

Dreaming on a Dominican Chicken Farm

A handsome black face with a thin mustache looked out at the curious from the wall of Port-au-Prince's Hotel de Ville in 1991. Fred Baptiste's image, along with other photographs of some of the victims of the Duvalier dictatorship, revealed nothing of Baptiste's guerrilla past. The young man next to Baptiste in the line of photographs, with a sheepish grin, was Reneld Baptiste, Fred's younger brother and a fervent follower. Missing from the ghostly gallery along the Hotel de Ville's walls evoking Haiti's recent past were other images of Fred Baptiste's small band of devoted anti-Duvalier Dominican-based rebels—*Les Kamoken.*

Fred Baptiste's war against Papa Doc is a reminder that successful guerrillas become heroes but those who fail are often condemned to anonymity. Like so many before and after him, Baptiste believed he could lead a revolution and become Haiti's new leader. Instead, his remains have long since been disinterred by dogs or the wind like so many victims of Ft. Dimanche.

A maverick revolutionary, free of the political ideology of either the doctrinal left or right, Fred Baptiste was born in Jacmel on December 29, 1933. He attended the town's *Lycée Pinchinat* and became a mathematics teacher at the Industrial School in his home town. (Years later, in exile in the Dominican Republic, Baptiste confessed to me that he would have liked to attend Haiti's Military Academy or to become an engineer, but that he did not have the marks that would have allowed him to enter the Academy or university.)

After Haiti's presidential campaign of 1957, Baptiste became obsessed with the desire to overthrow Duvalier. Like fellow Jacmelians, he firmly believed that Papa Doc had stolen the election. Jacmel was considered pro-Louis Déjoie, who had family and business in the town.

Baptiste undertook open guerrilla warfare against Papa Doc on June 9, 1959, with an attack on the Army post guarding Jacmel's small grass airstrip. His plan had called for disarming the soldiers, capturing the airport, and persuading the Haitian exiles in Castro's Cuba to fulfill their longstanding promise to invade Haiti and fight Duvalier. With a safe landing field, Baptiste believed the battle would begin. However his mini-uprising failed when one of the attackers froze with knife in hand over a sleeping sentry.

Fred escaped, but his brother Reneld, then 22, was captured and spent four months in prison. In September 1962, with installation of Juan Bosch as the first freely elected president of the Dominican Republic after the 31-year Trujillo dictatorship, the Baptiste brothers crossed into the Dominican Republic to join Haitian exiles in the struggle against Duvalier. They slipped over the frontier near the Dominican mountain border post of Aguacate.

They found that things were hardly politically verdant on the other side. The mostly young Haitian exiles assembled in Santo Domingo lived in a veritable cocoon, driven by powerful emotions that made the impossible appear not only possible but probable. With a few good men and rudimentary weaponry, they believed, they could duplicate Fidel Castro's success in nearby Cuba. But Haiti was not Cuba. Castro's rebellion against dictator Fulgencio Batista, launched in Cuba's jungle-shrouded Sierra Maestra, was not only popular but could draw on logistical support from friends in the U.S. as well as peasants. The Haitian rebels had no such logistical support and, in the barren hills of Haiti, the peasants were too poor and intimidated to offer aid.

While Baptiste's Kamokens enjoyed freedom to plot, their own survival in the Dominican Republic was tenuous. After the breakup of the first exile camp in Dajabon in May 1963, Baptiste and his colleagues had been dumped back in Santo Domingo and moved into a tiny shack on an embankment at 71 Calle Francisco Enriquez y Carvajal. They had to take turns sleeping on the floor after repairing the roof. They ate "refugee" corn meal distributed by CARE and by the Church World Service charitable agency.

"It was very cold and old, and at the same time, it was raining all the time, and we had to buy some tools to try to repair the chalet, if we can call it that," Baptiste told me a few months later. "We ate almost anything but mostly food distributed by the American people to calm the suffering of the poor. We couldn't sleep all at the same time. There was not enough space and so we took turns."

One Saturday, in early June 1963, Baptiste fell sick and had to be interned at the Padre Billini hospital in downtown Santo Domingo. He was diagnosed with a duodenal ulcer and was hospitalized for two weeks.

Shortly before Baptiste took ill, a Roman Catholic priest who had recently been allowed to leave political asylum in the crowded Dominican embassy residence in Pétionville for exile introduced himself to Baptiste. His name was Father Jean-Baptiste Georges. While Fred Baptiste was in the hospital, his brother Reneld and fellow guerrilla Montero Norbert accepted a proposal by Father Georges that he find a better house for the group. "Just to help you guys," Father Georges told them. The house was in the Villa Duarte neighborhood of Santo Domingo, very pretty, with beds and other amenities provided by the Dominican Red Cross. Fred Baptiste's first Dominican movement, the FLHL, Liberation Front of Free Haitians, was already a year old.

Father Georges had been the first chaplain of the Catholic University students in Port-au-Prince in the 1950s and had built a summer home in Kenscoff for them. While operating the *Maison des Etudiants* on Port-au-Prince's Ruelle Roy in 1956, Father Georges had hidden the then-presidential aspirant and political fugitive, Doc Duvalier, for a time under the strong-arm presidency of Gen. Paul Magloire. The priest and the doctor-politician had plenty of uninterrupted time together to discuss how to remake Haiti. Understanding Father Georges' enthusiasm and passion for education, Duvalier, following his 1957 election, appointed the priest education minister.

However, when Father Georges discovered what he termed the "other side" of Papa Doc, he quit. He finally escaped from house arrest in his hometown of Les Cayes, to asylum in the crowded Dominican embassy residence in Pétionville. Father Georges was eventually permitted to go into exile. His association with the Papa Doc, now wielding power, had turned the well-educated Roman Catholic priest into a rabid opponent who was prepared to devote the rest of his life to ridding Haiti of the man he called a "monster."

Father Georges became the active spiritual father of all anti-Duvalier invasions throughout the sixties. Early in 1964, Father Georges toured South America seeking funds for a liberation army. In Colombia, he told the media that a new invasion force was being prepared and would be in Haiti by year's end.

A graduate of Quebec's Laval University, Father Georges, 45, continued his priestly duties, saying mass daily at Santo Domingo's Altagracia church, where he preached in Spanish on Sundays. In April 1964 Haitian exiles living in Puerto Rico, Venezuela, and the Dominican Republic declared a week of mourning in memory of the "martyrs of Duvalier tyranny," and those who perished in the Duvalier bloodbath of April 26, 1963. Dominicans were invited to a special Mass at the Altagracia church by Father Georges on April 26. Among the attendees was the entire Kamoken force, wearing black arm bands.

Pierre L. Riguad, coordinator of the National Democratic Union (UDN), at a Santo Domingo news conference lamented the fact that the democratic forces in Latin America had "done very little to help the Haitian people rid Haiti of the tyrant Duvalier." Rigaud pointed out that Duvalier had removed himself from the ideals of the Organization of American States (OAS) by proclaiming himself President-for-Life. He charged that Latin American nations watched with "indifference the disintegration of a sister nation."

*   *   *

The fact that all the attacks led by General Cantave and launched from the Dominican Republic in 1963 had failed did not deter Fred Baptiste. He saw them as practical battle experience and felt encouraged to lead his own group against Papa Doc. Though the outcomes increased Baptiste's distrust of the military and politicians, in early 1964 he told the author in Santo Domingo, "Now it is our turn!"

But it was a different time—with Juan Bosch in exile, General Cantave in prison in Santo Domingo, and his penniless exiled officers living in a borrowed loft on the grounds of the capital's Hotel Jaragua, waiting for visas to the United States. The *Congos* had retrieved their machetes and returned to the Dominican *bateys* ("barracks") to cut sugarcane.

Without arms, money, or friends in high places, Baptiste found it essential to make alliances, no matter his personal distaste for the military and politicians. The distaste, in many cases, was mutual, resulting in anarchic disunity among the Haitian exiles. Haitian Marxists, for their part, distrusted Baptiste, viewing him as a dangerous *illumine,* a man who believes only in himself and his "mission." Right-wing exiles, led by former Senator Louis Dejoie, called Baptiste a dangerous communist, wished him dead, and consequently tried to sabotage his efforts to strike at Duvalier.

Moreover, the political climate in post-Cantave Santo Domingo had changed, and Haitian exiles could no longer count on the support of high-ranking Dominican military officers. (In December 1963, Manolo Taverez Justo, leader of June 14 Movement, had taken to the mountains with some of his men, only to be wiped out by the Dominican military. Emilio de Los Santos, the elderly head of the Dominican Trimvirate, had quit in shock as one of his nephews was among the dead. Donald Reid Cabral was named in his place, and his major balancing act became efforts to de-Trujilloize the military.) Finally, in early 1964, Baptiste, after numerous discussions, accepted the formal patronage of Father Georges and ex-Haitian Army officer and diplomat Pierre L. Rigaud. The former wore his Roman collar and the latter presented the imposing bearing of elevated military and diplomatic status. Both were fluent in Spanish. Once again the Baptiste movement underwent a name change. It became known by the grandiose title Haitian Revolutionary Armed Forces (FARH).

There was one small glimmer of outside encouragement. President John F. Kennedy had authorized the U.S. Central Intelligence Agency to proffer some assistance to the Haitian exiles in the Dominican Republic. Kennedy had also approved the training in the United States of young members of Jeune Haiti, the anti-Duvalier group founded in New York, at the CIA's "farm" training facility in Virginia.

*   *   *

Very little has been written concerning the depth and breadth of CIA or DIA (U.S. Defense Intelligence Agency) assistance to the Haitian opposition groups after Cantave's failed venture. The covert aid did appear to be little more than handouts of small stipends to some exiles, possibly with the sole purpose of monitoring their activities. President Kennedy may have decided to hedge U.S. bets in anticipation of a future move against Papa Doc, but this possibility ended with JFK's assassination in November 1963.

The author's own unanticipated introduction to the CIA operation in the Dominican Republic began on the day after my arrival in Santo Domingo in May 1963, to set up shop as a foreign correspondent. A muscular American came up to me as I entered the Hotel El Embajador where I was staying and introduced himself as Neil. He said he was attached to the American embassy and that his job description included trying to help the Haitian exiles. Neil made a point of explaining that he personally sympathized with the exiles' efforts to get rid of Duvalier, but that their efforts in launching attacks on Papa Doc depended on the "green light" from Washington. Apparently the light was then set at yellow.

It was evident that Neil was with the Central Intelligence Agency. I later learned that he had been a paramilitary type who had worked in some covert assignments from the islands off China. As usual, he wasn't telling me the whole story, nor did I expect him to. Neil wondered whether we could compare notes. Anything worthwhile, I replied, he could read in my dispatches in *The New York Times* or on the AP wire. He explained he just didn't want to be caught flatfooted, and would like to call me some time and compare notes. I agreed, as I also needed to know in advance when the light in Washington might turn green and he would be the first to know—at least that is what I believed.

But the light turned suddenly from yellow to green when Cantave made his first invasion in north Haiti and Neil and I were both caught flatfooted. Neil was not even on the island. In fact, he had temporarily left his post in Santo Domingo for the U.S. Virgin Islands on his honeymoon, having just gotten married, or so he said. Prior to departing Santo Domingo, he had asked me whether I knew of any action planned by the Haitian exiles. I honestly hadn't known of any. Neil returned extremely upset. He believed I had concealed the truth from him. I had not.

*   *   *

The following year, in early 1964, Father Georges found another ideal home and training center for Baptiste's Kamokens. It was an abandoned chicken farm twelve miles north of the capital in a rural area known as Villa Mella. The place was rented for the equivalent of $35 a month from one Mario Mathis. (Interestingly, Ramon Caceres, a member of the then-ruling Dominican Triumvirate, owned a neighboring family farm.) As I had a Volkswagen, I took it upon myself as a humanitarian gesture to pick up CARE and Church World Service bags of barley, wheat and cornmeal for the Haitian refugees. I regularly delivered these basic foodstuffs to the chicken farm in Villa Mella.

The Kamokens, with the little money they had, were able to purchase some meat and fruit. The owner of the abandoned chicken farm was surprised when he visited to find that the Haitian refugees, out of their sense of honor, had not stripped his fruit trees on the little farm. He made them a gift of some plantains. The troops slept in the chicken coops and learned the art of guerrilla warfare from a blackboard. There were no firearms in the camp. At night, the rebels played war games in the dark, "tracking" and "attacking" the "enemy" with their wooden sticks. Most, if not all, had been trained in the use of firearms in the Dajabon camps and in several attacks on Haiti. They shared their knowledge with those who had not. The camp learned Morse code but had no radio communications or medical unit or supplies. Nevertheless, spirits were high, especially when the ragtag guerrilla band learned that Fidel Castro had launched his revolution in 1953 from a chicken farm in Siboney, Cuba.

Every morning the Haitian flag was raised at the camp to the singing of the FARH hymn and lowered with ceremony in the evening. With lectures on behavior towards the peasants in the mountains, map reading, and how to find water, the camp could be easily mistaken for a Boy Scout camp but for the grown men assembled.

*   *   *

Another Haitian Roman Catholic priest, Father Jean-Claude Bajeux, then 33, came onto the Dominican scene in March 1964. He soon became the unofficial chaplain to all Haitians in the Dominican Republic. Extremely well-educated, Bajeux had studied theology and philosophy in France, collaborated on several books dealing with the problems of the national clergy in the Third World, and spent five years in Africa teaching and editing a newspaper in Senegal. His Holy Ghost Order sent him back to Haiti in 1962 to teach at Petit Séminaire St. Martial where he became an activist professor of philosophy, editing the Catholic cultural youth magazine *Rond-Point*, as well as directing the Catholic youth center. He helped launch another religious magazine, *Church on the March.*

In July 1963, Father Bajeux, searching for a rental house in which to reestablish the Catholic University student center which had been closed by Duvalier after its founder, Father Georges, became the "enemy," visited the old gingerbread Riobé family home next to Port-au-Prince's Sans Souci Hotel. The Riobés had recently completed building a new residence across from the Sacred Heart church and next to Mr. French's barber shop in Turgeau. Bajeux recalls his visit to Mrs. Riobé and her sister. The setting was a picture of the genteel past. They were seated in the salon which was graced with a grand piano and highly polished mahogany furniture. No, the ladies told the priest, they were not interested in renting the house and they were not sure when they would move into the new home.

Events suddenly changed. A month later Father Bajeux received an urgent message from Mrs. Riobé: "Please come and get the keys." When Father Bajeux and Father Jean-Paul Claude arrived at the Riobé house they found Mrs. Riobé and her sister in a shocked and anguished state, gripped by fear. Not only had Mrs. Riobé's husband been killed; now her only son had died fighting the Duvalier regime. Moreover, she had been made to act as a human shield to force her son to desist from attacking the army from a cave above Kenscoff. She found him dead. Mrs. Riobé and her sister begged the two priests to take them to an embassy. They obliged, but at the Mexican embassy, located above Pétionville, behind the Ibo Lélé hotel, the ambassador, Bernardo Reyes, bargained with them. He complained of the costs of housing refugees. Finally the fearful women, after much haggling, were granted asylum with a down payment of $2,000 cash.

When the two clerics returned to the Riobés' vintage gingerbread house, a Macoute emerged from the garden with his rifle pointed at them. A civilian by the name of Nelson, who said he was in the service of

Windsor Day, the prefect of Port-au-Prince, ordered the priests into a Volkswagen Beetle recently confiscated from Eric Tippenhauer, an earlier victim of the regime. As the prefect was not at his residence, the priests were taken to Ft. Dimanche where they remained from 3 p.m. to 9 p.m., when Archbishop Claudius Angenor arrived. He had gained permission from the Minister of Foreign Affairs and Cults to place the two clerics at the archbishopric under house arrest.

At Ft. Dimanche, Father Bajeux and his fellow priest experienced first-hand the bullying technique of Police Capt. Jean Tassy, who interrogated them while the enigmatic palace enforcer, Pastor Luc Désyr, looked on without moving a single facial muscle. At the archbishopric, Father Jean Hilaire, the palace chaplain, admonished Bajeux for purportedly wasting his time in what he was doing, and advised him to focus instead on acquiring a big new car with four good tires. Bajeux retorted to Hilaire, "If you ever end up in Ft. Dimanche don't call me." Hilaire protested to Papa Doc that Bajeux had threatened him.

After spending 21 days under house arrest, Father Bajeux was freed from confinement and ordered by his superiors to take up priestly duties in the Pétionville Parish. But by February 1964 he was in hiding at the Hotel Villa Kreyól, after Duvalier ordered all print shops not to print *Rond Point,* which Bajeux was editing. Finally, Bajeux was issued a passport and left for exile, initially and briefly in Guadeloupe, then Venezuela and New York.

In March 1964, Bajeux, having heard of the plight of his fellow Haitians refugees and immigrants in the Dominican Republic, arrived in Santo Domingo from New York. He soon established, with the help of prominent Dominicans such as businessman Guido (Yoyo) d'Alessandro, Ephrain Soler Herrera, Dr. Guariones Lopez, and Dr. Pablo Nadal, the "Friendship of Peoples Foundation," to aid Haitians with their myriad problems in the absence of a Haitian consulate. Father Bajeux also had assistance from CASC, the Social Christian Labor Federation based in Caracas, Venezuela. Soon Father Bajeux became a familiar face in Santo Domingo, in his flowing white robe, striding into police or army headquarters demanding the release of some hapless Haitian.

In a survey, Bajeux's Foundation reported that there were from 30,000 to 50,000 Haitians in the Dominican Republic. "Most of the Haitians live," he said in his report, "in the most pitiful conditions of filth and hunger around the sugarcane bateys. Incredibly crowded, the ancient, wooden shacks are totally without sanitation or running water. The mud floors are vermin-infested. The 'lucky' Haitian has a piece of corrugated cardboard to serve as a 'mattress' between him and the damp mud."

Duvalier bagmen were paid $15 a head for each Haitian cane-cutter delivered and received a portion of the cutter's wages—a near-slave trade that netted some $6 to $8 million to Duvalier and his henchmen.

*   *   *

Fred Baptiste's Kamokens were a diverse lot from different parts of Haiti and from various callings. Most had been involved in anti-Duvalier movements inside Haiti, had become suspect, and jumped across the border with the Macoutes on their heels. Some had been soldiers and tradesmen. One was a rural teacher, another a Port-au-Prince policeman. There was even a Haitian veteran of Batista's army. And of course, it was later discovered, one was a Duvalier spy. They were mostly black but several were mulattos and one was of a rich Cap-Haïtien family.

Like all Haitian exile groups the Kamokens suffered from sectarianism and regionalism and failed to build relations with any anti-Duvalierist organizations inside Haiti. Not that any clandestine opposition force in Haiti was prepared to make a pact with the little-known Kamokens. Nor were the groups within Haiti by any means united. The two young Marxist parties still argued dialectics and differences on future tactics to battle the dictatorship. Members of Catholic activist groups such as Haiti Progrès also debated among themselves ways to fight the dictatorship with something other than the mimeograph machine.

Outside Haiti, the exiles lived in an Alice-in-Wonderland environment in which many became delusional concerning the realities of trying to overthrow Papa Doc. One Haitian exile, an auto mechanic by trade, knocked on the author's door one morning to inform him that the American embassy believed that he, the auto mechanic, was the man to lead Haiti. So it was in the Dominican Republic and in New York in 1964.

One day in March 1964, Col. Luther (Fritz) Long, the U.S. officer assigned to the MAAG, the U.S. Military Assistance Group in the

Dominican Republic, telephoned. He needed to talk. "Your Haitian friends," the colonel warned, "have been denounced to Gen. Elias Wessin y Wessin as communists by that Haitian senator, Louis Déjoie." Colonel Long added that the chicken-farm exile camp could expect visitors within a day or two from General Wessin y Wessin's men. General Wessin y Wessin, the right-wing commander of the San Isidro airbase and the armored infantry brigade, was a leader in the coup that overthrew President Juan Bosch.

The news that another Haitian would denounce them did not come as a shock to the Kamokens. They knew that Déjoie was opposed to any Haitian exile group that was not under his leadership. General Wessin y Wessin, an anti-communist zealot, had been told by Déjoie that the Baptiste group was allied with both Castro and Duvalier.

On the same day after receiving the alert from Colonel Long, who was a good friend and a good source, I headed to the local U.S. Information Service (USIS) office. I had decided that the Kamokens needed some literature at the camp. The U.S. Information Service office had a wide range of pamphlets available dealing with President Kennedy's Alliance for Progress program for the Americas. There were some inspiring titles such as *Agrarian Reform in Latin America*. I delivered the U.S. literature, which was in Spanish, to the Villa Mella chicken farm. (Many of the Kreyól- or French-speaking Haitian Kamokens had already mastered Spanish.) Fred Baptiste ordered his men, if they happened to be reading Che Guevara, to "have it disappear."

On Saturday night, March 14, Wessin's soldiers raided the camp. In brutal fashion, they made arrests to the sound of their San Cristobal rifles cracking heads. The sweeping roundup included Haitians living at the Hotel Europa in the capital. The two French soldiers-of-fortune, Andre Riviere and Claude Martin, who were close to Jeune Haiti, were also arrested.

Advised of the raid the following morning, I took an early Sunday drive to Villa Mella to assess the situation. I was accompanied by my wife and our infant son, and also by Paul Arcelin, a coat-and-tie exile who taught French at the Dominican Naval Academy. As we drove by the Villa Mella police post in my VW Beetle, a policeman sounded an alert, crying out, "*Ahi viene el hombre del carrito.*" ("Here comes the man of the little car.") Ordered to stop, we were told that we would not be going further in Villa Mella, that instead a policeman would accompany us to National Police Headquarters in Santo Domingo.

Arcelin and I were escorted into the police palace while my wife was left in the car with the baby. For two hours she waited in the broiling heat of the Volkswagen. Finally, at my urging, an officer agreed that she and the infant should return home rather than suffer heat stroke in the police yard. When the police told her she could go home, she enquired how she was expected to drive the car and hold the baby—there were no baby seats in those days. A plainclothes detective finally drove her home to nearby Calle Rosa Duarte.

Having been denied a request to be jailed together with the Haitians to learn their condition, I was held in the police office. Shortly after midday a high-ranking national police officer arrived and escorted me to the residence of President Donald Reid Cabral. In a touch of high irony, the president had been advised of my arrest while attending a closing meeting of the Inter-American Press Association in nearby Boca Chica, where the topic was press freedom in the Americas.

Over the years I had gotten to know Donald Reid Cabral. A man of Scottish heritage, "Donny," as he was known, was generous, at least with his time. He had been among those who fought to free the country from the remnants of the Trujillo regime. His doctor-brother had been one of the regime's last victims. Donny always managed a smile no matter how tough the situation was. He quickly turned my apprehension into a joke. When, in the midst of our conversation, the British ambassador telephoned to learn "what has happened to Diederich," Donny informed the envoy, "Mr. Ambassador, I have him here with me and I am torturing him with Johnny Walker." (It was actually cognac.)

U.S. Representative Charles Porter of Oregon, known for his anti-Trujillo position in the U.S. Congress, was on a visit to the Dominican Republic and was in Reid's home when I arrived. Porter joined in the laughter. Agreeing to look into the "communist" charges against the Haitian exiles, President Reid Cabral requested that General Wessin send the material evidence to the president's residence right away. A Lieutenant Pou of G2 (Intelligence) of Wessin's forces arrived with an armful of the "communist" literature. It was Donny who, flipping over the pamphlets, discovered the name of the publisher: the "United States Information Service." There was a lot of laughter and considerable embarrassment on the part of Lieutenant Pou. Then came a shock for this author. Pou stated that General Wessin's men had also seized at the chicken farm camp a film of the Haitians being trained in Fidel Castro's Cuba.

The four of us—the president, Congressman Porter, Lieutenant Pou, and I—went to the *Voz Dominicana* broadcast headquarters to view the training film. I had no prior knowledge of this film, and was somewhat apprehensive when it began with scenes in San Juan, Puerto Rico, showing Kamoken Gérard Lafontant acting up for the camera. The next scene had us riveted to the movie screen in the large Trujillo-built radio and TV station. The footage was of easily identified Haitians preparing to fire a bazooka. Then into the frame strode two military officers in charge of the training. It was Lieutenant Pou's turn to be shocked. Pointing at the screen himself in complete surprise, he said in Spanish, "I recognize these officers, they are Dominicans . . . and that's Dajabon." Not wishing to draw Representative Porter into a long domestic intelligence discussion, Donny cut the movie short and announced that from the evidence he had seen the incarcerated Haitian exiles were not communists.

*   *   *

The following morning, I went to the National Palace. The president had ordered the Haitians freed. "Go and see for yourself," Donny said. "They are back at the farm."

Could the president, I asked, loan me a car so I could go and see? "I don't want to go in my little car, they might arrest me again." Before climbing into the back of the long, black presidential limousine and giving directions to the chauffeur, I asked Donny if Wessin's men could return the boots, clothing and equipment they had taken from the Chicken Farm. "I cannot ask them that . . . I can't antagonize them." By them, he meant Wessin y Wessin, his major supporter.

The chauffeur confirmed it was a car used often by *El Jefe* (Trujillo). However, President Reid, the chauffeur noted, was a car importer by trade, and was in no manner impressed with old presidential automobiles.

The limousine drew stares, and upon reaching the police post at Villa

Mella, I instructed the driver to slow to a crawl and stop. The policeman on duty actually saluted the car; I wound down the window and returned his salute. It was the same policeman who had stopped me and my family the morning before. He obviously couldn't believe his eyes, and appeared hopelessly perplexed. I made sure he and other policemen who had emerged from the post heard my order to the driver, "*Vamonos a la finca.*" On reaching the chicken farm I told the driver to enter. The gate proved too small and we uprooted a post with the right fender entering— to the cheers of the Kamokens who for a moment thought the president was honoring them with a visit. My visit in the presidential limousine afforded the Kamokens a certain amount of protection among the local constabulary, but it was good to return to Santo Domingo and my chartreuse Beetle.

*   *   *

Following this series of contretemps, Father Georges stepped up the Haitian rebels' operation. His priestly duties had taught him how to successfully collect funds, and the money he had derived from his Latin America trip helped in the purchasing of arms—rifles, munitions, and explosives—from a Cuban anti-Castro exile source in Miami.

Because of his fluency in English, Gérard Lafontant, considered the "intellectual" of the group, was assigned the task of taking delivery of the arms shipment in Miami and moving it to a safe house near the Miami River. Lafontant's adventures in Miami were not unlike one of the comedy movies he used to show at the Paramount, his family's Port-au-Prince cinema.

The Cuban exile gave Lafontant a garbage truck in which to move the arms. The illicit arms dealer was not a generous person, and Lafontant, who did not have a valid driver's license, ran out of gasoline on U.S. interstate highway I-95. Perhaps it was Lafontant's heavy Haitian accent and his cover story that he was shipping the garbage truck to Haiti in order to keep Port-au-Prince clean that persuaded the Florida Highway Patrol officer to "rescue" Lafontant. The officer didn't ask Lafontant for his driver's license or take a peep into the garbage truck. Lafontant completed the arms drop without further incident at a storehouse next to the

Miami River. The arms would later be loaded onto the 235-foot *Johnny Express,* a freighter belonging to the Antillean Marine Shipping Corporation owned by Teofilio Babun Selman.

On his return to Santo Domingo, Lafontant, carrying illegal communication radios and some small military items, was standing before a not-so-friendly Dominican customs officer at the Santo Domingo airport. As the agent was about to open his bags, Lafontant dropped a bottle of vodka that exploded into pieces, showering vodka all over the agent and Lafontant. The disgusted customs officer waved Lafontant on, fearful that the arriving Haitian passenger was a walking Molotov cocktail. Knowing Lafontant's fondness for hard liquor, neither Fred Baptiste nor other Kamokens believed Lafontant had sacrificed a full bottle of vodka merely to distract the customs officer from potentially incriminating baggage contents.

There was another arms delivery destined for the Kamokens, but it was hijacked by two members of the Haitian political left. Two thousand dollars had been paid on behalf of the Kamokens to a member of Jeune Haiti in New York to purchase four NATO-issued automatic FAL rifles and ship them to Santo Domingo in a refrigerator. The rifles arrived by ship in March 1964, cleverly hidden in the inner padding of the refrigerator. The accompanying ammunition was ingeniously stowed inside auto batteries. The guns and ammo were unloaded by the Kamokens, but a few days later were claimed by longtime Haitian exiles, poet Jacques Viau and Lionel Vieux, who threatened to blow up the house in which the arms were stored unless they were handed over. Not wishing to get into a fight, the Kamokens caved and relinquished the guns. Viau and Vieux were to use the guns fighting on the Constitutionalist side in the Dominican Civil War the following year.

*   *   *

Back across the border in Haiti, Duvalier's decision to become President-for-Life was expected. The only surprise in April 1964 was that he had not declared himself "Emperor François I," which was rumored.

With all political power concentrated in his hands, Duvalier triumphantly declared, *"Apres nou se nou."* ("After us it is us.") Haitian presidents traditionally riding the proverbial tiger use the excuse that they must remain in power in order to protect their followers from retaliation and prosecution for acts (read: crimes) they carried out in the service of the regime. Thus, Papa Doc's palace sycophants and Macoutes rejoiced at his decision to anoint himself "President-for-Life." It meant that they, too, now had life tenure in their jobs unless, of course, they crossed Papa Doc—as his own brother-in-law, Lucien Daumec, had done, and it had cost him his life.

The circus-like buildup to Papa Doc's presidency-for-life in April 1964 would have embarrassed the most adulation-hungry, megalomaniacal Caesar of ancient Rome. Each Duvalierist orator strove to outdo the other with slavish prose proclaiming Papa Doc the greatest leader of all time.

Papa Doc's endless series of speeches were self-adulatory and bellicose. He told his *milice* not to worry about the niceties of permission to kill, that they had the right to shoot enemies of the Republic on sight.

Haitian intellectuals—most of whom now in exile—were humiliated by the degrading spectacle of such rhetorical madness run amok in their native country. Many realized that only through revolution could they remove Duvalier from power. Exiles in the Dominican Republic and the U.S. rededicated themselves to the challenge—knowing full well that the alternative was their own exile-for-life.

*   *   *

The first to take up Papa Doc's latest gauntlet was Fred Baptiste. D-Day (Day of Departure) for Baptiste and his Kamokens finally dawned in Santo Domingo on June 27, 1964. Only Baptiste, Father Georges, and Pierre Rigaud knew the invasion plans. Although the rest of the guerrillas had not yet been filled in, against huge odds they were finally putting out to sea to invade Haiti.

In a well-planned ruse to protect secrecy, the 29 men were shuttled in a van in the early evening from the chicken farm at Villa Mella to a cocktail party at the apartment of Mr. and Mrs. Pierre Rigaud on Avenida Independencia in Santo Domingo. A Dominican medical student, Nelson Gonzales, who had spent time in Cap-Haïtien where his father had been

Dominican consul, befriended the Kamokens and provided the van. Even with a broken tail light, Nelson, who drove the van to the party, managed to elude the police as well as General Wessin's G2 (Intelligence) and other services that had the chicken farm camp under surveillance. At the Rigaud residence, the guerrillas hungrily gobbled up the dainty hors d'oeuvres. At the appointed hour, the Kamokens emerged from the rear of the windowless van to find themselves not back at the chicken farm as they had expected, but on the Dominican coast not far from the international airport, facing their invasion craft, the freighter *Johnny Express,* to which they were ferried in a small boat. (Two nights before the Kamokens launched their invasion, Father Georges asked me to drive him to a house in a poorer section of Santo Domingo. I left him there and later inquired as to whom he had gone to visit. Fred Baptiste said the good Father had arranged for a *mambo* to perform a ceremony for the success of the invasion. Father George was covering his bases.)

Though surprised, few of the Kamokens protested as they boarded ship. They welcomed action at last. As the *Johnny Express* got underway and moved out to sea, the guerrillas broke out the weapons from Miami hidden aboard the freighter. Their principal arms were a shock. They proved to be antiquated World War I British-made Enfield rifles. However, the vessel also carried the men's new U.S.-made camouflage uniforms.

As the *Johnny Express* passed Beata Island, the ship was hailed by a Dominican patrol boat. When the freighter's captain refused to heed the command, the patrol boat fired a warning shot. Saved by the dark night, the *Johnny Express* made its escape. The following day, June 28, heaving in heavy seas, the vessel drew as close as it could to the Haitian coast near the western town of Saltrou.

Handicapped by the rough sea, the disembarking proved difficult and the Kamokens suffered their first casualties. Guy Lucchesi, 24, a student who had volunteered to fight despite a crippled arm, fell into the churning waters and drowned. The second drowning casualty was a rebel known by his nom de guerre, "*Chien Méchant.*" Most of the detonators for their explosives were lost in the sea.

After the drowning of the two men, a fisherman brought his battered sailboat alongside and helped the others disembark. Once ashore, two members of the group quickly deserted, leaving a force of 25. However, the fisherman, learning they were anti-Duvalier Kamokens, left his boat and joined them, helping to carry their munitions.

On shore, the survivors, in their new American-made olive-green fatigues, appeared to local Haitians to be members of Papa Doc's army or *milice*. But the Army post commander, who observed the landing, had no such illusions. He promptly changed into civilian clothes and headed for Thiotte, a garrison town on a fair-weather road leading over the mountain to Port-au-Prince.

The Kamokens later told the author that a young army officer attempting to flee in civilian clothes had been captured, then killed trying to escape. They recounted that Fred Baptiste personally killed the officer.

The following day, Duvalier was informed of the presence in the Belle Anse area of the Kamokens. The resulting repression in the town of Belle Anse and the surrounding districts was immediate and terrifying. The landing had taken place a mile away. Anyone in the affected zone believed to be anti-Duvalier was taken from home and killed. (Townspeople confirmed 25 years later to Haitian Human Rights workers that 67 persons were executed on the town square and buried there.)

Because one of the Kamokens was identified as the 23-year-old schoolteacher Adrien Fandal, the Macoutes hunted down and killed everyone in the area with the name Fandal. Few had time to change their names. The Macoutes seized the land of the victims. (For years afterward, the killers and relatives of the victims lived almost side by side in Belle Anse.) The largest town on the coast, Jacmel, was sealed tight as a drum. Not even food provisions were permitted to enter. People lived in fear as suspects were arrested.

In Port-au-Prince, Papa Doc took personal command of the armed forces. He ordered Army Maj. Sonny Borge to take command of a U.S. Marine-trained force from the Dessalines Battalion, equipped with mortars and automatic weapons, and to pursue the invaders. Borge, who himself had trained at the U.S. Army's Fort Benning in Georgia, liked to use mortars in action and numerous times thought he had the Kamokens surrounded. He would pummel the target hill with mortar rounds only to find that the guerrillas were somewhere else.

For three weeks it was terror for the peasants in the battle-theater mountains. There was no choice for the subsistence farmers. If they welcomed the Kamokens they were later summarily executed by the Macoutes. If the Kamokens found them to be Macoutes they were likewise executed. There was an ongoing debate among the Kamokens as to this harsh wartime policy.

Duvalier's small Air Force made daily sorties while truckloads of militiamen were being sent into the mountains. Roadblocks halted traffic above the capital on the route to Jacmel. The invasion appeared to be evolving into a sustained effort.

Duvalier quickly put into action other countermeasures. He personally went to Ft. Dimanche in uniform and ordered Madame Max Adolphe, who was then the prison warden, to choose 21 prisoners. The president's casual manner did not reveal his intention. Madame Max, as she was known, thought Duvalier planned to free some of the prisoners as a gesture. She picked those she regarded as friends. Papa Doc then ordered them executed. The following day Duvalier sent a high official to the U.S. embassy to informally advise the Americans of the executions. The purpose of the macabre episode was to demonstrate Papa Doc's seriousness in dealing with the invasion. Duvalier believed that the U.S. was in some way involved and wanted Washington to know that he could act, as well as talk, tough.

In a long complaint to the United Nations Security Council on July 3, Haitian Foreign Minister Chalmers accused the Dominican Republic of aggression. "The invasion forces," he charged, "made up of Haitians and Dominican elements landed on June 29 at *lagoon des huitres*, a rural section of the commune of Belle Anse (Saltrou) in the Department of the Southwest, and at once made for the mountains, armed with automatic weapons, grenades, wireless receivers and a large store of ammunition."

The invaders, the foreign minister said, planned to blow up bridges and gasoline tanks as part of a general campaign of arson and sabotage and "assassination of the closest collaborators of Haiti's chief of state."

Chalmers declared that prominent exiles were behind the invasion. He named Louis Déjoie, Henry Clermont, and Father Georges. He even accused Gen. Leon Cantave and ex-president Magloire, both living in New York at the time.

The author himself got tied up in the denunciation at the United

Nations, accused of providing the Kamokens with identification. Emanuel (Manny) Friedman, foreign editor of *The New York Times*, one of the author's reporting clients, demanded to know whether I had dropped journalism and become a guerrilla. I explained that I had indeed photographed the Kamokens and made a study of their backgrounds, which was after all a journalistic effort to learn more about these young men fighting Papa Doc. However, I had not provided them with IDs.

Back in Haiti, the UN complaint was censored out of all arriving publications, but word of the invasion in the Southwest spread quickly throughout the rest of Haiti.

It was not until July 8 that Duvalier finally allowed official mention of the Kamokens in his controlled media. The first reference was highly colored: "They [the invaders] were armed with M-I rifles, .45-caliber revolvers and grenades. They were harassed as soon as they landed by peasants of Belle-Anse wildly devoted to the person of His Excellency Dr. Francois Duvalier, President-for-Life of the Republic. They left five dead and had to flee to La Selle peak, where, harassed day and night by the population, surrounded by the detachment of the armed forces and of the corps of the Volunteers of National Security, without water or food, they have no other alternative but an unconditional surrender or pure and simple annihilation without delay.

"From interrogation of prisoners fallen into the hands of the loyal forces it was found 1) The rebels left from Boca [Chica] about 30 kilometers from Santo-Domingo. 2) They were organized earlier in a militia training camp prepared with the assistance of the Dominican authorities and placed under the direction of Rev. Father Jean-Baptiste Georges and Pierre L. Rigaud, both traitors to the Haitian motherland and in the pay of a foreign power. 3) They are backed by the Dominican parties of the left and mostly the *14th of June Movement* of Castroite obedience. ..."

When the Dominican government received news of the invasion of Haiti, President Reid Cabral countered Duvalier's charges with one of his own, accusing Duvalier of lying, and declaring that no invasion force had left from Dominican territory.

Summoned to the palace, I found a smiling President Reid feeling good about having accused Duvalier of prevarication. Fellow Triumvirate member Ramon Caceres looked on with an amused look. The elderly

General Miguel Angel Ramirez, one of the military leaders of the Caribbean Legion (1946-59), was present. It appears that the general had been asked to keep an eye on my apartment building, as he lived opposite on Calle Colon. Donny suddenly realized that I hadn't said a word.

"Those Haitians are still in Villa Mella?" Donny asked. Then, when I shrugged, the painful truth dawned on him. "Oh no, no! And I've just protested to the OAS. How did they do it?" Donny asked. It was a temporary embarrassment for Donny.

Even angrier than the Dominican president was Vince Blocker, the CIA's man at the U.S. embassy in charge of watching the Haitians. The night the Haitians left on the *Johnny Express,* my wife and I attended a diplomatic party at Blocker's home. We knew a few of the details of the scheduled invasion departure but were sworn to secrecy by Fred Baptiste. We did watch the clock and stayed late at Blocker's house, knowing that if anything happened, his police sources would notify him. There was no telephone call. But when Blocker heard that the rebels had landed in Haiti he burst into our first-floor apartment and wanted to know, "What the hell is going on?" I asked him what he knew, and he left in a huff. His actions confirmed that all the CIA was interested in was keeping tabs on the exiles and he obviously had been shaken by the fact that the first word had come from Haiti. He had probably received a "rocket" from his Langley headquarters.

A week later Haitian Foreign Minister Chalmers reiterated that his report on the invasion was still correct, and when asked if he had anything to add, he replied, "Did Castro issue a statement at *Playa Giron* [Bay of Pigs] until victory was achieved?"

*   *   *

Duvalier's forces were not eager to venture too far into the mountains and face a guerrilla force of unknown strength. Papa Doc's troops and Macoutes contented themselves with occupying farm marketplaces and exacting vengeance on any who were suspected of helping the rebels. It was sound strategy, for the hills were barren and yielded little in the way of food supplies for the guerrillas. One rebel invader who ventured into a marketplace forgot he was wearing boots. The footwear marked him as a Kamoken and he was executed on the spot.

Other guerrillas were more fortunate. In the pleasant little village of Mapou, the Kamokens were greeted with cries of *"Vive Fignolé."* When they took over the village store, they distributed goods and cash to the impoverished peasants, as well as a bundle of mortgage notes to peasant lands found in the store. In a formal ceremony, the guerrillas burned the papers before the astonished eyes of the peasants.

The store owner herself was accused of being a Duvalierist, and one angry Kamoken, who had witnessed a Macoute drag his mother from their house by the hair, allowed revenge to get the better of him and he killed Mrs. Bernadette, the store owner. The killing of Mrs. Bernadette was a blot on the Kamokens' war against Papa Doc, whom they accused of the same type of atrocities.

They were forced to discourage recruits, having neither arms nor food to offer them. The people in the mountainous region were themselves pitifully poor, too poor to afford even a dollar machete, and sometimes cultivated the land with their hands, scratching between rocks to plant millet. Water was also a problem. During 16 days of crossing Morne La Selle and other rocky mountains dotted with scraggly pines they found little food or water to purchase. Several peasant women joined and did their shopping for them, often walking three days to find food. To quench their thirst and hunger the guerrillas ate chocolate-coated laxatives for temporary relief from hunger, but the result was predictably disastrous.

Baptiste was a tough leader and, overcome with quasi-paranoia, he forced his men to move miles at a time and forbade them to drink from water holes, fearing poison.

Schisms developed within the small guerrilla group, such as regional rivalries. Those from Jacmel didn't always get along with others from the north. On the plus side, the guerrillas moved around sufficiently to give the impression they were larger in number. For the peasant, the Kamokens soon acquired a legendary status in the countryside. They had taken on the mystical attributes of the fearsome nocturnal *loupgaru.* They were everywhere and nowhere!

On the morning of July 21, a Kamoken contingent was astride the Haitian-Dominican border. A heated discussion broke out when Baptiste commanded his men to cross back into the Dominican Republic to find rations. Gerard Lafontant, whose weak physical state belied his quick mind, disagreed. Neither Lafontant nor Baptiste mentioned the ensuing scene to the author, but other members of the guerrilla group said that it proved to be ugly. Lafontant was adamant that they remain in Haiti territory and continue the fight. Angered by Lafontant's insubordination, Baptiste decided it was an act of mutiny and, according to several Kamokens, leveled his rifle at Lafontant's head at point-blank range, then pulled the trigger. Nothing happened. The gun had misfired. The sick and hungry guerrillas buried their weapons in Haiti in preparation to return to Dominican soil. Kicking and protesting, Lafontant was dragged away and across the frontier back into the Dominican Republic, where the rebels were taken prisoner by a Dominican Army patrol.

The Santo Domingo daily *Listin Dario* reported only that a group of Haitians had crossed into the Dominican side and were believed to be in search of food to deliver to guerrillas fighting in Haiti.

The rebels were detained at a Dominican Army fort in the town of Neyba. Their future hung in the balance for a few days. President Reid Cabal did have Admiral Tomas Cortinas, head of the country's newly formed DIN (Division of National Information) intelligence agency, ascertain that there were no communists in their ranks, as Duvalier charged. Only one member was said to have been a Marxist, Gerard Lafontant, who had belonged to Haiti's Popular Socialist Party as a youth, but all were given a pass.

Two weeks later the Dominican Army deposited the Kamokens in the mountain region of the border without arms and with only a few rations supplied by their supporters in Santo Domingo. No one was sure whether the Dominican Army officer in charge of the zone had acted with President Reid Cabral's permission or on his own in agreement with Pierre Rigaud, the Kamokens' patron. It was generally assumed at the time that President Reid Cabral was not opposed to allowing the Kamokens to return to Haiti.

The Kamokens retrieved their weapons from their cache and resumed operations. Their numbers had remained the same, thanks to new Haitian peasant recruits.

CHAPTER 9

The Littlest Victims

On July 3, 1964, Maurice Duchatelier left his Texaco Oil Company office in downtown Port-au-Prince and picked up his wife Ghislaine at the Air France office where she was secretary to the manager. As was their habit, the couple drove home for lunch. Maurice had earlier worked for Pan American Airways for many years, and was a warm, genial, handsome man with wavy gray hair. Ghislaine Edeline Duchatelier was a beautiful woman, and both she and her husband were well known because of the public nature of their work. Maurice had four sons by a previous marriage.

There was tension in the city. It was flooded with rumors that the Kamokens were battling government forces in the Southwest. Travel to Jacmel and even to Kenscoff, the mountain resort, was restricted.

Ghislaine's sister Jacqueline was married to Army Lt. Francois Benoit, who remained in asylum in the Dominican ambassador's residence. Jacqueline herself had given birth to a nine-pound son, Pierre Randolph, while in asylum in the Ecuadorian embassy. Fortunately, Ecuadorian Ambassador Antonio Bustamante found the wife of another diplomat to assist in the delivery. The ambassador received congratulations from fellow diplomats—it was the only happy event of the time in the diplomatic circles of Port-au-Prince.

After Jacqueline Benoit and her infant son were allowed to depart for exile, her brother, Army Lt. Claude Edeline, and his wife Josselyne and their children were also accepted at the Ecuadorian embassy, even thought it was small and overshadowed by the palatial mansion of former Police Chief Col. M. Prosper across the street.

In spite of their temporary safe haven, the Edeline couple's thoughts, like those of many Port-au-Princiens, were never far from the bloody events of Thursday, April 26, 1963. Claude's mother, Mrs. Georgette Edeline, 50, and other members of the family had managed to escape over the back wall of their home on Ruelle Robin in the Bois Verna neighborhood, when the Benoit residence was attacked by Duvalier's Presidential Guard under the command of Col. Max Dominique and Macoute chief Justin Bertrand. It was then that retired Supreme Court Judge Joseph Benoit and his wife Louise, both 67, having just returned from Mass at the nearby Sacre Cour church, were machine-gunned to death. Also shot to death were longtime family retainer Amanie Sincere, Paulette the family cook, another helper, and a young man who happened to be visiting. The house was then set on fire. It was then too that Col. Max Dominique took away Francois and Jacqueline Benoit's 18- month-old-son, Gerald.

On that bloody Thursday of 1963, René Edeline, 54, the father of the family, a prominent personage with an auto repair and car sales business, refused to run, declaring that he had no reason to be afraid as he was not involved in politics. It didn't matter. An Army officer and Macoutes arrived in a jeep and beat him over the head when he protested his innocence. They carted him off to Ft. Dimanche, which had been turned into a human slaughterhouse and where he joined the long execution line. Nor did it matter that René Edeline was a good friend and hunting partner of the powerful Macoute Lucien Chauvet.

*   *   *

A year later, on July 3, 1964, Maurice Duchatelier and wife Ghislaine finished lunch at their home. Eleven-year-old Georges Edeline (Ti Joe) was not at home. He was having lunch with his aunt Jeanette Edeline Romain, wife of retired Army Col. Louis Romain. The Duchatelier couple kissed and hugged their adorable 18-month old baby, Philippe-Morris, and left to return to work.

It was then that it happened. As Maurice Duchatelier backed his car out of their house in the Delmas neighborhood, their exit was suddenly blocked by two automobiles. Capt. Harry Tassy of the Presidential Guard, well known for his sadistic zeal, was accompanied by Duvalier's personal hatchet man, Elois Maitre, and plainclothes soldiers. Tassy ordered Maurice and Ghislaine out of their car and into one of the palace automobiles. Tassy, Maitre, and their contingent entered the house and began ordering family members out. Grandmother Philomène Blanchard protested and was left bleeding on the floor.

Ghislaine's 13-year-old sister Guerda had the presence of mind to flee nextdoor with baby Philippe-Morris, her godson. There, Mrs. Coicou received Guerda and the baby Philippe-Morris with Guerda's younger brothers Eddie, 10, and "Ti-Maurice," the son from Duchatelier's earlier marriage. Mrs. Coicou was not only the mother-in-law of the tough Maj. Franck Romain, but was mother of Lt. Serge Coicou, then an officer of the Presidential Guard.

Driven away and never heard of again were Ghislaine, her husband Maurice, her mother Georgette, her brother Robert, 20, and her sister Gladys, 18. Within five minutes Tassy returned, realizing he had not seized all the family members. He had his orders. The children hiding at Mrs. Coicou's were terrified. Tassy, a wiry little man, this time approached Mrs. Coicou and demanded to search her house. Mrs. Coicou told him defiantly, "You are forgetting who I am." She refused to be intimidated and continued to stand her ground. Tassy hesitated; he knew her powerful Duvalierist connection but he had his orders. Annoyed by the woman's refusal to allow him to search her house he suddenly turned his attention to a maid holding the baby Philippe-Morris. In hiding Guerda heard Tassy demand to know whose baby it was. Realizing the true identity of the baby, Tassy seized the child from the maid, ignoring Mrs. Coicou's protests. As Tassy left with the infant, she tried to hand him the baby's bottle. The scowling officer refused it, snapping, "Where this baby is going he will not need a bottle."

The three other children were crying. Fearful that Tassy and Elois Maitre would return, Mrs. Coicou sent the youngsters to hide, first in the chicken coop behind the house, then in the woods farther back. They were terrified, but teenage Guerda, though shaking, held enough composure to try to comfort Eddie and Ti-Maurice Duchatelier as they huddled in the tall grass in the woods. Mrs. Coicou got word to friends of the family to pick up the three children. Around 10 p.m. a family friend, Mrs. Laura Dulix Epstein, went out into the darkness and found the three in hiding. She made them lie in the back of her car and took them into more secure hiding.

But it wasn't over yet. Thirty miles south of the capital, Raymond Edeline, 31, the eldest Edeline son, who worked for the American Reynolds Bauxite Mining Company at Payan in the hills above the town of Miragoane, was unaware of the drama unfolding in Port-au-Prince. Unknown to him also was that Capt. Jean Beauboeuf had been dispatched from the capital in a jeep with Lt. Edouard Guilliod of the Criminal Research Bureau of the police. They arrested Raymond Edeline. En route back to Port-au-Prince a tire of the jeep was punctured. After it was fixed, they executed Raymond Edeline, declaring later that he had been shot while trying to escape.

The odyssey of the three remaining Edeline children had just begun. Following their fearful night, they were taken in at the French ambassador's residence in Bourdon. Then Guerda was taken to live with Doctor Pape and his family in Kenscoff. Georges Edeline, known as Ti Joe, who had been away at lunch with his aunt on that fateful day, joined his brother Eddie, and they were hidden, disguised as priests, at the Salesian Father's residence and school in Pétionville. When school started the two boys were moved to the Turnbulls' Baptist Mission church and residence in Fermathe.

One day, on a fundraising trip to the U.S. for her Baptist Mission in Haiti, the outspoken Eleanor Turnbull chided a group of potential donors at the Yonkers, N.Y., racetrack, saying, "Here you are enjoying yourselves and in Haiti people are suffering." Encouraged by the group to tell her story, she mentioned the predicament of the Edeline children. One of those who listened intently was a U.S. Central Intelligence Agency operative.

A few weeks later, the CIA operative arrived in Port-au-Prince and set about arranging the youngsters' escape to the U.S. The sons by Maurice Duchatelier's earlier marriage remained in Haiti with their mother. The three Edeline children were spirited out of the country in a masterful coordinated operation. The French Ambassador's wife, Madeline Legenissel, invited the children to a birthday party aboard the ship *Le France*, which was on a Caribbean cruise and had anchored in the bay at Port-au-Prince. When the party ended and the rest of the guests came ashore, the Macoutes who had counted the children as they arrived for the party noted that three children were missing and demanded to search the ship. The captain of *Le France* categorically refused to allow them to do so. There was nothing the Haitian officials could do: The ship was French territory. The CIA agent had arranged the papers for the children to enter the U.S. They steamed off to Puerto Rico and then on to the mainland United States, carrying with them the terrible nightmares of having witnessed the destruction of their family. Captain Tassy, it was later learned, had been acting on the president's orders, and that was why he was able to stand up to Mrs. Coicou.

*   *   *

For years the three young survivors suffered post-traumatic stress. After the Duvalier dictatorship went the way of all such tyrannies, collapsing in 1986, Claude Edeline returned to Haiti in search of Philippe-Morris. During his search he met Tony Guilliod. The Guilliods and Edelines had grown up in the same neighborhood. They were all childhood friends. During their 1987 encounter, Tony Guilliod told Claude Edeline that it was Capt. Beauboeuf who had killed Raymond Edeline, not Tony's brother, Lt. Edouard Guilliod. (A few years later Beauboeuf, who may or may not have killed Raymond Edeline, committed suicide. He shot himself in bed with his own .45 pistol. Lt. Edouard Guilliod lives in retirement in South Florida with his many terrible secrets.)

As best the story can be pieced together, Papa Doc had murdered an innocent family, including an infant, because one of his spies in New York had erroneously reported that exiled Army Lt. Claude Edeline had disappeared from New York and was with the Kamoken invasion force that had landed near Saltrou. (U.S. Representative Cornelius E. Gallagher, a member of the House Foreign Relations Committee, once said he had evidence that Duvalier might have a "Gestapo of Americans" monitoring Haitian exile activities in the United States.)

"Dumont Bellande, living in New York, called me that same day, July 2, 1964," Claude Edeline recounted to the author in an interview in 2003, "and told me to go immediately to report my presence to the Haitian consul André Elie. I was just coming back from the Hospital Immaculate Conception where my son Patrick had emergency surgery, having been hit by a car that same day—he was three weeks in intensive care. I met with the consul Elie the same night and he immediately called President

Duvalier to tell him that Claude Edeline was in New York."

It was already too late. Foreign Minister Chalmers had told a group of Latin American diplomats who had inquired about the Duchateliers and Edelines that it was possible that Claude Edeline had participated in the invasion and flown back to New York on a regular flight out of Port-au-Prince.

When Francois Benoit, still in asylum at the Dominican embassy residence in Pétionville, heard of the arrest of his in-laws, he sent a message to New York. Benoit wrote with lemon juice, invisible ink that turned brown when heated over a stove. Through the embassy driver, a longtime friend and a courageous Dominican-Haitian named Manuel, he managed to get a message to Claude in New York urging him to make known his presence there to prove he had not joined the rebels.

Claude Edeline got a job teaching French, Latin, and Spanish and serving as varsity soccer coach at Gilman High School in Baltimore. The three young survivors have never returned to Haiti. Today they are married with children of their own, but are still traumatized by those terrible events of forty years ago.

No one—retired Haitian Army officers or Claude Edeline's Military Academy classmates, including Max Dominique, or hatchet man Elois Maitre—would tell Claude, even after so many years, what really happened to Philippe-Morris in order to bring some sort of closure. Is he in fact alive somewhere? They would not say.

*   *   *

In 1964 Papa Doc's terror had a Hitlerian quality of all-encompassing, mindless reprisal. An unknown number of peasant families from the village of Mapou, and more than 64 identified persons in Belle Anse, were executed because they were suspected of welcoming the arrival of the Kamokens or having relatives among the guerrillas.

During the same period, in Port-au-Prince, a special target was the family of exiled Catholic priest Father Jean-Claude Bajeux. Published reports in Dominican newspapers had described Father Bajeux as helping Haitian refugees in the neighboring country. In Port-au-Prince's genteel old Bois Verna neighborhood, Father Bajeux's mother, Mrs. Lise Bajeux Montas, 62, was deathly afraid. She had a premonition that bad things were going to happen. Well aware that her son, Father Jean-Claude, was in the Dominican Republic, Mrs. Bajeux worried for the safety of the family. Her eldest son, Yves, had been imprisoned in 1958, accused of being part of a bomb plot against Papa Doc. He spent months in prison. There he had been savagely beaten there under the supervision of the prison commander, Col. Gerard Constant, according to the testimony of other prisoners. Yves had eventually been granted his freedom but quickly fled into asylum in the Venezuelan embassy and later into exile, knowing full well that he was a marked man.

Mrs. Bajeux's anxiety was not only that of a mother. She had witnessed what happened to her neighbors in Bois Verna on that bloody Thursday, April 26, 1963. Fearful of what might occur next, she sought advice from the papal nuncio, Msgr. Giuseppe di Andrea, who resided nearby. The *Petit Nonce*, as he was known because of his size, told Mrs. Bajeux, according to her neighbors, that she should not worry because her son was doing the work of God in the Dominican Republic. He confirmed that Father Bajeux was certainly was not in the rumored invasion force that was said to have come from the Dominican Republic. However, the Vatican's ambassador noted that Father Bajeux had recently been delegated by the Dominican bishops as the chaplain of the Haitians in Santo-Domingo. A photograph published in the Santo Domingo daily, *El Caribe*, of the dedication of the "Friendship of People" center (Foundation for the Promotion of Haitian Refugees and Immigrants in the Dominican Republic) headed by Bajeux and located on Santo Domingo's Juan Pablo Pina Street showed the Papal Nuncio to the Dominican Republic speaking before the archbishop of Santo Domingo, representatives of the American embassy, and other diplomats. Only Bajeux's forehead was visible on the sideline with other participants. Unfortunately, the most prominent figure in the photo was Pierre Rigaud, standing next to the Papal Nuncio, and Rigaud was on Papa Doc's dangerous enemies list.

Still fearful, Mrs. Bajeux, whose late husband had retained French citizenship, went the same day to ask for help from the French ambassador, Charles Legenissel, at his Manoir des Lauriers residence. The envoy agreed with Nuncio di Andrea that there did not appear to be any reason to be afraid. Instead of offering the distraught woman and her family a token of diplomatic protection at his residence, which he had done for others, the French ambassador had Mrs. Bajeux driven down the hill to her Ruelle Berne home and to what she correctly feared would be her imprisonment and "disappearance."

At 11 p.m. that night, Macoutes and police agents converged on the Bajeux house on a narrow Bois Verna street. Neighbors watched in horror from their darkened homes as the principal enforcers of the regime arrived. The presence of Lucien Chauvet, Elois Maitre, Sub. Lt. Gregoire Figaro, and the Macoute Ti Cabiche was the most ominous of signs. Years later several neighbors related to Jean-Claude Bajeux the events of that tragic night. There were no niceties, they said. The defenseless Bajeux women in their nightdresses—Mrs. Bajeux and her daughters Micheline, 32, and Anne Marie, 42—were cursed and beaten like common criminals as they were pushed and dragged away to a waiting truck. Anne Marie was engaged to be married and had come home to comfort her mother to relieve her anxiety. Albert, 37, the eldest son, and his brother Maxim, 24, were also beaten as they were dumped in the truck.

In shock, the neighbors, some praying for the Bajeux family, would only stare in disbelief or turn their eyes away from the Bajeux home, which became ghostlike after Papa Doc's enforcers had left. The lights remained on but no one ventured near the house. Finally Macoutes returned with two trucks and looted the house bare. Some months later, members of Duvalier's civilian militia moved into the confiscated Bajeux home with their families. They were officially given the house by Ft. Dimanche commander Madame Max Adolphe as a reward for their devotion to Papa Doc.

The Bajeux family was taken to Ft. Dimanche and never heard from again. One inmate, Dr. David Innocent, later recounted that he heard from his cell the voice of Elois Maitre: "Bring the Bajeux women, too," which Dr. Innocent took to mean they were to be executed.

CHAPTER 10

Papa Doc's Counter Coup

There is no presidency for life without gunfire. Join your soul to those of the ancestors to understand me well because I am no sentimentalist.
—FRANÇOIS DUVALIER ON BECOMING HAITI'S
"PRESIDENT-FOR-LIFE" IN 1964

On August 5, 1964, Fred Baptiste and his fellow Kamokens returned to their old base camp, on Haiti's *Morne La Selle*, at 7,899 feet the highest mountain in Haiti. Their camp, which still contained their cooking utensils and other necessities, was set amidst a few surviving pine trees only a stone's throw from the Dominican border post at El Aguacate. The Dominican soldiers had orders from their commander to ignore the Haitian guerrillas' reentry into their country and their continued proximity.

Retrieving their old firearms, Baptiste's ragtag force acted on this second incursion more like disciplined fighters, according to recollections of Gerard Lafontant, who had become the second-in-command of the guerrillas.

Baptiste sent out columns on forays against Macoutes and military targets. On August 11, a column led by Lafontant sabotaged the Pine Forest sawmill and logging equipment belonging to Maj. Jean Tassy, the brutal Criminal Research Bureau officer who had risen to occupy Clément Barbot's office in the National Palace. Lafontant later described to the author the special satisfaction he and his men had in destroying Tassy's sawmill. "Not only did it belong to *un des assassins les plus feroces de Duvalier*," Lafontant said, but Tassy was destroying precious Haitian pine trees without regard to the environment.

Four days later, a column led by "Renard" and "Rommel" (their

Kamoken noms de guerre) carried out a successful night attack on the Haitian military border post at Savane Zombi. The soldiers and Macoutes fled, leaving behind their equipment and, more importantly, the post's archives. The guerrillas set fire to the post and two houses belonging to the Macoute chieftain of the region. That same afternoon another Kamoken column ambushed a truckload of Papa Doc's militia traveling slowly over the rugged mountain road that led from Thiotte to Port-au-Prince by way of Fonds Verrettes. The guerrillas inflicted four casualties on the *milice*. A Duvalierist congressman, Deputy Hugo Paul of Saltrou, escaped another attack by the Kamokens, but his son suffered wounds. The congressman later died, reportedly of shock.

A small convoy of soldiers was sighted but the Kamokens decided not to attack because the convoy was heavily armed. Later, however, on examining the records seized at the Savane Zombi post, the guerrillas learned that the convoy they had spared was that of Duvalier's Army chief of staff, Gen. Gerard Constant, who was making an inspection tour.

Duvalier, a frustrated general himself, was told that Maj. Sonny Borges' mortars could not be effectively used against the Kamoken because they were perched on a mountain too close to the Dominican border. Mortar shells landing in Dominican territory would provoke yet another diplomatic incident. More importantly, Maj. Borges and his troops were required on the southern peninsula to confront the Jeune Haiti exile force that had landed August 5. During the second week of August Papa Doc's Dominican exile Trujilloist advisors suggested a plan that appealed to Papa Doc's sense of intrigue. Duvalier had given refuge to a group of former Trujillo SIM agents, several of whom acted as advisors on Dominican issues. It was only years later, though interviews with Duvalier insiders and Jean-Claude Duvalier, that the author learned of the full extent of the scheme which they said Papa Doc considered ingenious.

Papa Doc's Dominican advisors—one of whom was identified as Col. Tuto Anselmo

Colon—had persuaded him to use the Dominican exiles, some of whom were living in a Port-au-Prince bordering house at government expense. His plan of action was designed not only to attack the Kamokens but also to destabilize the ruling Dominican Triumvirate.

The Dominican exile force would attack and destroy the Kamokens, as well as the Dominican border post of El Aguacate. Once this was accomplished the exiles would declare that they had seized Dominican territory and were setting up a provisional government. Several Dominicans who hatched the plan actually believed that some Trujillo military elements would seize the opportunity to oust the ruling *Triunvirato*. For Duvalier, the action by his Dominican exile force based in Haiti would at least frighten Donny Reid Cabral and force him to curb the activities of the Haitian exiles in the Dominican Republic.

Some of the details of Papa Doc's fanciful plot were revealed on August 21 in Santo-Domingo by one of the participants. The Dominican military high command introduced to the press a 37-year-old former Dominican Navy non-commissioned officer, Themistocles Vicioso Abreu, who declared he had been forced to participate in the action against his country but had then deserted.

Vicioso Abreu related how he and a group of ten other Dominicans, whom he described as former policemen and *Calies* (Dominican Macoutes), had been forced into the conspiracy headed by President Duvalier. He described how they had been rounded up and brought before President Duvalier by Col. Tuto Anselmo Colon, a onetime Trujillo rural police chief, who he identified as working as an advisor to Duvalier.

"We were brought before Duvalier and each given the equivalent of $160 in Haitian gourdes," explained Vicioso Abreu. Duvalier instructed them that they were to fulfill a special mission. They were to attack the 25th company of the Dominican border patrol and burn down the El Aguacate post. The Haitian President, he explained, promised that they would be supported by a well-armed Haitian force. He ordered the Dominicans be issued olive-green fatigues, two Thompson submachine guns, two .45-cal. pistols, and eight incendiary and fragmentation grenades, along with a quantity of gasoline and cotton to make Molotov cocktails to burn down the border post.

The force of eleven Dominicans, including himself, Vicioso Abreu said, were escorted to the border on August 15 and told to attack the Dominican post. Instead, they wandered around the hills for a while and then returned to inform the Haitian Army captain at the Haitian frontier post of Malpasse that they had gotten lost. The group was taken back to

Port-au-Prince and imprisoned at Ft. Dimanche. On August 17, Vicioso Abreu related, they were taken once more before Duvalier, whom he described as "frantic with tears in his eyes, because we had failed our mission. He gave us another chance and issued new arms, five revolvers, two .45 pistols, five Thompson submachine guns, and a 7 mm caliber rifle." Two of the eleven didn't go because "one had fever and the other was sent on another special mission." (Vicioso Abreu didn't know anything about the other mission.)

"We were taken to a little abandoned peasant hut approximately three kilometers from the El Aguacate post, where we rested from 7 p.m. to 10 p.m. and then set out to attack the post," Vicioso said. Shortly before midnight on August 17, he and the others approached El Aguacate. "We threw several grenades, and then fired our Thompson submachine guns before retreating when the Dominican sentries opened fire," explained Vicioso Abreu, who declared that he had given himself up to the Dominican border guards because he hadn't wished to fulfill his mission. Dominican Army Chief of Staff, Gen. Salvador Montas Guerrero, told the press conference that he was still trying to determine whether the ex-Navy man had surrendered voluntarily or been captured. The other Dominican members of the attack on El Aguacate, he said, had returned to Port-au-Prince, as they had a criminal record in the Dominican Republic. Vicioso did not.

In Santo Domingo, President Reid Cabral dismissed the raid on El Aguacate as a minor incident, designed, he said, to stir up trouble. He said privately to the author that he was not falling into that trap and the incident wasn't worth protesting.

Nevertheless, Papa Doc ordered the operation to proceed and on August 18 a United Press International news bulletin, datelined Port-au-Prince, reported that Dominican exiles had captured a portion of Dominican territory near Barahona and had set up a provisional government. According to the UPI dispatch, a "great battle" had taken place, either as a result of an invasion or mutiny.

There was no truth to the story. It was pure fabrication and UPI attributed the story to a Haitian government source.

A single telephone call to Barahona sufficed to kill the story and Papa Doc's invention.

*   *   *

Several days later, a messenger arrived in Santo Domingo from the Kamokens encamped on Morne La Selle with a request for guerrilla reinforcements, plus arms, food, medicine, and winter wear. Night on the mountaintop was bone-chilling, as temperatures plunged. In Santo Domingo, friends of the Kamokens supplied sweaters, which they had dyed dark green. Food and medicine were no problem but there were no heavy weapons. Fred Baptiste said he had been assured by both Pierre Rigaud and Father Georges that once he and his band had carried out the landing in Saltrou and set up a base of operations in Haiti, reinforcements and heavy arms—including machine guns—would be sent to them.

The author volunteered transportation, since it was a unique chance to learn firsthand about the Kamoken campaign. As my VW Beetle was too small for both passengers and the supplies, I appealed to a friend, Amadito Barletta, a Cuban exile and owner of Santo Domingo Motors, an auto dealership in the Dominican capital, for the loan of a car for the weekend. (The Barletta family had published the newspaper *El Mundo* in Havana.) He offered a deal: If I would repossess an automobile that a fellow Cuban exile had refused to return to Barletta, "the car is yours for the weekend." With two burly Haitians in tow, I had no trouble repossessing the late-model stylish car. The repossessee politely handed over the keys to the big, sporty American sedan.

At midday on August 24, loaded down with food, clothing, and medicine but no heavy weapons, three Haitian friends and I left Santo Domingo for El Aguacate as Hurricane Cleo approached the south coast of Hispaniola. The sun had disappeared. It was as if night were falling. The thunderclouds were streaked with an eerie yellow. Racing the Caribbean hurricane along the coast in gusting wind and heavy rain was exhilarating until we reached the mud-soaked mountain road to El Aguacate and the car began at times to slide backwards. Despite the hazardous stretch, we finally made it to our destination.

Without mentioning me, Pierre Rigaud had arranged with his Dominican military contacts permission for our access to the border post. (If the military had known a journalist was driving the car, approval would certainly have been denied.) When we finally drove into the military compound of El Aguacate, sentries ignored us.

We had hardly turned off the engine when Fred Baptiste strode out of the mountain fog, accompanied by a squad of fellow Kamokens. They appeared completely at home in the post, which consisted of a neat cluster of olive green wooden huts in the saddle of the pine-clad mountain. No Dominican officer approached us while the goods were handed over to the Kamokens. For their part, they handed over several rolls of film to be developed in Santo Domingo and provided to the media to illustrate the guerrilla war against Papa Doc.

"Where are the arms?" Baptiste was crestfallen when he heard that there were no machine guns in the boot of our car. He believed that Rigaud had been capable of convincing the Dominican military to release the guns that General Cantave had received in the airdrop at Dajabon. "Tell Rigaud that we urgently need arms and munitions to go on the offensive," Baptiste instructed the Haitians accompanying me. He had been presented with a .45-caliber pistol but he shrugged as he placed it in his belt, saying, "A lot of good this will do."

There was no time for further discussion of the campaign. Hurricane Cleo, bearing down ever closer, was beginning to turn the mountain road we had just negotiated into a river. Bridges might soon be swept away and leave us marooned in our deluxe American automobile. And indeed, as we arrived in the town of Bani the waters proved too high. The car stalled and its engine died. We managed to find a bus back to Santo Domingo. The following day, Barletta in Santo Domingo was informed that his repossessed car had "conked out" in the town of Bani during our weekend drive.

The developed film of the Kamokens posing as a tough guerrilla force in the Haitian mountains was passed on to Paul Verna, the former Haitian diplomat-turned-public relations guru for the rebels. He had begun to publish, in a full-color political sheet he called *Haiti Libre,* a highly imaginary account of the Kamokens' "successes." One chilling picture showed a supposed Macoute with a hangman's rope around his neck.

On October 5, 1964, a Kamoken knocked on our door in Santo Domingo. He delivered a letter from Fred Baptiste. The latter's cry for help was a shock. Baptiste announced in his note that he was hospitalized in the Dominican Army barracks in Azua, and that the remaining members of his guerrilla band had been interned in the army's *fortaleza* in Neyba.

(3 Octobre, 1964

Bien Cher Ami,

Je suis sur de vous et de votre appor a notre cause. Je ne sais que vous dire. J'amla jambe enflée et une rupture à la peronée. Imaginez-vous combien cette histoire me ronge, moi avec une rupture dans l'impossibilité d'agir!

Hélas! L'inaction me tue et je ne suis puis rester d'avantage dans la Fortaleza de

Azua. Faites de votre mieux pour moi. On ne peut pas laisser tomber la lutte; que nous importe les avions du "Doc". Nous sommes jeunes, nous mourrons ou nous vaincrons.

Quand je nous verrai, l'on causera...Bien des choses à Sulzan! J'ai besoin d'aller à la clinique òu j'étais, je ne peux pas manger la nourriture de la prison. On me soignait mieux à la clinique. Je ne marhe que difficilement à l'aide d'un bâton sur un seul pied pour aller au bain.

Je crois qu'il est nécessaire que les gars de Neyba reçoivent l'attention de tous car ils ont beaucoup souffert.

Pentolite au moins, pourquoi ne vient-il pas nous voir. Nous l'éspérons.

Il nous faut sortir de la Fortaleza de Azua cette semaine et que les gars soient déplacés.

Jaimerais vous voir aussi, mais je sais que c'est difficile, mais si vous voulez, vous viendrez avec autorization pour faire le nécessaire pour nous...

Jérôme, [Fred's nom de guerre]

P.S. Salut en la liberté d'Haiti.

*   *   *

Fred Baptiste's personal war was over. Yet, in spite of his broken leg (fractured in two places) he was dreaming of returning to fight Duvalier. "I must get out of the Azua Fortaleza this week and the fellows must be moved," his note read. "Alas, the inaction is killing me; I cannot stay any longer in the Azua Fortaleza. Do your best for us. We cannot let go of the struggle. ... We are young. We will win or die." His words proved prophetic, for years later Fred and his brother Reneld would both die in Ft. Dimanche, Duvalier's gulag.

Mystery surrounded the routing of the Kamokens from their mountain base. Around noon on August 30, according to Baptiste and other members of his force, they had heard voices coming from across the valley on the Dominican side of the border. The Kamokens identified them as those of Spanish-speaking Dominicans. Two hours later a Kamoken sentry became alarmed. He observed some two dozen men dressed like Dominican soldiers approaching through the pine trees into Haitian territory in an offensive posture. When the sentry fired into the air to sound the alarm, the approaching force opened up with what the Kamokens believed was a .30-caliber Machine gun.

There was no question of fighting the intruders coming from the Dominican side of the border, and the alternative was to split up into small groups and retreat further into Haitian territory. Fred Baptiste fell over a precipice and broke his left leg in two places.

For the next two days the weary Kamokens left their hiding places inside Haiti and straggled in twos and threes back across the Dominican border at different points. Fred, his leg swollen and inflamed, was helped across the frontier by his brother, Reneld. Once again they were taken prisoner and interned into the Dominican Army *fortaleza* in the dusty little town of Neyba. Because of his injuries, Fred was transported to another fort in the town of Azua.

Who had attacked the Kamokens? Speculation focused on Dominican Gen. Elias Wessin y Wessin, who feared that the Haitian guerrillas might cause an escalation of trouble with Papa Doc. The Kamokens conjectured that he may have sent a unit from his garrison at the Barahona airfield to clear them out of their camp in Haiti because it was too close to the Dominican border for comfort. That version has never been confirmed by the author. At the time, the top command of the Dominican armed forces was divided. A group of high-ranking officers supported exiled President Joaquin Balaguer; another opposed to the overthrow of President Bosch was in favor of a return to constitutional rule. Only Wessin y Wessin was in full support of President Reid Cabral.

On September 2, Dominican Armed Forces Minister Víctor Elby Viñas Román had announced at a press conference that on the previous day, Haitian troops from Malpasse had attacked the Dominican border post at Jimani, slightly wounding a sentry before they were repulsed. The Minister reported that later the same day, a Haitian aircraft had flown over the frontier area at Jimani. News correspondents in the area report-

ed that the Dominican armed forces had reinforced the border and moved
up tanks. (The Kamokens believed that the Haitian troops from Malpasse
had been pursuing Kamoken stragglers trying to reach the Dominican
border.)

President Reid Cabral had ordered the border reinforced, but refused
an army request for additional tanks to be moved to the frontier. Privately,
President Reid told the author that he was concerned that rival military
groups might be trying to have Wessin y Wessin disperse his tanks around
the country in order to weaken his force in Santo Domingo and bring off
a coup d'état. In early March 1964, Reid set off a minor controversy in
the Dominican media and military when, at the urging of the OAS, he
suggested it might be a good thing to reestablish relations with Haiti,
even at a consular level, to learn what was happening in Haiti.

There was another version of the attack on the Kamokens, according
to which Papa Doc's Dominican exile recruits may have been the ones
who actually assaulted the Kamokens disguised as regular Dominican
soldiers and speaking Spanish.

In any event, only 24 Kamokens returned from their war. The fate of
the other four was never known. They were recorded in the guerrillas'
lore as missing in action.

Nevertheless, for the typical Haitian peasant and for exile propagan-
dist Paul Verna in Caracas, who was editing *Haiti Libre*, the Kamoken
war continued in all its glory, winning fictitious victory after fictitious
victory. Disinformation, psychological warfare, and wishful thinking
combined to make Verna's *Haiti Libre,* published in French in Caracas in
color, a remarkable document. Verna sought to keep the guerrillas fighting, at least in his imagination, describing their triumphs and the enormous casualties they inflicted on the Duvalierist enemy. It was propaganda so blatantly false as to be embarrassing to many of Papa Doc's
foes. One issue appeared in September 1964—less than a month after the
guerrillas were imprisoned—pronouncing 1964 as the year of liberation
of Haiti.

Such wishful thinking was possible in large part because, for the
Haitian peasants, the rebel Kamokens had taken on all the mystical attributes of the nocturnal airborne werewolf, the *lougarwu.* Like that night-
time fearful blood-sucking phantom, the Kamokens—at least in the

Haitian popular imagination—seemed to be everywhere and nowhere. The Macoutes also feared that the Kamokens were still in the hills. However, as events were to prove, the Kamokens were more unnerving than potent, and they won far more victories in the minds of the enemy than on the battlefield.

* * *

For the Dominican military, the Haitian detainees in the military prison of Neyba didn't exist. The Army allotted neither food rations nor funds to supply non-existent prisoners. Hungry, sick, and depressed the Haitians were indebted to the prison commandant, Capt. Pedro Rivera, a 30-year veteran of the Dominican Army, who gave the 24 men a daily rice ration of 12 pounds from his own prison allotment. The Kamokens cooked the rice at night, with a little salt and an occasional plantain. They gradually sold off their clothing and boots to Dominican soldiers to survive. Their home for seven weeks was a dark room filled with the stench of open latrines. The little bedding available was cast-off, bug-invested prison mattresses. They had no toothbrushes or soap and there was no electric light, but there were swarms of voracious mosquitoes that one Kamoken joked "found it difficult to find any blood in any of us." At least five of the guerrillas needed medical attention, one for a broken arm and the others for malaria and depression. The group's morale was understandably rock-bottom, and most believed they would be handed over the border again, this time into Duvalier's hands.

President Reid Cabral was receptive to my appeal to release Fred Baptiste for specialized medical treatment. Reid listened patiently as I explained other problems being experienced by the imprisoned Haitians. He summoned his Army chief of staff, General Salvador Montes Guerrero, who, on the president's instructions, addressed a note to the commander of the Neyba garrison giving permission for the bearer to see the Haitian prisoners. The note was handed to me by the General. The general was not a very good letter writer but his instructions in Spanish were legible. Reid asked me to report back to him to see what could be done for the Haitians.

At Neyba, the prisoners were paraded before me in military fashion.

They stood at attention outside the high prison wall. They resembled World War II concentration camp victims, emaciated, barefoot, and with the little clothing they wore reduced to rags. When I went among them, they uttered no concern about their own shocking physical state; nor did they complain. They were desperate for news from Haiti and asked about their chances of being released. I told the prisoners I would return and assured them, based on what the president had said, that they would not be sent back to Haiti, as was rumored in the prison—and that we would get Baptiste medical help in Azua.

On Sunday, October 11, Father Bajeux and the author drove to Azua with the authorization of the president to transport Fred Baptiste to a clinic in Santo Domingo. Baptiste was checked in under a fictitious name at Dr. Abel Gonzales' clinic, a private general practice facility. Baptiste's fictitious name was necessary because of Papa Doc's spies, and also as he was opposed by Louis Déjoie and other exiles. Dr. Hoffiz, one of the best orthopedists in the country, reset the leg, which was broken in two places. The doctor said Baptiste would have to wear the plaster cast for at least six weeks. I assumed the cost of the operation—$180—which I could hardly write off as an expense. Though a foreign correspondent's expense account can sometimes appear bizarre, listing "medical operation for a Haitian guerrilla" would have been a bit much for any accounting department. After Baptiste was released from the hospital, he convalesced in the author's apartment office, sleeping next to the Telex machine and playing with our infant son.

CHAPTER 11

Tales from a Lunatic Asylum

President Reid was sympathetic to the plight of the Haitians, but once they were released from military custody, where to put them? When eventually the president suggested that they be interned in the insane asylum near the village of Nigua, fourteen miles from Santo Domingo, it sounded like a bad joke. Indeed, Hispaniola itself, with its volatile and violent politics, often during that period evoked images of a mental institution. But Reid assured me that the asylum had been abandoned for many years. The last occupants were lepers. There were stories that Trujillo had used this government institution as a gulag to lodge political prisoners and worse. Set amidst fields empty except for African zebras that had been imported by Trujillo and were still roaming the area, the asylum exuded a Graham Greene-like aura of Caribbean tragicomic opera. Nevertheless, Reid offered assurances that the place was both habitable and available.

Beginning on Oct. 19, 1964, the 24 Kamokens were trucked from prison to their new home. They quickly ejected the goats that were wandering the premises. The window frames and doors of the long dormitory barracks had disappeared. The interiors of the buildings were heaped with goat dung. Digging out the dung became a major chore, and a dirty one.

Meanwhile, on the previous October 18, Gen. Léon Cantave had been released from being held incommunicado at Dominican Army headquarters. He was escorted to the airport and placed on a plane bound for New York. Next to leave the country, at the request of the government, which was under pressure from the OAS, were the Haitian exile political leaders, including Pierre Rigaud and Louis Déjoie. The latter complained bitterly that the Dominicans had no right to expel him, while Rigaud, the graceful diplomat, thanked the Dominican people for their hospitality.

Father Bajeux was exiled to a sugar mill parish far from the Haitian border.

Déjoie's protests once again illustrated the serious division among exiled Haitian groups. Declaring that he had done nothing to deprive himself of his right to asylum in the Dominican Republic, Déjoie, in a letter to Dominican Commerce Minister Pompilio Brower, denounced other Haitian exiles who were actively trying to overthrow Duvalier. President Reid Cabral, shocked by Déjoie's broadside, gave me a copy, commenting, "It is pitiful."

Dated November 17, 1964, Déjoie's letter to the Dominican minister stated:

> I am writing to you to tell you that I am not sure of the government's word. It appears that I am the only one who is going to leave the Dominican Republic.
>
> I see that Pierre Rigaud and all the others are still here [Rigaud had not yet departed] and no effort has been made for them to obtain their papers and passports to leave the country.
>
> I have never involved myself in any activities, and I have never embarrassed the government, and yet it is I who has to go when the others who have been causing trouble for the Dominican government are permitted to remain here.
>
> I will leave when Jean-Claude Bajeux, who is the representative of Father Georges and Father Bissainthe, leaves and the others go; Pierre Rigaud, who organized the attack on Saltrou and Malpasse; Athis, a Fignolist, Paul Arcelin, a communist, Louis Charles, the former Haitian consul and a Duvalierist spy, Lieut. Raymond Montreuil, who is in charge of Bajeux's camp, Maurice Lacroix, a Duvalier spy, Arnold Salnave, assistant to Father Bajeux, Frantz Armand, a guerrilla captain training Bajeux's men, two guerrillas, Gerard Lafontant and Fred Baptiste who are in a clinique on Avenida Independencia who were brought there from Aguacate and Malpasse, Madame Jacques Wadestrandt, the wife of a guerrilla in Jérémie area who has been here 15 days.
>
> We know and the Dominican people know that it is these people who have been causing the government trouble and not me. I am denouncing these people. I am sick today. I cannot see you.
>
> Regards and we are confident of the Future: Louis Déjoie.

Three weeks later, on December 10, 1964, Déjoie and six other Haitians, including Pierre Rigaud, left the Dominican Republic. Father Bajeux, assigned to a sugar mill community, finally departed of his own free will for Mexico in March of 1965.

*   *   *

The Kamokens were basically restricted to the Nigua complex, although the Dominican soldiers guarding the state property were flexible, and before long some of the exiles were commuting back and forth to the capital. The loads of goat manure excavated from the institution's decaying buildings were used as fertilizer for vegetable gardens the Kamokens quickly created in the extensive grounds of the asylum. In no time, they had recovered their health and had model vegetable gardens, watered by an aqueduct made of local bamboo. They organized an educational center for fellow Kamokens and invited children of the Dominican soldiers guarding the property to attend, teaching them to read and write in Spanish. (When common-law wives of the Dominican troops asked to join the Haitian literacy classes, permission was granted but it was decided to conduct the educational sessions in the open under a mango tree under the jealous eyes of the soldiers.) The Kamokens fished, made furniture, and were helped on their farm by aid from occasional visitors, such as Graham Greene, who supplied $30 for the Kamokens to purchase chicks to start a poultry farm. President Reid made a contribution of double-decker iron beds manufactured at what had been a San Cristóbal arms factory.

CHAPTER 12

Thirteen against the Tyrant

Their firefights were fought in places that have no names on any map. They fought their way over the length of Haiti's rugged Southern Peninsula against the full force of the dictator's might, winning some battles, losing others, until they were whittled down from 13 to two. The two were taken prisoner and given a very public execution.

It was the longest guerrilla war in Haiti since the Caco rebellion against the U.S. Marine occupation in the 1920s, and the end of the last battle typified its tragic trajectory. In desperation, two brothers fought and died together, firing away to the last bullet. The last three on the field threw rocks after their ammunition was depleted. And they had not planned on fighting a guerrilla war!

They landed by boat in Haiti on August 5, 1964. By October 26 it was all over, except for the execution of the two prisoners. The heads of the last three Jeune Haiti fighters, all of them exiles from New York City, were severed as trophies and delivered to Papa Doc. He ordered the heads to be photographed and published as a prop for the subsequent Port-au-Prince executions of the remaining two fighters.

Duvalier's U.S. Marine-trained and equipped Army triumphed over thirteen commandos, the majority of whom had themselves been trained by the U.S. Central Intelligence Agency at its secret facility in Virginia, known as "The Farm."

If Le Groupe de Treize, as they were to become known in Haiti, had landed near the Jérémie airport, their original objective, their families—including women and babies—might not have been murdered on orders from the National Palace, then buried on the scrub fringes of the grassy airstrip.

As an advance commando unit for a planned larger incursion aimed at toppling Duvalier, their immediate objective was to seize and secure the small Jérémie airstrip. That would have permitted reinforcements and supplies to pour into Haiti for the battle against the dictatorship. And if the "Thirteen" had not succeeded, they expected to be withdrawn to fight another day on a more tactically favorable battlefield.

However, their well-laid plans were doomed to failure when they were put ashore much too far from their airport objective. Every Latin American "national liberation" group at the time recalled the example of Fidel Castro finally reaching the Sierra Maestra with only a dozen survivors after his landing from Mexico. What these revolutionaries elsewhere often overlooked was that Castro quickly established his base. Within a short time, his sympathizers from Cuba's cities were joining him in the mountains with arms.

Such was not the case with Haiti's beknighted Thirteen. They lost the element of surprise and were thrust into a guerrilla war they could not win. To cap their disastrous landing, they lost their vital communication equipment.

Haitian Army records tell very little of the extraordinary story of the thirteen Jeune Haiti guerillas. Legends on the peninsula began to flourish soon after their landing. Rumors portrayed them as marathon men who could cross from one end of the peninsula to the other and inflict casualties on the Army and VSN at will. Overnight, the rumors mutated into a hundred myths. For that reason, years afterwards it was impossible to separate the fertile local imagination from reality in the region. For the area peasants, it was an epic guerrilla war that harked back to the time their ancestors fought under the banner of the invincible guerrilla leader, Jean-Baptiste Perrier. Known as Goman, Perrier was a brilliant guerrilla tactician who, in 1807, took up arms against the central authority of President Alexandre Pétion in Port-au-Prince. Goman's insurrection lasted 13 years, and he never was captured.

The long, mountainous stretch of land jutting southwest from Port-au-Prince to Dame Marie is normally a region in which verdant valleys are checkered with banana fields, coffee bushes flourishing under giant shade trees, and, on the plain outside Aux Cayes, sugarcane plantations and thriving cattle. However, ravished in October 1963 by Hurricane Flora, and the following year by Hurricane Cleo, which literally passed over the Jeune Haiti guerrillas, the peninsula had become a grim land, largely cut off from the rest of the country by confusion, lack of communication, and government apathy.

Hurricane Flora had been more deadly than Cleo. When Flora slammed into the area on October 3, 1963, leveling dwellings, destroying crops, and leaving devastation and death in its wake, the scope of this disaster anywhere but Haiti would have propelled the government into immediate emergency action. Not so with Papa Doc, whose major concern was his regime's security. He had stalled a full-scale U.S. relief operation for almost a week, fearing that Washington might be scheming to use Flora's tragedy to overthrow him. Duvalier temporarily barred U.S. military assistance and kept his own armed forces on the alert in the capital, instead of dispatching them to the Southern Peninsula.

When finally helicopters from the U.S aircraft carrier *Lake Champlain* were granted permission to fly aid into the stricken region, they could not lift off because of bad weather.

There was no accurate count of the final toll on the peninsula, but it was believed that more than 5,000 died and at least 125,000 were left homeless. Most of the region's livestock was destroyed, along with at least half of the coffee trees representing the country's major export.

Hurricane Cleo the following year compounded the misery. Taken together, the two hurricanes turned the terrain into an ugly patchwork of brown, flooded fields, with the hills scarred by vicious brown streaks from water cascading down onto humble flimsy homes and little farms of impoverished peasants. In some villages—where even in normal times only faith would enable one to survive—it was faith that was hardest hit, as Flora's winds lifted off church roofs and gutted other houses of worship. The rains that accompanied the winds left a sea of mud. The countryside was deep in mire and filled with the nauseating, malodorous stench of death as corpses of pigs, goats, and chickens littered the villages and slowly decayed.

Anti-Duvalier youth in Port-au-Prince, and even in provincial towns, were not just uninformed about the landing and identity of the rebels; with all possible information, there would still have been no way to join the elusive Jeune Haiti guerrillas. As soon as the landing was confirmed, all roads to the area came under control of the military and Macoutes. Travel to the South was possible only with special police permission.

*   *   *

The Thirteen left no diary or oral history. For reasons never fully explained, their radio transmitter either was lost on landing or did not work. Without communications, they were doomed, although they did not realize it. They had no way to arrange for reinforcements or to be evacuated. They had no choice but to fight.

The month before he went ashore in the "invasion," Jacques Wadestrand visited the Dominican Republic with Col. Pierre Armand's son, Frantz. Their mission was to arrange for Franz Armand to meet with Eduardo Cabral in Santiago de los Caballeros and arrange for radio reception from the Thirteen, after their landing in the South of Haiti. Cabral had attended Harvard University with Wadestrand and agreed to help. But as Cabral was unable to establish contact, it was believed the radio was disabled or lost. The two guerrillas taken prisoner provided no clue, in their published interrogation, as to what happened to their radio transmitter.

The Haitian government's communiqués about the incursion came only at the end of hostilities, contained few details, and gave no hint of government casualties. Nor did the coded messages between Duvalier and his field commanders, intercepted in Santo Domingo, tell much of what was transpiring.

All but two of the Thirteen learned commando tactics at the Central Intelligence Agency's "Farm." President Kennedy ordered training for a series of anti-Papa Doc Haitian commando teams, but with JFK's assassination on November 22, 1963, the project came to an end. The CIA continued, however, to help Jeune Haiti financially, as its members waited impatiently for another "green light" from Washington. Meanwhile, the Haitian commando team continued its marksmanship practice at a deserted farm field on New York's Long Island, with commandos' wives and girlfriends transporting their weapons under long dresses.

Rev. Father Gerard Bissainthe, a Catholic priest, had helped assemble the young Haitian exile activists in 1963 after arriving in New York as an exile. They adopted a political platform and program for a new Haiti, publishing their own magazine called *Lambi* (the conch shell used to spread the alarm in rural Haiti).* Father Bissainthe, 34, a Holy Ghost priest, and son of a prominent Port-au-Prince lawyer, had studied in France and served as a teacher and chaplain of a student group in Port-au-Prince. In their paper he described Jeune Haiti as favoring a system of socialist-oriented cooperatives in the style of Israel's *kibbutzim*. Jeune Haiti's published platform called for social change, including compulsory civic service of six months to one year for all youths between 18 and 21 years of age.

When Jeune Haiti first received financial assistance from the CIA, Father Bissainthe tried but failed to set up a camp for the group in the Dominican Republic under President Juan Bosch. Henry Clermont, who left his studies at Fordham University in New York City to join the movement, traveled to the Dominican Republic and opened a refugee house with some support from the Dominican Red Cross. Clermont added to what aid was available by taking a job at Wimpy's supermarket in Santo Domingo. Some members of Jeune Haiti, including Roland Rigaud, son of the "disappeared" dentist George Rigaud, survived harrowing escapes across the border from Haiti and participated in Cantave's invasion. Roland Rigaud had done so even though he was married with a baby daughter. He was one of the Thirteen.

The members of Jeune Haiti were by no means quixotic revolutionaries out to change the world. Many came from privileged families in Haiti and had college degrees. They had promising careers and peaceful family lives ahead of them in New York or elsewhere. But they had been radicalized by Papa Doc's tyranny and the unspeakable horrors inflicted by his regime. They also pined for their homeland. Driven by all this, they were now prepared to fight to return. They knew that Papa Doc intended his dictatorship to last a lifetime and beyond.

*   *   *

---

* The *Lambi* published by Jeune Haiti should not be confused with another publication of the same name, *Lambi*, published by the Haitian Communists; the latter began to appear in February 1968 as an *Organe exterieur de la lutte révolutionnaire du people Haitien*. Its address was a post office box in La Chaux de fonds, Switzerland.

Duvalier's immediate reaction in early July 1964, after the Kamoken landing in Saltrou, had been to reach deeply into the public treasury and send agents to the U.S. with orders for an impressive line of anti-guerrilla armament that shocked even Washington. On July 13, quoting a reliable source, a Dominican radio station stated that Duvalier was seeking the purchase of fifteen T-28 armed fighter training planes. On July 4, Duvalier transferred dollars via a letter of credit drawn on the Commercial Bank of Haiti to a bank in Mexico as down payment for the purchase. The Dominican radio report stated that Arismendi Trujillo, brother of the late dictator, was said to have had a hand in the Papa Doc deal. The bank notified Duvalier that the planes he sought were in Texas.

Correspondent Tad Szulc reported from Washington in *The New York Times* on July 16 that Duvalier's shopping list also included an impressive, but hardly realistic, armada of "24 naval craft, including 10 cannon-armed PT boats." Szulc's dispatch noted that the "Haitian specification emphasized that equipment such as radio, radar, sonar and diesel engines should be identical in all the crafts if possible."

"It was reported authoritatively," wrote Szulc, "that the Johnson Administration would refuse to license for export any surplus naval craft that Haitians might obtain in this country, just as it blocked last week licenses for 30 T-28 trainer aircraft that the Duvalier regime had purchased in Texas."

The figure of 30 such aircraft might have seemed to be financially out of Papa Doc's reach; nevertheless, Szulc added in his report, "The chief purchasing agent for military equipment for President Duvalier is Clemard Joseph Charles, a 41 -year-old president of a Port-au-Prince [Banque du Commerce] bank. He has been in the United States for several weeks first negotiating the aircraft transaction and now is reported shopping for naval craft."

Papa Doc's impressive shopping list of military hardware was said to have worried Washington. Such an amount of armament, if delivered, might have given Duvalier ideas about destabilizing the already shaky Dominican government of Reid Cabral. Did this motivate the change of heart in Washington? Inexplicably, the Jeune Haiti group in New York in late July 1964 believed they had received the green light.

Yet it seemed improbable that the new American president, Lyndon B.

Johnson, would himself authorize an operation in Haiti. In Asia, he had his hands full with Vietnam, and close to home he feared above all "another Cuba" in the Western hemisphere. LBJ didn't want Fidel Castro moving into the inevitable vacuum the U.S. State Department believed would follow in Haiti upon Papa Doc's exit. So once again U.S. policy toward the tyrannical Papa Doc, on the highest level, became "cool and correct." Moreover, in April 1965, President Johnson dramatically demonstrated his concern over Communist encroachment in the Caribbean by ordering 22,000 U.S. troops into the Dominican Republic to prevent "another Cuba." It appeared to many observers at the time that the Thirteen—along with their CIA advisors—were caught by the shifting winds of top U.S. policy. Tragically so, for the Thirteen had already set out for Haiti, and it was too late to turn them back to New York.

Father Georges, their transportation master, reassured the Thirteen that they were not alone. Fred Baptiste's Kamokens were active in the hills above Port-au-Prince, and some in the New York group believed that they would in effect be opening a second front.

*   *   *

Nevertheless, in the dark hours before dawn of August 5, 1964, the group reached Haiti at last. They were put ashore by the captain of the MV *Johnny Express* at Petite Riviere de Dame Marie at the tip of Haiti's southern peninsula, some 140 miles from the Haitian capital and 50 rugged miles from their objective immediate: Jérémie. They numbered thirteen because at the last moment in New York some of their colleagues could not be found and others withdrew, calling the expedition lunacy.

Father Jean-Baptiste Georges remained aboard the Antillean Line's *Johnny Express*, returning to Miami and then traveling on to New York to collect arms and reinforcements. Father Georges later reported that he and the Jeune Haiti fighters were furious with the captain of the *Johnny Express*, who literally had left them on the beach, miles from their agreed disembarking site at Bonbon. Why the captain of the freighter, who made regular cargo trips between Miami, Port-au-Prince, and Santo Domingo, had been unable to locate Bonbon has never been explained.

In an endeavor to patch together the story of their campaign, the author spoke with as many knowledgable sources as possible, but the full story is known only to the Thirteen: eleven interred on the mountains of the southern peninsula and the two prisoners who were dumped into an unmarked grave somewhere near Port-au-Prince.

The group decided that their only chance of success was to approach Jérémie through the mountains. The small coastal town of Dame Marie was not a target. They walked through the town, where officials, hearing of the guerrilla presence, had suddenly disappeared. Proceeding inland, the Thirteen moved expeditiously and halted at a farm school at a place called Lesson. There they sought out the residence of Father Lefevre, a Canadian missionary of the Catholic Oblat order. Following a meal in the mission yard they moved on to their next objective, leaving, according to the interrogation of the two prisoners, a box of munitions and several raincoats in storage at Father Lefevre's residence.

Having lost the element of surprise and realizing that their presence would soon be reported to Duvalier—who would order his army and Macoutes to track them down—the Thirteen made a forced march to Chambellan, a town in the hills some 20 miles west of Jérémie.

The group's leader—although it appears decisions were discussed among all Thirteen—was 28-year-old Gusle Villedrouin, of Jérémie. He had served in the U.S. Air Force and was one of the founding members of the New York-based Jeune Haiti. His father, Army Col. Roger Villedrouin, was beaten to death in April 1963 by Macoutes. Gerald Brierre, 30, the group's second-in-command, had trained in exile Senator Louis Dejoie's camp in Cuba in 1959 for the Dejoie invasion that never materialized. An anti-Duvalier activist while in Haiti, Brierre managed to escape, but his brother, Eric, was not so lucky. He was tortured to death at Ft. Dimanche.

Young, strong, healthy, and dedicated to their cause, the thirteen Jeune Haiti fighters were all mulattoes, with one exception. Their excitement at returning to their native soil was tempered by the knowledge that they now had to fight a different guerrilla war from the one they had planned, and they knew the odds against them were dramatic.

They reached a hill overlooking Chambellan without incident, aside from several sprained ankles from trudging over the rough mountainous terrain, and they camped the night of August 6. They had made good time, but they didn't move on to Chambellan until the next night, a Friday. With a local peasant as a guide, they slipped into Chambellan unopposed. Saturday morning, they devoted themselves to liberating food stored at the mayor's office. They relieved Papa Doc of his local tax money kept in a safe at the Tax Office, which they blew open with explosives. Again, the town's officials and military post were absent or had taken refuge behind closed doors. With rented pack horses carrying their equipment, and three of the group with sprained ankles, they made good time traveling south and crossing the Grand Anse River that winds its way down to the coast.

One member, Reginald (Bobby) Jourdan, who at age 16 had fought in Fidel Castro's rebellion against Cuban dictator Batista, was in his element. Another of the Thirteen, Charles-Henri Forbin, a reservist of the U.S. Army's 82nd Airborne Division, in which he had served on active duty, was among the best trained. While both men were scouting the area, they spotted the enemy: Government troops from Jérémie were crossing the Grand Anse River in their direction. On the afternoon of August 8, three days after landing, Jeune Haiti guerrillas fired their first shots in what was to be a long guerrilla war. The government soldiers took cover and did not return fire.

Receiving word of a hostile landing in the south, Papa Doc immediately cried "communists" and set his creative propaganda machine to work. The U.S. embassy in Port-au-Prince was notified by Duvalier that his intelligence network had reported that 300 of Castro's Cuban guerrillas had landed on the southern coast. The Cubans had been ferried ashore from a large vessel, the National Palace said. U.S. Ambassador Benson E.L. Timmons III agreed to a Haitian government request that the U.S. Navy make surveillance flights along the Windward Passage and coastlines of Haiti and Cuba to ensure that no further landing force was en route.

Duvalier was said to have been concerned that a small landing in the south was only a diversion, and that that the major attack could be launched on Port-au-Prince. He was relieved when informed that the U.S. Navy reported no suspicious vessels had been sighted. The Cuban government denied that any force had left Cuba. But, interestingly, the Haitian government reported finding a discarded American-made

Browning automatic rifle and other American-made equipment at the Jeune Haiti landing site.

*   *   *

In the meantime, news reports out of Port-au-Prince quoted unofficial sources as stating that the number of "rebels" was eighty, and that they were divided into at least two columns.

Troops from the Army's tactical battalion at Casernes Dessalines were ordered to Jérémie under the command of Col. Breton Claude. The commander at Aux Cayes, Col. Henry Namphy, soon took command of the entire operation. The reinforcements in Jérémie sealed the city and the search for the guerrillas began.

The Garde-Côtes d'Haiti had been the beneficiary of the loan of patrol boats belonging to the U.S. Coast Guard. Each carried historical names but not all were in fighting shape. They were: the *Admiral Killick, La Crête à Pierrot,* the *Vertiere,* and the *Jean-Jacques Dessalines.* The main problem facing the Haitian Coast Guard was that most of its capable officers and men had been victims of Papa Doc's frequent purges, and so its ships were undermanned, and several could not put to sea. The Corps de Aviation had five P-51 Mustangs, an effective World War II-vintage fighter plane, but only one was said to be operational at the time. There were two AT-6 aircraft, converted trainers, and three transport-type C-47s used for Coharta, Haiti's only domestic passenger air service. Hundreds of VSN joined the battle against the 13 Jeune Haiti fighters, assisting in tracking the guerrillas. The VSN also helped by garrisoning the ports and beaches while those elements of the Coast Guard that were functioning patrolled the shoreline.

From testimony gathered years later by the author, it is evident that, in spite of Papa Doc's claims, much of the population was sympathetic to the young fighters. This was an area that had already suffered for backing Duvalier's opponent, Senator Louis Déjoie, during the 1957 election. Some farmers and their families fed and otherwise aided the rebels, while others risked their lives as guides, even though the penalty for aiding rebels was death.

On August 23, in the wake of Hurricane Cleo, young men more accustomed to the apartments and restaurants of New York City were forced to live off the land, sleep in the open, and eat roots and lizards except when they were lucky to share the meager food of poor peasants. There were mountains to climb and rivers to ford, but mountains turned to mud and rivers became dangerous, cascading floods. Hurricane winds and rain were followed by scorching sun.

Even before his forces' first clash with the rebels, Papa Doc was recorded (in a Dominican intercept) making an urgent appeal from the National Palace: "The supreme commander of the armed forces to the command in the field. 'Get one, just one prisoner, repeat, one prisoner.'"

Despite their first sighting of the government troops coming from the direction of Jérémie, the guerrillas continued their advance on Pre'vile, a rural section of the town of Moron. The rebels' second-in-command, Gerard [Geto] Brierre, decided to go to Latiboliere to contact the priest of the region for information and, with a little luck, find a radio to make contact. Brierre was accompanied by Commander Gusle Villedrouin. They left the other men to continue their march onto Pre'vile. On the night of August 11, the group camped amid coffee trees near Pre'vile.

The following morning, Brierre and Villedrouin rejoined the camp after having spent the night in Pre'vile. They had been unable to find the local priest. But scores of people from the region arrived at the Thirteen's camp, laden with gifts of oranges, bananas, coconuts, and other fruits. As captured guerrilla Marcel Numa later described in his interrogation, the people had recognized one member of the group, Milou Drouin, who had once worked in the area. The crowd grew dangerously large to the point where it had to be dispersed by guerrillas firing into the air. Unsurprisingly, the crowd attracted the attention of government troops.

That afternoon, a government reconnaissance AT-6 flew over the guerrillas' position several times. Numa declared that Villedrouin lost his cool and began firing at the plane. It was a tactical error, as it further gave away their position. (The plane, piloted by Antonio (Toto) Fénelon, was hit but was able to make a forced landing in Jérémie.)

Suddenly, bursts of machine gun fire began striking coffee trees near the group's position. The war had begun in earnest. It was the rebels' seventh day in Haiti. As they prepared to move out of their Pre'vile position, a peasant arrived and told Milou Drouin that his family had been arrested in Jérémie. Three of the group decided it was not a government trap to entice them into Jérémie and left with the intention of trying to free the Drouin family and any others who had been arrested. Not everyone was in agreement, and as Charlie Forbin, Jean Gerdes, and Mirko Chandler set out on their Jérémie rescue mission, Milou himself decided to remain.

Unknown to the Jeune Haiti, the killing of their family members in Jérémie had already begun. The flagrant brutality of the Papa Doc regime had previously concentrated largely on the murder of political opponents, military officers deemed untrustworthy, students, and anonymous peasants. As of July, it had begun to strike down members of prominent families with supposed blood links to guerrillas. Now, for the first time, Papa Doc, by ordering the public murder of Jérémie mulatto families, was killings innocent people because of their skin color. His goal was to terrorize the living.

As the guerrillas were moving out of their camp above Pre'vile, a Haitian Air Force P-51 Mustang suddenly appeared. As it dove down on them, the guerrillas took cover under the coffee trees. The plane strafed their position three times without inflicting casualties.

But as it flew away, bullets from government troops ripped through the coffee trees. Yvan Laraque, who had been on point duty, provided covering fire as government troops attacked and the group began its withdrawal. Forbin, Gerdes, and Chandler, who had heard the shooting, managed to rejoin the group. They brought with them the sad tidings that they had suffered their first casualty. The trio was carrying Yvan Laraque's guns. The first casualty is always the saddest, and that was especially the case for Laraque, at 33 the oldest of the group, who had left a wife behind in New York. Moreover, unknown to him, his ten-year-old son living in Port-au-Prince had been arrested when it was learned that his father was one of the rebels. The boy was imprisoned in Ft. Dimanche. Laraque was a well-known soccer player who captained Excelsior, one of the football clubs of Port-au-Prince. Dedicated to maintaining the secrecy of the anti-Duvalier incursion, he had left to fight without telling even his wife where he was going. There were stories, repeated by government soldiers who admired Laraque as a footballer, that he had died heroically covering the retreat of the rest of his group with a grenade attack against them. This was not surprising to those who knew Laraque. As Jacques Auguste recalled to this author, "Laraque played in Excelsior and I was one of his teammates for a short period. He wasn't that big of a man but he imposed respect because he was fearless. His position, I recall was 'demi-center,' with all the stamina and responsibility it requires and he fulfilled that duty very well."

*   *   *

Duvalier didn't have a prisoner, but he had a body. On Duvalier's orders, Laraque's corpse was shipped to Port-au-Prince, where it was placed on public display at a main intersection in the capital. Naked except for undershorts, Laraque's bloated, decomposing cadaver was displayed in a sitting position at the busy intersection of the Grand Rue and Somoza Avenue, which led to the city's Bowen Field airport. Close by was a Coca-Cola stating, "Welcome to Haiti." To call the scene a macabre government exhibit would be a colossal understatement. The body continued to swell in the heat and was covered by flies. The offensive odor had motorists and pedestrians holding their noses. The body slipped off the wooden garden chair on which had been tied by police on specific palace orders. A sign had been hung on the body by the government, stating: "Chief of the traitors to his fatherland killed at Grande-Anse." The putrid, ballooning corpse remained there on the roadway against the chair until the Liberian ambassador complained to the Haitian Foreign Ministry that the exhibition was a disgrace to all Africans, and should be removed.

Meanwhile, in the Grand-Anse, the remaining 12 Jeune Haiti fighters managed to extract themselves from the surrounding government troops and move into the hills. Their first engagement they called the "battle of Pre'vile." It also spelled the end of any thought of attacking Jérémie, as the area was now infested with government forces. Pre'vile was the closest they would get to Jérémie.

In turning away from their original objective, they had to decide on their future moves. They knew it was now a guerrilla war. It was agreed among them that Bobby Jourdan was the only one with experience in guerrilla warfare. He replaced airman Villedrouin as commander.

There also appears to have been a discussion among the group on whether to move to Pic (Peak) Macaya, Haiti's second-highest mountains, at around 2,255 meters. A majority decided that Peak Macaya was too distant, so they headed for Mazenod, where they hoped to establish their camp, map subsequent strategy, and receive supplies. They had heard that the Roman Catholic priest at Mazenod had a radio transmitter and talked daily to people in Boston. There was also the growing realization that if they did not receive supplies and reinforcements soon, the incursion would be a lost cause. Some members of the group, according to the government's interrogations of the two prisoners, were already suggesting the best policy would be to extract themselves and return to New York. How true it was, there is no way of telling. Geto Brierre, Milou Drouin, and Gusle Villedrouin were said to be set on remaining and continuing the fight no matter what.

The intrepid Father Georges was said to have kept his promise and was reportedly transporting arms to Miami when, on September 1, he was arrested by U.S. Customs agents and charged by the Bureau of Alcohol, Tobacco, and Firearms with "conspiring to export munitions of war for revolutionary purposes." A trailer with $11,000 worth of arms allegedly had been transported from New York to Miami. Father Georges allegedly had a key to the trailer. He was released on $1,000 bond, and the charges were eventually dropped. Duvalier was described as elated with the news of Father Georges' arrest.

Meanwhile, Duvalier's smuggling efforts were bearing fruit. Two T-28 aircraft had been flown out of the U.S. to Haiti in violation of half a dozen U.S. federal laws, including munitions control, the Neutrality Act, and a specific law under which no military training aircraft could be exported without a special license. When the planes arrived in Port-au-Prince from Texas, Papa Doc's joy turned to anger when he learned that the aircraft were not fitted with aerial gunnery or bomb racks. Finally, Duvalier's agents in Miami found an armaments mechanic in South Florida who knew how to convert the T-28 to fighting machines. But when he arrived in Port-au-Prince, he discovered that there was a lack of tools and equipment to do the job. He returned to Miami, where he was arrested and detained briefly. The unnamed armorer could have been a witness for a pending U.S. State Department case against Papa Doc's consul in Miami, Rudolph Baboun, but, according to information obtained by the author, the CIA stepped in and put the armorer's case on hold. He had done work for the CIA in the past, and the intelligence agency did not want him on the witness stand.

Baboun was later charged with shipping arms to Haiti, mostly small lots of pistols, without an export license, and was told to either leave the country or face trial. He also was reportedly implicated in the smuggling of the two T-28 planes to Duvalier's government. Duvalier gratefully appointed the Syrian-Haitian Baboun as Haiti's ambassador to Mexico.

When another shipment of arms bound for Haiti was seized at the Fort Lauderdale, Florida, airport as it was being loaded onto a plane, Haitian-born dentist Carlo Mevs was arrested. The arms shipment, including 50,000 rounds of .30-caliber ammunition, was valued at $100,000. Mevs was released in an unofficial prisoner swap, under which Haiti released three American citizens who had doing historical exploration work aboard their yacht, Fairwinds, and had sailed into Haiti's southern war zone. They had been taken to Port-au-Prince and held for 19 days.

With government troops moving onto the peninsula, it was obvious that the dozen surviving Jeune Haiti fighters had lost their momentum, but they were still to prove themselves the best guerrilla fighters Duvalier forces had faced.

Working their way across the peninsula, the rebels faced hunger as they spent two days moving through an area without farms, houses, markets or water. They survived on a diet of lizards. When they reached the mountains above the town of Les Anglais, peasants informed them that there were many government troops in the costal towns below. Haitian Coast Guard ships patrolling the coast were visible from the mountains.

On August 18, eight of the guerrillas, in search of food, surprised a unit of government troops who were preparing to dine. It was a well-coordinated attack. Three soldiers were killed and a fourth wounded while others fled to the coast, believing a second landing had taken place. This action not only gave a moral lift to the rebels; it replenished their arms supply with a captured machine gun and rifles, plus additional ammunition. The soldiers' dinner included two containers of rice, a guinea hen and a small pig, which the rebels enjoyed.

However, the Jeune Haiti guerrillas concluded that, given their plight, their priority was no longer to search out and destroy the enemy. They decided to fight only when Army troops got in their way or stumbled into

their path. They urgently needed to set up communications. They needed
to create a base and communicate with their pre-arranged Jeune Haiti
contact in the Dominican Republic to arrange for supplies and reinforcements. They had been joined by two able peasants who proved excellent
scouts.

On August 29, at Caliot, in the hills above Port-a-Piment, guerrilla
leader Bobby Jourdan, scouting ahead with Charlie Forbin and one of the
peasant scouts, learned that government troops were moving in the guerrillas' direction. Armed with captured Army weapons, the Jeune Haiti
guerrillas ambushed the troops with such firepower that again the latter
thought the rebels had been reinforced.

The rebels claimed to have killed five soldiers, among them the
machine-gunner, and seriously wounded three in the ambush. Jourdan
called a cease-fire and ordered the officer commanding the unit, Lt. Leon
Achille, and his remaining troops, to surrender. They did. The most seriously wounded soldiers were treated and sent with peasants to Port-a-
Piment for further medical care. Also captured were three mules, arms,
binoculars, medicines, maps, and a large quantity of ammunition.

In his interrogation, rebel prisoner Numa stated that Lieutenant Achille
had been killed by having his throat cut, as reported to him by Max
Armand. It was not true. Achille, who had suffered a double facture of his
left thigh, was left behind with the knowledge that the Army was on the
guerrillas' trail and would rescue him. On September 8, Achille was
indeed found by the Army. He was carried to the coast and transported to
Port-au-Prince, where Papa Doc greeted him as a hero. The President-for-
Life went to Achille's bedside in the military hospital and personally
pinned decorations on him.

(Achille went on to become a colonel in Duvalier's army. His last post
was head of the Port-au-Prince fire brigade before he was discharged by
Papa Doc's son and successor, Jean-Claude Duvalier. Achille died in
Port-au-Prince on January 25, 1984.)

The Haitian Army reported that, following the Caliot skirmish, the
guerrillas moved across the Macaya Mountains and, at a locality known
as Dallest, on September 8 they encountered units of Duvalier's tactical
battalion, commanded by Capt. Williams Regala and whose officers
included Lt. Prosper Avril. In that engagement, the Army had the men and

firepower and Jeune Haiti lost three of its ablest fighters. Killed were Gerard Brierre, second-in-command; Charlie Alfred Forbin, 23, the former U.S. paratrooper and son of Col. Alfred Forbin, who had been seized and executed in April 1963; and Jacques Wadestrand, 29, a former classmate of Edward Kennedy at Harvard University. (On a chance encounter with ex-U.S. President Harry Truman, Wadestrand said that he intended to go to Haiti and fight. "Don't get you killed," Truman advised him. He left a wife and son behind.)

At Pic Formond, on Sept. 14, the rebel brothers Jacques, 26, and Max Armand, 25, were killed. Their father, Benoit Armand, had been murdered by Macoutes in April 1963 because his first name resembled the last name of Lt. Francois Benoit. Jacques and Max Armand both had degrees from New York University, Jacques in economics and Max in electrical engineering from NYU. Jacques's daughter Lisa was born after he was killed.

On September 27, guerrilla Marcel Numa, 21, disguised as a peasant, walked into the coastal village of Coteaux and was taken prisoner as he tried to purchase supplies. Numa was the son of a black Jérémie coffee planter. He had studied diesel engineering at the Bronx, New York, Merchant Marine Academy. Duvalier had his prisoner. He later gloated that the captured Numa had told his interrogators that the rebels were low on food and munitions and that their morale was also low.

At Mount Sinai, on September 29, another engagement took place. Rebels Mirko Chandler and Jean Gerdes were seriously wounded. Chandler, according to Louis Drouin, who was later captured, pleaded with his best friend, Bobby Jourdan, to end his agony, and Jourdan did so with a well-placed bullet. The wounded Jean Gerdes, the Jeune Haiti artist who had been a late recruit to the group, destroyed all their papers and a case of munitions before ending his own life.

The remaining four rebels pushed eastward to Pic Tete Boeuf where, on October 4, Roland Riguard, 32, who had once tried to assassinate Duvalier, was wounded in a clash with Papa Doc's militia. Some two weeks later, on October 16, the militia pinned them down again, wounding Louis Drouin, 28, who told his companions to leave him. Drouin could not bring himself to take his own life and was taken prisoner three days later. The mulatto son of a Jérémie baker, he also had served in the

U.S. Army. He had studied finance in the United States and worked in several New York banks.

Gusle Villedrouin, Roland Riguad, and Reginal (Bobby) Jourdan, 26 (one of the few remaining relatives of Hector Riobe), fought their last battle on October 26 at Ravine Roche, a few kilometers from L'Asile. With their ammunition exhausted and surrounded by a horde of militia and regular troops, the three remaining Jeune Haiti fighters used stones in the final effort of a long and lonely war.

On orders from the palace, the heads of the young rebels were severed and transported to Port-au-Prince, where they were photographed to publicize Papa Doc's victory. There were summary executions of peasants said to have aided the rebels. How many died in total? Duvalier hid his own casualties.

*   *   *

Geraldine Carro, a slim, sophisticated blonde American magazine writer who was engaged to Max Armand, is quoted in an article published in the April 1970 issue of *True* magazine:

> When the first team landed in the south of Haiti, Max was second-in-command. After the first few days they ran into Duvalier's militia all around Jérémie and there were fire fights almost every day. Then their radio conked out, broke or was lost, we don't know; we just couldn't communicate with them. It gradually became obvious that unless something was done these boys were cooked. And we tried— listen, the CIA really tried—to get some help to the boys or somehow save what was left of them. And we couldn't do a thing. Washington just shut down on us; it was like running into a stone wall—nothing. All the boys were killed. My fiancé, too. I have since found out how he died, but I don't think I can talk about it. Anyhow, the CIA guys—the people who trained and equipped the boys—were terribly bitter, and said someone was pulling strings behind their backs to destroy the expedition. The only thing they could do was chip in just like an office collection, and pay for a requiem mass, a memorial service for the dead. It was right here in New York, on 14th street. I went too. All the CIA guys and families and girls of the dead boys were there: the aisle was a river of tears.

The story of Jeune Haiti is the tragic saga of young men who had everything to live for. One of their number, who acted as medical corpsman—Jacques Wadestrand, 28—had, together with Jean-Claude Assali and Jean-Claude Aime, been the first Haitian-born graduates of Harvard University. Wadestrand had abandoned his medical studies to join the political movement against the Duvalier dictatorship. He married in 1962 and a son was born in August 1963. He had been chosen as Secretary General of Jeune Haiti and volunteered to join the invasion, even though he had no military training and had not attended the CIA camp.

Realizing that something was wrong with the group's radio transmitter in Haiti because they had not been able to communicate with the assigned receptor in the Dominican Republic, Wadestrand's wife, Sylvie, made a desperate effort to send them a radio transmitter and reinforcements. She recruited volunteers and opened a training camp in Samana, in the eastern part of the Dominican Republic, and even managed to hire a landing craft in Miami. But the plan quickly unraveled when the Dominican government denied permission to refuel the craft. The volunteers were also having second thoughts about their mission. Even before her efforts collapsed, it was already too late. The war was over.

Papa Doc's Televised Execution Show

Early on the morning of November 12, 1964, businesses and schools in the Port-au-Prince were ordered closed. Students and government employees were instructed by radio announcements to go to the Port-au-Prince cemetery to witness a public execution of two rebel guerrillas. The 7 a.m. the event was scheduled before the 12-foot cemetery wall.

Crowds of obedient Duvalierists had already formed when Marcel Numa, 21, and Louis Drouin, 31, were led from a police van by Maj. Franck Romain and Lt. Francois Delva. As the two were tied to the pinewood poles, a murmur of surprise, as well as gasps, came from the crowd. It was only then that they realized that not all anti-Duvalier rebels were *bans;* one of the condemned bound to a pole before them, the younger and taller of the two, Marcel Numa, was black. The other, Louis Drouin, was a light-skinned mulatto.

There was heavy symbolism in the spectacle—perhaps more than

Duvalier himself realized. The scene, witnessed by a schoolteacher and described to this author, was reminiscent of an execution in 1790 when Vincent Oge, a mulatto, and J-B Chavanne, a black man, had faced what was to be a terribly torturous public execution at the wheel on the Place de Armes in Cap François (today's Cap-Haïtien) after their abortive uprising against the French colonial masters had failed. They, too, had an invited audience: slaveowners and slaves.

The two survivors of the thirteen Jeune Haiti invaders—who had what now seems a utopian dream of liberating their fellow Haitians from dictatorship—had been found guilty of treason by a military court martial sitting in the Caserne Dessalines for a day and a half (November 2-4). Their execution order was signed by Armed Forces Chief of Staff Gen. Gerard Constant, Assistant Chief Col. Jacques Laroche, and Maj. Franck Romain. It was Papa Doc's decision to execute the two guerrillas and make it a public spectacle.

Haiti's only television station, privately owned Tele-Haiti, was ordered to televise the execution. The government radio station, Voice of the Republic, was also on hand, transmitting its description live. The two condemned Haitians faced a nine-member firing squad showing no emotion. Small solace, perhaps, was the fact that hundreds of victims of the Papa Doc had been executed in secret in the dark of night at Ft. Dimanche. Numa and Drouin at least had a public execution.

The radio announcer described the scene of the actual execution step by step, in much the same blow-by-blow manner soccer matches were broadcast from nearby Sylvio Cator stadium. During the Roman Circus-like event, blue leaflets—like programs—were distributed to the crowd. Their content indicated that Papa Doc's macabre machinations were not yet concluded. The programs featured the severed heads of the three decapitated Jeune Haiti guerrillas and the U.S-made identification photos of the other member of the 13 invaders. The I.D. photos had been somehow removed from the Jeune Haiti headquarters in New York and forwarded to Duvalier. Several Haitians said to be in the pay of Duvalier in New York reportedly managed to take possession of the photos, but no investigation was ever carried out to learn the truth.

It was on October 28, after the campaign of two months and 20 days against the rebels had ended, that Duvalier revealed the grisly photographs of the three severed heads of the last Jeune Haiti guerrillas. The release of the photos was in part Papa Doc's grotesque idea for a victory statement. According to a rumor at the time, after the severed heads were presented to Duvalier, Macoutes and soldiers had played football with them in the backyard of the National Palace.

One of the heads was used for another practical purpose. The shocking incident was recounted to the author by a well-known Haitian activist, Robert Benodin, in Orlando, Florida, in 2003. One day before the heads were disposed of, Benodin said he had been in his electronics shop, which he operated at the time at the corner of Rue Champ de Mars and the Grand Rue in Port-au-Prince, when a man he knew came in carrying a flour sack. "He said he had something to show me." Benodin explained that he had a passing acquaintance with the man, who had been assigned by Duvalier to take care of former Dominican SIM agents who happened to be living in a lodging house behind the Bertoli building where he had his shop. Benodin said he told the man to come to his office on the mezzanine. The door had hardly closed, he recalled, before the visitor opened the flour sack to expose a matted bloody human head. "This is the head of Jourdan!" the man said. Benodin, shocked, said the head was unrecognizable but he took the man's word. When the visitor left, Benodin said, "I realized the caller had shown me Jourdan's head as a warning—because my wife, Mireille Brutus, was a cousin of Bobby 'Puchon' Jourdan. She packed up and left for the United States as soon as possible." The foreboding atmosphere under Papa Doc had become too much for Benodin. He closed up his electronics shops and left for voluntary exile in the U.S. the following year. Edouard Jourdan, Bobby's father, and other relatives of the Jeune Haiti fighters living in Port-au-Prince went into hiding or took refuge in Latin American embassies. Bobby Jourdan's father died in hiding, supposedly of a broken heart.

A written victory message by Papa Doc was handed out as part of the program at the staged public execution; it declared:

> Dr François Duvalier will fulfill his sacrosanct mission. He has crushed and will always crush the attempts of the anti-patriots. Think well, renegades! Renegades! You will not enjoy the gold with which they filled your pockets. Here fate expects you and your kind. They will not pass. Duvalierism . . . the living forces of the nation, will

crush you and any sacrilegious invasion of the sacred soil of the fatherland. . . . Thus will perish the anti-patriots who want to again put the Haiti of Jean-Jacques Dessalines under the whip of the colonials. It carries the strength of a torrent. ... The Duvalierist revolution will triumph. It will trample the bodies of traitors, and renegades . . . !

The two young Jeune Haiti rebels, Numa and Drouin, were tied to the stakes; a young French priest, Father Menard, was ordered to the execution site to hear the condemned men's confessions and give them absolution. The young Breton had only recently arrived in Haiti and been assigned as vicar at the Cathedral. When he arrived at the crowded cemetery wall, he mistook a person for one of the condemned men; the person quickly rebuffed him. Menard left. A police officer caught up with him and ordered him to return. As Father Menard met with each of the condemned men, an Army officer tried to listen to their confessions. When the priest rebuked the officer, he said, "They may be giving away secrets." As confessions in the Roman Catholic faith are confidential, only Menard knows what the condemned men said.

The dramatic suspense continued. When Lt. Pierre Albert, commanding the firing squad, gave the final orders, "load, aim," a hush fell over the huge crowd as TV and still cameras recorded the scene. People visibly winced when Lieutenant Albert barked the final order: *"Feu!"* ("Fire!") The two youths fell forward, slumped at their posts. Then, as photographs recorded, an officer carrying books, Col. Franck Romain, stepped forward and administered the coups de grace.

Broadcasting live from the cemetery wall, the government radio announcer was heard to pause and hold the microphone clear so his listening audience could hear the rifle volley and then the coups de grace. At the end, the loudspeakers called upon the crowd to move to the National Palace and there demonstrate their support for Papa Doc. On cue, Duvalier appeared on his palace balcony, waved, and smiled the smile of the victor. Jean-Claude said he did not see the footage of the execution.

For a week the televised execution carnival was rebroadcast to viewers on Duvalier's orders. The print account of the executions in *Le Matin* was similarly vivid: ". . . and this morning one should have seen this huge crowd, this feverish crowd communicating in a mutual patriotic exaltation, this crowd with only one heart, one soul to curse adventurism and brigandage; this crowd made up of the people, workers, functionaries, businessmen, all the forces of the nation standing, manifesting their total adhesion to the politics of peace of the Duvalier government . . . "

"One cannot control the painful sentiment felt when one sees debased sons soil the fatherland," *Le Matin* added, "our fatherland so dearly conquered by the numberless sacrifices. . . . They have not thought of the fatherland. They have never loved it. That is why they have tried to bloody it, to bruise it, to annihilate it. They have paid and let us throw a veil over this abominable act that nothing can erase."

Few Haitians could erase the memory of the executions of the two rebels. While it was a public spectacle, Haitians well knew that there had already been countless executions hidden from the public view at Ft. Dimanche, and in the darkness of night in untold other uncelebrated places.

The official accusation against the Thirteen was that they had lived in the U.S., been equipped by a foreign government, and "after having undergone intensive military training in a military camp of this foreign state" had landed in Haiti in an attempt at treason. Duvalier did not accuse the U.S. officially but he left no doubt that he believed the U.S. had backed the Thirteen.

Decorated by Duvalier for their part in the war against the Thirteen were 129 members of the military, VSN and police. At the same time, Duvalier decorated his two favorite spy chiefs, Luc Désyr and Elois Maitre, "for exceptional bravery on July 14, 1963," the day Barbot brothers were killed.

Duvalier also decreed that 14 persons be stripped of their Haitian nationality and condemned to "Civil Death." According to the decree, the 14 individuals lost all their civil rights, and their belonging and properties were to be confiscated by the State. It was all rather academic since all of those so condemned had already been murdered in Jérémie.

The weekend following the executions, 40 U.S. travel agents were welcomed to Port-au-Prince, with tourism director Gerard De Catalogue speaking for Duvalier in telling the agents that all was peace and quiet on the magic isle and not to believe sensational newsmen who were opposed to the march of progress in the little country of blacks. De Catalogue, known to the foreign media as the "White Bear," declared smugly, "We have no Harlem, Rochester, or Little Rock. Here everyone is safe."

*　　*　　*

The story of "The Thirteen"—or as least as much of it as is known—is one that many Haitians would rather forget. The barbarism that was inflicted on innocent families in Jérémie stands as one of the most shocking acts of Papa Doc's tyranny. The young men who fought and suffered extreme hardship died along with their dreams of achieving a better Haiti. In 1986, following the end of the Duvalier dynasty—with the flight of Papa Doc's son, President-for-Life Jean-Claude Duvalier, into exile—a monument was raised at the side of the Jérémie airstrip where entire families of Jérémie were murdered, one by one.

The 13 and the Dates of Their Deaths

August 12, 1964
　　Yvan Laraque, 33 years old, at Prévilé
September 8
　　Gérald Brièrre, 30 years old
　　Charles Alfred Forbin, 23 years old
　　Jacques Wadestrandt, 29 years old, at Dallest
September 14
　　Jacques Armand, 26 years old
　　Max Armand, 25 years old, at Pic Formand
September 29
　　Jean Gerdès
　　Mirko Chandler, at Mont Sinai
October 26
　　Guslé Villedrouin, 28 years old
　　Roland Rigaud, 32 years old
　　Reginald (Bobby) Jourdan, 26 years old, Ravine Roche, close to Asile
November 12
　　Marcel Numa, 21 years old, at wall of Port-au-Prince's cemetery
　　Louis Drouin, 31 years old, at wall of Port-au-Prince's cemetery

CHAPTER 13

Jérémie 1964:
The Terrible Wrath of Papa Doc

It was one of the prettiest provincial towns in Haiti, famous for its poets and patriots. On the east coast of the southern peninsula, in the early days of the Republic, Jérémie was in many ways closer to Europe than to Port-au-Prince. It was connected by both commerce and culture, and many Jérémians sailed to Bordeaux on passenger or cargo ships without ever calling at Port-au-Prince.

Historically, this had been part of the old mulatto south of Gen. Andre Rigaud. It had had the largest mulatto population of any Haitian provincial town. The merchants lived above their stores, situated mostly around the Dumas square in the upper part of town. In the hills farther above the commercial section of town was Borde, a district with cooler temperatures and the delightful gingerbread summer homes of the clannish entrepreneurial class.

Mornings in town were delightful. There was no need for an alarm clock, or for that matter any clock. In the early morning there was the melodious song of the coffee *marchanne*, calling "*min gro konet . . . cafe griye*." The freshly ground coffee was wrapped in paper like an ice cream cone.

By the late 1940s and early 1950s an exodus of members of the large mulatto families to the capital had begun. Jérémie had begun to prove too distant by road to Port-au-Prince for business and other purposes; it was a tortuous trip of a day or more of local travel. There was an overnight boat trip, but even that could be adversely affected by weather and other unforeseen circumstances.

The day following the 1957 presidential election, correspondent Peter

Khiss of *The New York Times* and the author were taken by Army Col. Andre Fareau, member of the military junta, to Jérémie to prove that the September 22 elections there were fair. It was laughable. Local Duvalierists had been organized and were waiting for us. They turned our visit into a Duvalierist victory parade. There were no mulattos in the crowd of prancing poor in Jérémie that day.

*   *   *

Seven years later, the terrible events took place in Jérémie. To learn what had taken place in Jérémie that summer of 1964 I turned years later to a survivor, a man whose word I knew could be trusted.

In July 1988, my interview with Methodist Pastor Alain Rocourt took place in his temporary office in the United Methodist Church in Miami's "Little Haiti." Pastor Rocourt was in temporary political exile from his homeland recuperating from the violent elections in Haiti the year before, in which he was a leading member of the country's electoral council and a target of military thugs.

A slight, wiry mulatto with a palpable sense of social justice, Pastor Rocourt recounted in English Duvalier's terrible reprisals known as the "Vespers of Jérémie" as if they were a bad dream not easily revisited. His account:

> It's a bit hazy in my mind, but one can never forget those terrible events that took place in Jérémie during the summer of 1964 when the 13 young men landed near Dame Marie, about 50-odd kilometers from Jérémie. I was a pastor in Jérémie. My family was there and immediately the whole area was under curfew. I remember very well at six o'clock the first night not even a candle was allowed. There was complete blackout. Our two children asked repeatedly, "Why should we have to go to bed so early?" It was during that first night I was nearly killed.
>
> I was living in Borde, the residential area of Jérémie, and I had two colleagues with us, an Irish minister, Patrick O'Connell, son of the old O'Connell who spent much of his life in Haiti, and a man from Switzerland, called Gardel. He was a member of the Swiss team that was working in Jérémie at the time, on our rehabilitation project. We had dinner that night together, at the back of the house, with a single candle, and we kept talking when about 9 p.m. I heard

the noise of cars in my neighbor's yard. They were the Jerome family, not related to the military officer Abel Jerome by any means, but the old Jerome family of Jérémie. In fact, Georges Jerome was a businessman who had a store in Jérémie. He was actually the main layman in my church, responsible for the business administration of the church. His ailing mother was in the house with grandchildren who had come to Jérémie to spend the summer holidays.

Hearing these car noises I said, "Surely it is strange that George is going out at this hour when there is a curfew. It must be that his mother is very sick, so let me go out and see what I can do." My house was at the end of a long alley, so I came out of the house and approached the fence in pitch darkness, but I knew my way very well. My eyes became accustomed to the darkness, and as I approached the fence I heard some voices. "Hands up!" said the voices. So I put my hands up and then they commanded me to "Come over, come over." I replied, "But how can I climb a barbed wire fence with my hands up?" "You do it, you do it," came the command. To this day I still bear the marks of where the barbed wire cut into my body from climbing over that fence.

My neighbor's house was full of heavily armed people. When I entered I was facing Astrel Benjamin, the chief of the Tonton Macoutes from Les Cayes. In a rough voice he demanded, "What were you doing there?" I replied, "Well I heard some noise and this is the house of my neighbor, my church people. I wondered if my neighbor's mother who is an old and sick lady had any trouble. I had come to see what I could do." The Macoute chief screamed at me, "You must be a traitor." At the moment when he began to shout at me, I saw two of his henchmen pouring gasoline onto the wooden door of the house. They were about to set the house on fire. When they heard their chief talking to me, they quickly put aside their gas can. You could smell the gas. I think it was a providential thing that I had appeared at that very moment. The house was filled with young children, and the old lady was there.

I didn't know then that old Georges and his brother-in-law, Westley Clerie, my cousin, had already been arrested and were in jail. As the Macoute was shouting at me, he stripped me of my belt and led me outside. As I am a very thin and a light-weighted person, the Macoute had no trouble picking me up and throwing me into his jeep. Before we drove away, a car appeared. The Macoute shouted, "Who is there, identify yourself." The person in the car replied, identifying himself. It was the assistant mayor of the town. The assistant mayor saw me in the jeep. "Pastor what are you doing there?" I replied, "Ask the man here, he has arrested me."

Then the assistant mayor addressed Astrel Benjamin. "Don't you know he is Pastor Rocourt, Methodist pastor in the town of Jérémie, and very well known?" Benjamin barked back, "I don't care, bishops are betraying Duvalier, and pastors even more." He revved the engine of the jeep and we were off. As we drove down the hill into town we passed the infamous Sanette Balmir—*fillétte Lalo* (name for a female Macoute)—who was the woman in charge of the town. Benjamin stopped the jeep and Sanette asked him, "Who do you have in your vehicle?" Benjamin replied boastfully, "I've got one of them. I'm going to kill him, his tomb is already dug."

He wasn't lying. The graves were already dug near Number Two (the name of the locality is Number Two) at the little airport, a few miles from town. But when he got to the front of the Army barracks, he changed his mind about going to the killing place at the airport. "Let's go to the barracks first," he said to his fellow Macoutes.

That hesitation saved my life. If he had taken me straight to the airport where they were digging the graves where they buried most of those who they were murdering, I would have been dead.

Benjamin took me inside and he sat down and I remained standing. It was his grand moment, his great opportunity to humiliate me. The place was full of Macoutes, most of them from Aux Cayes, who had come to burn the residential sector of the city. I stood there. He then ordered, "Take off your undershirt, take off your pants, and take off your underpants." He wanted to have me naked but he wanted to do it gradually to enjoy his triumph. As he was doing this, I was facing the staircase leading upstairs to the headquarters. I saw Abel Jerome who was the Captain in charge of Jérémie. He came down the stairs and threw up his hands, and he came before Macoute chief Benjamin: "Why are you doing this to the pastor?" He turned to me and said, "Pastor, put on your clothes."

The Tonton Macoute was furious, and there was a dangerous exchange of words between the two, and the Macoute felt that Jerome was taking his prey away from him. Jerome ran back upstairs and the Macoute threw me into a cell. In the cell were Georges Jerome (again, no relationship to Abel) and Westley Clerie, my cousin. It was only then I knew they had been arrested. Benjamin was furious. Then the door of the cell opened and Abel Jerome said very politely, "Pastor will you come upstairs with me please." So I went upstairs, and found myself in a room with high-ranking officers of the Army, including the secretary of Duvalier, Pierre Biamby.

They were all very polite. There were colonels, majors, and cap-tains. I didn't know them, but Biamby was the one who spoke and the others were shaking their heads. Biamby apologized very, very much on behalf of the government, saying, "Pastor, we are very sorry this thing happened to you, these things do happen at times like this." . . . He then said, "We'll have people take you back home, please don't blame the government for doing this," and he said, "Do you have something you wish to say to us?" I said, "Yes, two things: First of all, I'm not going back without the two people who were in the cell with me, Mr. Jerome and Mr. Clerie, who have done nothing wrong as far as I know. . . . I want them to go back with me and I want to tell you about this action." I explained to him that if the government wants to alienate the population they are doing that but if they want people to believe in them, then it's exactly the wrong way to go about it. And if they want to fight those whom they said have invaded the country, it's not the way.

They sent me back home with my two friends. We had an officer and a sergeant accompany us home. We were the only people who were arrested and not murdered. The 27 other people arrested during the two months that followed were all murdered, including women and children.

In the town, it was a horrible situation. Night after night you heard the terrible sound of the DKW jeeps, the hallmark of the Macoutes since Barbot's days. We became so accustomed to the noise of terror, that every time we heard it, my wife had to close her ears, and up till now, 24 years later, she just can't hear the sound of the DKW because she lost good friends being dragged to their grave in that death jeep.

Astrel Benjamin was originally from the mountains above Jérémie. He was the archetype of the tough, angry, and frustrated person that became a Macoute. He was 35 years old, of average height but well-built, a natural bully. He had asked Duvalier for the privilege of coming to Jérémie and to burn it—he had a chip on his shoulder—he wanted to burn residential Jérémie to the ground.

*   *   *

In my 1988 interview with the Rev. Rocourt, he continued:

Jérémie was in quarantine, you couldn't leave the town. The whole peninsula was cut off. Why Abel Jerome saved me from Astrel Benjamin is a Haitian story of the time. Some months earlier, I had received from the Church World Service 83 bales of clothing.

I had made a careful survey of all the places where we had churches, some thirty of them. I checked people's height, size, and so on, and in this I had been helped by the church volunteers. We were going to make packages for individual families. That is what we had planned. When we received those 83 bales of clothing, Jérémie was in a very difficult economic situation. The consequences of the devastating 1954 Hurricane Hazel were still being felt. There was widespread poverty.

When the 83 bales arrived in Jérémie, the head of the Customs received a telegram from Port-au-Prince, from Duvalier, ordering him to confiscate the bales of clothing. Just because he had received a report from the civil authorities in Jérémie that if (we learned this later) he had allowed the Methodist church to distribute so much clothing to people all over the place, then the Methodist church would get the credit for helping the people, and Duvalier wouldn't be seen as the Father of the Nation. So they were confiscated.

Now the wife of the Mayor of Jérémie, Mrs. Sajous, was a cousin of mine. She was furious about the confiscation of clothing and came to see me about a month after it had been confiscated. She said, "Why don't you write to Duvalier to complain about this?" "No," I said. "I won't write a word to him; after all, he claims he wants the good of the people, and yet look at what he is doing. Let them discover who is doing bad things."

Anyway, she came after me a few times. Finally I said, "Okay, let's make a bargain. If you want me to write to him I won't sign the letter, you will. You know him, he holds you in high esteem, you are the wife of the mayor of the town, Mrs. Sajous. But on one condition: Let me tell you all I think". She said to do it. "I'll take the letter."

So I wrote a very strong letter to Duvalier under the name of Mrs. Sajous and— posing as Mrs. Sajous—I told him what I thought of the civil servants in Jérémie, who were out to get what they wanted, and not to help the people. And I explained what the church wanted to do. The church was doing nothing politically. In fact, if he wanted to strengthen his action by helping the people, etc. I know he received that letter on Monday at 9 a.m. because a colonel in the Army took the letter to him at the palace. It went by boat on Saturday and the colonel received it on Sunday and the letter was on Duvalier's desk at 9 a.m.

At 10 a.m. in the morning I saw the head of the Customs. He drove into my yard and said, "I want to see you . . . pastor," in a low voice. "I've received a telegram from President Duvalier, and this is it, and he has ordered me to give back immediately all the bales of clothing to Pastor Rocourt. Are you going to pick them up today?" I said no, they had been there for a month; they can remain there a few more days. I enjoyed that moment.

A month after that, a Swiss team [that] we had invited . . . to Jérémie for a work camp arrived. On the wharf I went to meet them. The political situation in the country was tense. There were rumors of an invasion. Nothing had taken place. A group of nine white people—that was an event for the small town of Jérémie. Capt. Abel Jerome appeared at the wharf and told me, "Pastor, you shouldn't have these foreigners here." I said, "Why not? They went to Gonaïves and St. Marc, they went to Jacmel, for work camps. Why shouldn't they come to Jérémie?" "No, no, no," said the captain. "It's not allowed."

I said, "Well as you know I can't send them back to Port-au-Prince, there is no boat and no plane. I'll have to send them on the next boat or next plane." "Okay, okay," he said. "But keep them in your house," he ordered. But, I said, they were heading to the countryside at Léon where they were to camp and help build a school with us. "You keep them in your house; I'll come to you to tell you what to do." So they spent the weekend with me not knowing what to do.

Monday morning at 8 a.m. Captain Jerome drove into my yard. I greeted him and asked him to come in and he said, "No, pastor, I want to see you."

So, thinking the encounter was to be in private, the reverend took the officer into his small study. The captain, Rocourt said, was extremely polite:

"You know, pastor, I did not know you were a good friend of the president. When I left you I telephoned the commandant in Cayes"—I think he said Col. Henry Namphy—"who in turn, knowing that sometimes the president has his particular reasons, called the president. I have received a telegram from the president and here it is." The telegram read, "Pastor Rocourt is a personal friend of mine. [I had never seen the man.] Give him all the protection he needs, let the Swiss do all the work they want to, they are under my own protection." It was a month later that Captain Jerome found me in the Army barracks naked before the Macoute chieftain from Cayes.

The mayor, who was with the group of officers at the Army barracks, repeated later to me what Captain Jerome had said: "Do you know what the fool Astrel Benjamin has done? He has arrested Pastor Rocourt, who is a personal friend of François Duvalier, and he has stripped him naked."

*   *   *

Clergyman Rocourt went on in our interview:

Dr. Jacques Foucand stayed in the residential part of the Jérémie hospital. He did that to make people believe he was not taking part in the massacre. He was from Jérémie. He went to see the Villedrouin family, a family he knew very well—he grew up with Victor and Guy Villedrouin. He knew them well; they had been young together. Foucand told them not to worry, to assure them that no harm would come to them, to any member of this family, but he was said to have been the one who told Duvalier to get rid of them. He was a sinister man.

Sanette Balmir was a terrible woman. It's hard to find words to describe her low morals. Now dead. She was one of the lowest prostitutes in Jérémie. Her brothel was the lowest of the low. Duvalier made her the "Marie Jeanne" (leading woman) of the town of Jérémie. The Duvalier revolution gave power to all the worst, most terrible human elements. It was a way to debase the good people.

It's not that Sanette actually participated in the killings; she was there, she was part of it. She attended. As for Capt. Abel Jerome, the Macoutes, and mostly the Macoutes from Cayes, were doing the arresting, helped by the Macoutes of Jérémie. Astrel Benjamin was head of it all. Abel Jerome took part in the arrests, and in the looting of the stores, particularly of Sansaricq's store. The day before the public looting, he went at night and took Pierre Sansaricq, the owner of the largest hardware store in town, and made him hand over all the money he had in his safe, and all the precious stuff he had in his store. The following morning the public was permitted to loot.

Pierre's arrest was terrible. From 6 p.m. until 6 a.m. the town was under curfew. It was between 9 and 11 p.m. that they arrested people they decided to murder. We saw Sansaricq, he lived just 200 yards from our house—they sent Macoutes to get him. One Jérémian was forced to guide them. He said he was the one who every Saturday used to go to Mrs. Sansaricq to receive some money for his family. She said to the man, "Is it you who have come to arrest me?" and he claims to have said, "Well what could I have done, Mrs. Sansaricq? They sent me." He testified later that she then said, "God forgive him, for they don't know what they do." She went with them and was murdered at the airfield.

After that, in a piecemeal way, they took Mrs. Villedrouin's two sons, Victor and Guy, and afterward they took their families, their wives and children. Old Mrs. Villedrouin was 85 years old and a faithful member of the Methodist church. She was left in her house alone. There was nobody else. Even her maid who had been with her for many years, Hermas, she had to leave the yard because they told her if she remained she would be killed. She was a black woman, a very faithful sort. But the poor old lady was there alone, so my wife used to send her meals three times a day. I went to see her as often as I could until one day some people sent word from town to warn me not to go and see Mrs. Villedrouin.

"Tell the people who have sent you that I'll resign as a minister before I stop visiting her. As long as I'm a minister I'll go and visit her." I visited her the last time one Sunday evening at 6:30 p.m. because I wanted to have cloisters at 7 p.m. I had service with her, prayed with her and gave her communion. At 9 p.m. that night they came and got the old lady. Neighbors say that when they threw her into the jeep a leg was left outside and they slammed the door so hard that it broke her leg. She was still alive when they drove away. Whether she was alive or had just fainted en route to the airport, she was thrown into a pit and covered up. She was the grandmother of Guslé Villedrouin, one of the 13 guerrillas. Her son was Col. Villedrouin, who had been arrested the year before and beaten to death by Macoutes.

So they took Mr. and Mrs. Pierre Sansaricq and their only daughter, two married sons, and the youngest son working with their father in the store. The wife of one of the sons was a leader in the girl guides, she was four months pregnant. She had her children murdered before her and then she was murdered. She was said to have been taken by a terrible rage when she saw what they were doing to her children. There was one man, Renash, a rascal who had been working in the post office, and he is the one who sent into the air an 18-month-old child and received the child on a bayonet. Another child was asking permission to do "pipi" when Capt. Sonny Borge ground a lighted cigarette into his eyes. As far as I know, 27 innocent souls were murdered at Jérémie.

The local Macoute chief, Saint-Ange Bontemps, went to Mrs. Louis Drouin's home. She was a frail old lady who knew her embroidery and Catholic Church. Devout, she went to Mass at 4 a.m. every morning. Bontemps threw her down the staircase and snapped her spine in half a dozen places. She was carried off with her husband, Louis Drouin, and murdered in cold blood. For two months Jérémie knew nothing but terror, absolute terror.

Nicole Studley, a cousin of the Villedrouins, a terrible girl, survived. She took advantage of the situation to steal the Villedrouin jewelry. She reportedly went to Abel Jerome and told him he had forgotten one, one of the Villedrouin girls who was mentally ill. They came back and took her and killed her and the Villedrouin name disappeared completely from Jérémie.

A small tailor from the lower part of town one Saturday afternoon went down to the wharf and climbed aboard one of the boats that was about to leave. You had to have a special pass to leave the town. He didn't have one. When they ordered him ashore he refused. Soldiers and Macoutes tried to drag him off the boat, but he found some incredible strength and shouted for all to hear, "My children are dying of hunger! I can't earn anything because this town is damned because of the terror!" For some reason the soldiers and Macoutes were taken back, suddenly afraid. They released him and let him sail away without a pass, knowing perhaps they would have to kill him to get him off that boat.

Outside Jérémie the countryside was even worse. No one could go out of the town, peasants were not allowed to bring their produce into town. Lay churchmen were the ones who brought the news of terrible things happening, the systematic killing of peasants accused of harboring or helping in any way, even selling produce to, the Jeune Haiti guerrillas. Whole peasant families were wiped out, leaving no witnesses to the terror.

The rebels came to Chambellan, some 30 kilometers from Jérémie, to purchase supplies. The soldiers returning from patrols in the countryside said they were fighting like lions. The Army confiscated all four-wheel-drive vehicles for its campaign against the 13.

There was one man, a *chef de bureau* at the Public Works Department—everyone had to show they were Duvalierists and get their hands bloodied or else they were suspect and could be killed. You couldn't be lukewarm; the Duvalierists wouldn't accept that. This man from the Public Works was a good friend of Pierre Sansaricq, and he was so horrified by the killings that he took sick. When he went to see Dr. W. Ferrier, the doctor said he had nothing wrong, just high blood pressure. But the man confided to the doctor, "Wily, Wily [the Doctor], they have killed Pierre Sansaricq." The poor man kept repeating, "They have killed Pierre Sansaricq. It's not possible." He collapsed and died. He couldn't take it.

Concluding his story of what happened that summer of 1964 in Jérémie, Pastor Rocourt sighed with sadness, adding:

There was sun but it no longer shone on Jérémie. It was as if the town was under a thick, dark cloud. The killings lay heavily on the town. Although some people had participated in the massacre, they were asking themselves, "Did such a terrible thing ever take place?" Because the houses belonged to the murdered mulattoes, no one would touch them. They were left there as a reminder, witness to the horrible things that had happened. Jérémie was forgotten by Duvalier and left to decay and die.

Duvalier's Macoutes and Army were like a Mafia. They had a code of silence that if broken they knew it would implicate them and too many other people.

I must bear witness to that terrible time. Please publish what I have told you, it is the truth.

"It is perhaps God's will," he said, and he added in an almost religious tone that it was Jérémie that gave birth to the youth movement that sparked the popular rebellion that finally ended the Duvalier dynasty in 1986.

Pastor Alain Rocourt died in Port-au-Prince in December 2002. His chilling account of the murderous "Vespers of Jérémie" serves as a reminder that the term "dictatorship" signifies not only a tyrannical, often faceless national government. For the helpless humans living under it, particularly in a small community where everyone knows everyone else, dictatorship can be as up-close and personal—and terrifying—as the neighborhood spy living next door; the sadistic local cop exhorting, beating, and raping; the gunshots and screams in the night; the abiding fear that oneself will be the next to be dragged into the darkroom.

Col. Abel Jerome lives quietly in retirement at Lafond, some five miles from Jacmel, his hometown.

Years later, I heard that there was another person who had miraculously escaped the massacre. I learned of the story of young Mrs. Mona Ambroise Sansaricq, pregnant and prepared for bed in their Jérémie home when they came that night and ordered her and her husband, Fred, to climb onto the back of a truck. It was a scene akin to trucking cattle. They rattled over the rutted road from town to their freshly dug mass grave at the small, grass-covered airport.

Fred Sansaricq, an auto supply store owner with a fuel-storage tank, sold diesel and gasoline. Occasionally, the Haitian Army was a customer.

That was the couple's only connection with the military.

Some were praying, others were holding tightly to the sides of the truck as they headed like lambs to the slaughter. That night of infamy saw Papa Doc's blood-sated killers, on precise orders from the National Palace, execute all aged people and infants in the most barbaric and beastly manner, disfiguring their victims with unspeakable savagery.

On the way to the mass execution site, Papa Doc's killing field, an army officer stopped the truck on which Mrs. Sansaricq was a prisoner and ordered her to get off. She obeyed and was left by the roadside, alone in her nightgown.

Mona became a rare survivor of the Jérémie massacre. That night she eventually reached home. Her husband, Fred, and old and young members of his family continued on to the airport to be brutally butchered to satisfy Papa Doc's thirst for revenge.

Mona suffered a miscarriage and eventually got out of Jérémie and Haiti with her nightmare to join her parents who were working in Africa. She later married a Frenchman in Bamako, Mali, where they had three sons. Today they have four grandchildren.

CHAPTER 14

Dominican Civil War

For the Kamokens, the Dominican civil war of April 1965 had an almost innocent beginning. One Saturday, most of the Kamokens had taken a break and gone to the capital. A group that included Gérard Lafontant was seated before a pharmacy playing dominos in the cool shade on a hot evening. There had been reports of disturbances, and that Radio Santo-Domingo had been seized but that the government had taken it back. There was tension, but coup rumors had been so regular that many people did not give them much credence. Suddenly a group of civilians appeared, moving down the street and throwing rocks. They were followed by the *Cascos Blancos*—the white-helmeted riot police. Shop doors closed and those left in the street were victims of the nightsticks. Gérard Lafontant received a billy-club blow to the head which later required half a dozen stitches. Four of the Haitians were dragged off to the Ozama fortress, headquarters of the Cascos Blancos, but were released Sunday afternoon.

Most of the Kamokens were caught up in the tide of rebellion. Those remaining at Nigua scattered as soldiers moved in and seized their belongings. Events moved swiftly. Back in Santo-Domingo, a .50-caliber machine gun had been placed on a rooftop by a group of pro-Bosch rebels, but it was jammed. The Haitians took charge and quickly had the heavy machine gun in working order.

These events caught the author en route home from New York after warning editors of *The New York Times* and *Time* magazine that a Dominican coup was imminent. The coup happened on April 25, 1965, and all Dominican airports were closed tight. In Puerto Rico, following an interview with the exiled President Juan Bosch, the author joined other newsmen in hitching a ride to Santo Domingo on the U.S. Marine Corps landing tank ship USS Wood County.

In Santo Domingo, Gérard Lafontant and a group of Kamokens had made sure that the author's family was safe. They had offered to guard the apartment, but my wife said she felt secure. Meanwhile, U.S. President Johnson ordered American troops to land, and the conflict changed direction. Constitutionalists in Santo Domingo faced not only the right-wing Dominican military but also 22,000 U.S. troops, later to be dressed up as an OAS force that included token contingents from Central America and Brazil.

The day after the U.S. landing, several of my reporter colleagues and I ventured downtown into rebel territory. We found a much different atmosphere than that described by the U.S. embassy as a frightening reign of terror similar to the French Revolution or worse. On Independence Plaza, a U.S.-educated Dominican military officer stood beside a captured tank with the newly painted sign "Pueblo." The sound of Kreyól drew us to a group of Kamokens busily fixing ancient arms for the anticipated battle to come, under the supervision of Lafontant. Concerned about our safety, they quickly painted *Prensa* (Press) on the side and roof of our car.

Before long the Kamokens, under the leadership of Fred Baptiste, were integrated into the Dominican constitutional forces. The Haitian commando was located on a second-story building on Santo Domingo's Independence Plaza. Later, the commando moved across the plaza to the expansive Arab club.

During the early days of fighting, while I was sending a cable to *Time* from the RCA office on Calle El Conde, a commotion outside brought me to the door. There was Fred Baptiste, with a bazooka, moving down the street toward the Fortaleza Ozama. He led his men marched proudly toward the target, the besieged, hated Casco Blanco Police Headquarters in the ancient fortress. It was clearly Baptiste's finest hour. He had an audience and the attack had succeeded. The Cascos Blancos inside were imprisoned by the Constitutionalists for the duration of the war.

At the end of a press conference in the Constitutionalist Copello building headquarters during the war, Colonel Francisco Caamano Deno called me aside. He had a worried look. "*Mira*, we have a serious problem," he said. "I have been told that the Haitians had executed one of their own. It happened only yesterday. Do you know anything about it?" I did not. Caamano said he would have to take action against whoever was responsible. Later, I was able to explain to Caamano what had happened at the Haitian commando.

The Haitian commando was in a state of mourning when I arrived. Jean-Claude Romain, whose Kamoken nom de guerre was Puma, was dead. Puma was one of the most likeable human beings. Educated and without fear, he had often crossed into Haiti on missions for Pierre Rigaud. Puma, Fred Baptiste said angrily, had foolishly played Russian roulette and lost. It was true that many of the Kamoken had become despondent, wanting to take their constitutionalist arms and return to fight in Haiti. Baptiste refused to discuss the earlier death of a Haitian believed to be a Duvalier spy who had wandered into the constitutional sector, been seized by the Kamokens, and been "shot while trying to escape."

Another Haitian-born hero of the Dominican war was Jacques Viau. He had spent most of his life in the Dominican Republic, where the family had taken refuge in 1947 because of a well-known tragic incident in Port-au-Prince. Jacques Viau's brother, enraged over an article published by an editor of then-President Estimé's government newspaper, shot and killed the editor. In turn, Viau's young brother was lynched by a mob. Jacques grew up in Santo Domingo, became a schoolteacher, poet, and member of the June 14th Movement. He was among the first to join the Dominican rebellion of April 1965.

Viau opposed most of the Haitian exiles and specifically Fred Baptiste on the grounds that they lacked any political ideology. A Marxist himself, he sought the overthrow of what he termed the fascist dictatorship in Haiti and at the same time fully supported the Dominican Constitutionalist war. The Dominican cause came first. On June 15, 1965, when U.S. forces encircling the city were ordered to advance, Viau was defending a section of the Constitutionist front line, commando B-3, located in an old school building only four blocks from the advancing U.S. troops. With disregard for his own safety, Viau fought on until a shell from a 106 mm recoilless rifle tore off both his legs. He did not survive and died in his adopted country.

*   *   *

After peace was finally signed in September 1965 and Dominican provisional president Héctor García Godoy took over, the Haitian combatants had to surrender their arms. One day a group of them reported to the author that they had been at the San Luis sugar mill looking for work when a Haitian in Dominican uniform, accompanying a group of Dominican soldiers from the San Isidro base in a jeep, recognized Fred Baptiste and gave a cry of, "There he is!" Baptiste and the others managed to escape but they took it as a warning that they were being targeted by right-wing death squads.

It was only after several such incidents that Fred Baptiste, as well as his brother and Gérard Lafontant, agreed to go into exile. It was only a matter of time before relations with Papa Doc would be reestablished, and then they would face dual enemies: Macoutes as well as right-wing Dominican death squads. Alfredo Ricard, the chief of cabinet of President García Godoy, took on the task of finding funds and a country or countries that would receive them. Fred Baptiste, wearing a gift suit made of tough Irish tweed, finally, with his brother Reneld and Lafontant, departed for Belgium.

Eventually, moving to Paris, the Baptiste brothers joined with Lt. Sean Pean, a former Haitian military academy instructor, and top of his Academy class in 1956. In Europe, Fred Baptiste began seeking funds for what he termed "his" revolution. Along with Lieutenant Pean, he visited the author Graham Greene in Antibes during the filming of the movie version of *The Comedians* in the rugged French Riviera mountains nearby. Greene introduced them to the cast of *The Comedians,* to whom Fred pleaded for funds. Director Peter Glenville demurred, saying that he had already contributed generously to Father Georges for the Haitian revolution.

In his letters from Paris to me (by then I had been transferred to Mexico City), Fred Baptiste made known his frustration but also his determination to continue his fight.

In February 1969, I returned to the Dominican Republic to report for *Time* magazine on President Joaquín Balaguer. Shortly after my arrival, I was sought out at the Hotel Embajador by a former aide to the onetime

Haitian presidential candidate Sen. Louis Déjoie, who had since died following his exile in the Dominican Republic. How the ex-aide knew I was in the country remains a mystery, but he appeared extremely well informed. Fred Baptiste and his brother Reneld had been arrested, the man explained, upon their return to Santo Domingo a few weeks earlier from Europe in possession of false passports. Fred Baptiste had later been released but some of his old Kamokens still living in the Dominican Republic had been rounded up and jailed. Two of those arrested were identified as aging former Haitian army soldiers. While the informant didn't know why Fred Baptiste had been freed, it was suspected that Balaguer's well-organized secret service had let Baptiste go for the express purpose of learning more about his intentions.

The next news I received of the Baptiste brothers was contained in a dispatch by correspondent Jeremiah O'Leary, datelined Port-au-Prince, to *The Washington Star* on February 24, 1970, reporting that they had returned to Haiti!

> The two leaders of the anti-Duvalierist group had been in custody until recently. . . . Evidently Balaguer, who had troubles of his own with a presidential election coming up in May, was anxious to convey to Duvalier that the Dominicans were not responsible for helping the rebels cross the frontier. The Communist band is led by Fred and Reneld Baptiste, who are brothers and who took an active part in the Dominican civil war of 1965 on the side of the leftist rebels.
>
> Fred Baptiste went into hiding when he was released on bail and Dominican authorities subsequently learned that he was gathering men and arms. Last week, Santo-Domingo intelligence officials say, the brothers plus seven other armed men made their way into Haiti in the vicinity of Jimani in the south. Evidently hoping to round up the Baptiste band quickly, Duvalier has not announced to his people that they are in the country. The Dominicans similarly have not made public disclosure about the incursion. The Baptistes are tough and well-trained. In the past their small group has accepted financial assistance from Fidel Castro and Moscow.

Precisely how the Baptiste brothers ended up in Papa Doc's hands remains a mystery. Dr. Claude Simon, a native of Jacmel and son of deputy André Simon, who practiced medicine in New Orleans, in an interview with the author in 1992 on his return to Haiti recalled that he had been relaxing in the home of Army Capt. Noel, the commander of the Thiotte district about February 9, 1970, when he and his host were interrupted.

"'Commandant, they have brought rebels to the Caserne,' a soldier reported," Simon recounted. "The captain laughed and then got angry at the interruption—as he was playing the guitar. He cussed the soldier: 'What the hell are you doing annoying me with such old tales? . . . Get out of here.'" Rebels were a thing of the past in the zone, reflected Simon. "They are seeing ghosts," Capt.Noel told Simon. But then the post's sergeant arrived and said, "'Commandant, it is true they have brought eight rebels.' The officer swore again, 'What the hell is this shit!?'"

Simon related, "We went to the Caserne and I recognized Reneld. I knew him when we were kids together in Jacmel. I pretended not to know him because both brothers were high on the wanted list. Reneld pleaded for water. The soldiers were highly superstitious and the Kamokens had taken on a supernatural character in this mountainous region. The soldiers refused to give water, believing the water might make him disappear or something."

A corporal from the little border post at Gros Cheval in the mountains had escorted the nine prisoners. It was an implausible story, Dr. Simon said. Peasants, the corporal stated, had reported to the two-man military border post that there were rebels in the area. The two soldiers, armed with old Springfield rifles and only a limited amount of ammunition, had supposedly surrounded the eight rebels and captured them after a firefight. How could two soldiers capture eight rebels and tie them up? Dr. Simon believed that the rebels had been handed over, already tied up by the Balaguer Dominican intelligence service agents. The two soldiers at the Haitian *avant post* had taken delivery and marched the guerrillas across the mountains to Thiotte. Supporting this version was a brief dispatch from the *Agence France Presse* (AFP) news agency out of Santo Domingo on January 13, 1970, reporting that the Dominican Army patrols had been sent to the vicinity of Barahona after guerrillas believed to be "unsatisfied Dominicans" were noted in the area near the Haitian border.

Several years later, the leader of the Popular Dominican Movement (MPD), Máximo Gómez, passing through Mexico City en route to exile in Europe (he had kidnapped the USIS Barbara Hutchinson and freed her in exchange for exile), told the author in an interview that he had provided Fred and Reneld with some old firearms. The firearms were almost useless, the MPD leader said, but the Baptiste brothers were desperate.

Whatever the circumstances, Fred, Reneld, and the rest of the Kamoken band were bound even more securely and, under heavy guard, placed on a truck and sent to the Haitian capital, said Dr. Simon, who was an eyewitness. Reneld recognized Simon and turned to him to plead for water. The soldiers would not permit Simon to intervene.

In Port-au-Prince, Papa Doc decided that the Baptiste brothers should die a slow death in Ft. Dimanche. (There is no record of how their companions presumably died.) According to released political prisoner Marc Romulus, who survived Ft. Dimanche and compiled a list of some of the prisoner's deaths, Fred Baptiste, 41, died on June 16, 1974. His corpse was reportedly dragged feet first from his cell and dumped near the sea to rot and be eaten by dogs. Romulus records that Reneld, 35, died on July 19, 1976. Both where said to have contracted tuberculosis and Fred had become insane.

Curiously, O'Leary had labeled the Baptistes "communists." In 1964 they had been given clean bill of health by the CIA and DIN as non-communists. It was only later revealed that Fred Baptiste in his quest to find funds for his revolution had become a quasi-Maoist and traveled to China during the Cultural Revolution. There are various versions that disagree about whether Red China in fact supplied Fred Baptiste with his funds and, if they did, whether the funds were stolen. It is true that Fred was left with only a Maoist cap which he had worn proudly in Paris.

Author Graham Greene wrote their epitaph:

"I am proud to have had Haitian friends who fought courageously in the mountains against Doctor Duvalier . . ." (*London Daily Telegraph Magazine, December 3, 1976*).

CHAPTER 15

The CBS Invasion

By 1966 the Rev. Father Jean-Baptiste Georges had become desperate—so desperate that he failed to foresee the consequences of allowing Cuban exiles in Miami to take over what would have been his last attempted invasion of Haiti.

The anti-Duvalier Roman Catholic priest had already been caught moving weapons from New York to Miami to be used to reinforce the 13 Jeune Haiti fighters. Nor had he been able to find reinforcements to relieve the Thirteen before they went to their death.

No freelance military expedition could approach the island of Hispaniola in 1965, as U.S. President Lyndon Baines Johnson, paranoid about Cuba and to prevent the rise of another Castroite Communist regime in the Dominican Republic, had landed more than 22,000 U.S. troops there to put down a rebellion. The country had literally become a U.S.-defended fortress with American land, sea, and air forces patrolling the coasts, waters, and skies to repulse any Castro-aided infiltration of the Dominican Republic from Cuba. Washington was also closely watching restive Haiti.

However, by the spring of 1966 Father Georges had gathered the men, money, and arms to once again prepare an incursion into Haiti and attack his nemesis, Duvalier. It was the largest and most bizarre invasion ever planned and organized in Miami, a town accustomed to preposterous happenings. Indeed, the grim seriousness of Father Georges's mission was diluted somewhat by the cast of characters involved in his military expedition. These characters could have come right out of a sequel to Woody Allen's 1970s movie *Bananas*, a madcap film satirizing Latin American revolutionaries.

Many of the "troops" joined because they heard reports that preparations for the "Big One" were being filmed by the Columbia Broadcasting System (CBS). There was also word on the streets that this time Haitian exiles had the "green light" from the CIA to get rid of Duvalier. Some involved in the anticipated expedition even bragged that they had "company" (CIA) connections. Also, the ultimate target of the Cuban volunteers was Cuba's Fidel Castro. Once Papa Doc was "history" and Father Georges was installed in the National Palace in Port-au-Prince as "President" of the "Free Republic of Haiti," the Cuban exiles were planning to use that country as a springboard to invade Cuba. (It was learned later that the CIA, FBI, U.S. Customs, and Bureau of Alcohol, Tobacco, and Firearms [ATF] were well informed of the progress of the invasion, but that it was not sanctioned by the CIA. In fact, these agencies were waiting for the plot to hatch before pouncing on it. On the other hand, Father's Georges' brood saw the fact that the agencies were made aware of the operation and had not broken it up as their covert support of the conspiracy.)

"Miami: Casablanca of the Caribbean" was the colorful but apt headline of an article in *The Miami Herald's Tropic* magazine in April 1976. Authored by staff writer John Dorschner, it recalled what he described as the "drama and farce" of the 1966-67 invasion effort against Duvalier. However, the international intrigue of the Moroccan city during World War II would probably have paled by comparison to the Miami of the 1960s. The South Florida city, rapidly filling up with thousands of newly arrived exiles from Castro's still recent takeover of Cuba, in addition to newly arriving Haitian refugees, was seething with intrigue. The gangs of "cocaine cowboys" with links to Colombia and elsewhere in South America had yet to arrive.

*   *   *

Thirty "soldiers of fortune" who had joined the expedition (since they were not paid they could not be called mercenaries) were mostly former U.S. soldiers and Marines still thirsting for adventure. They were confident they could liberate Haiti; they had the expertise and daring to whack the dictator's forces. The only things the soldiers of fortune worried about were good weapons and reliable transport to Haiti. (In the end, some of the soldiers of fortune brought along their own rifles.)

The invasion plot's political leader, Father Georges, 48 years old when he initiated it, hardly looked the warrior. Well educated in Haiti and Canada, he was from an old bourgeois provincial (Aux Cayes) family, and he preserved his old-fashioned parsimonious ways. In replying to one or another of the brawny ex-Marines requesting weapons parts, Farther Georges would place his fingers on a cheek in thought, shaking his head, and then ask, "Can you get them cheaper?" "We would look at each other," one Marine recalled, and shake our heads.

By mid-November, the invasion force for "Operation Istanbul" (some believed the code name was "Instant Bull") that had gathered in and around Miami had reached its planned full strength and was ready to ship out. The only problem: There were no ships to carry the troops to Haiti. The force was said to be one of the largest assembled in Miami since the ill-fated 1961 Bay of Pigs invasion. The roll call numbered 200 Cubans, 30 Haitians, and 30 American soldiers of fortune.

It was a disparate band described by one member as a mixture of "saints and sinners." An illustration of just how desperate Father Georges had become was his acceptance, as military commander of the invasion force, of a notorious former Batista henchman, Rolando Masferrer Rojas.

Masferrer, 49, nicknamed "El Cojo" (the lame one) because of a limp, had been called many things, few of them laudatory. He had started life in his native Cuba, like many youths of the period, demonstrating as a schoolboy against the dictatorial president, Gen. Geraldo Machado. Born in Holguín, in Cuba's Oriente province, on January 12, 1918, Masferrer had been attending school in San Antonio, Texas, in 1933, the year Machado was ousted. Young Rolando went on to make his rebellious mark in the Spanish Civil War (1937-1938) at age 19, as a member of the leftist Abraham Lincoln International Brigade. In Spain he became a Communist and was wounded in the foot in one of the last great battles of the Civil War, at the Ebro River in 1938—hence his nickname. Back in Cuba, his toughness was recognized by the Cuban Communist Party. However, he was ultimately expelled from the party in 1945 as uncontrollable. He then moved to the extreme political right, establishing his own political party called the Movimiento Socialista Revolucionario (MSR).

"Operation Instanbul" was not Masferrer's first involvement in a plot to invade the island of Hispaniola. His first attempt had been as a member of the "Cayo Confites" force which, in 1947, aimed to end the reign of Dominican dictator Generalissmo Rafael Trujillo. That invasion force was led by Dominican exile Juan Bosch and included, in addition to Masferrer, another Cuban volunteer, Fidel Castro. The force gathered on Cayo Confites off the coast of Cuba's Camagüey province. It was squashed when Trujillo protested to the Organization of American States and U.S. President Harry Truman in turn warned the then-Cuban government to put an end to the expedition. Havana complied. By 1956 Masferrer had become not only a member of the Cuban Senate but a powerful Batista *cacique* in Oriente province, with his own private army known as Los Tigres. No single henchman in Batista's Cuba was as notorious as Rolando Masferrer.

As Batista and his entourage of aides fled to Ciudad Trujillo on January 1, 1959, Masferrer decided it was prudent to put to sea. Offices of his newspaper, *Tiempo en Cuba,* had been smashed by victorious urban rebels in Havana on January 2, 1959. On January 6, Masferrer arrived in Florida on his yacht with an exile nest egg of $17 million, according to historian Hugh Thomas in his book *Cuba: The Pursuit of Freedom.* Thomas states that the money was impounded by U.S. authorities. Masferrer was later barred by the CIA from participating in the April 1961 Bay of Pigs invasion of Cuba because of his past connection to the Batista dictatorship. In exile in Miami, Masferrer opened *Libertad,* a Spanish-language newspaper, and liked to hint of links to the CIA, something that infuriated members of the Miami CIA station, who denied any such links.

Others involved in the Haiti invasion conspiracy likewise resembled characters drawn from Hollywood casting. Their resumes were lengthy and, to say the least, colorful.

One participant was Mitchell Livingston Werbell III, a licensed arms dealer from Powder Springs, Georgia, near Atlanta. He was said to have been with the Office of Strategic Services (OSS) during World War II and was fresh from the Dominican Civil War, where I knew him as a conspicuous figure, striding around war-torn Santo Domingo in khaki shorts and a pith helmet, carrying a swagger stick, and allegedly reporting to the

CIA station across the street from the U.S. embassy. (To his credit, when U.S. Marines at a Santo Domingo checkpoint opened withering fire on a taxi carrying two *Miami Herald* newsmen—reporter and photographer—it was Werbell who, waving his swagger stick furiously at the Marines, persuaded them to stop firing. Werbell then helped the badly wounded photographer, Doug Kennedy, and reporter Al Burt from the bullet-riddled vehicle.)

In October 1966, Father Georges and Haitian colleague René Lilavois began hunting for a boat to transport their invasion force to Haiti. Virtually all of 1966 had been taken up by the Miami invasion force's preparation and training. By November 1966, they were ready to go, and no one was more anxious than Father Georges. So obsessed had he become with the conviction that he was morally right in using any and all means to over-throw the Duvalier dictatorship that the priest lost sight of the possibility that his actions might lead to the rise of yet another monster.

Father Georges had written a "Proclamation to the Haitian People," to be published once the invasion force landed in Haiti. Left blank on the proclamation were the place and date of its issuance from the "Headquarters of the Revolutionary Army." Formally addressed to the Haitian people, civilians and military, the proclamation declared in French:

> Over the course of nine years of an unfeeling dictatorship, the infamous regime of François Duvalier has inflicted all sorts of humiliations on our country, demolished all national institutions, accumulated a considerable number of innocent victims, and violated all the laws of the Nation. The hour has at last come for you to terminate the fury of this tyrant. The first group of the invasion forces of the Revolutionary Army has landed, composed of civilians, military of the Haitian Army, and other elements dedicated to an idea of justice and liberty. They carry the combat to the very soil of Haiti. This army fights in your name and at your sides to help you to free our country from gangsterism, from anarchy and ignorance, and to instill in the Peace, in Union and Fraternity, an era of Liberty, Justice and of Progress.
>
> The town [followed with a blank line] has spontaneously, and as one person, joined forces with the forces of liberation. With us they assure the victory of the democratic forces which bring you full

enjoyment of your civil and political rights denied you for nine years. Without delay, take your place beside the revolution. The time for action has come. We make an appeal to the officers and soldiers of the army, who have been humiliated and ill-treated for the past nine years. We appeal to the military, baffled and exploited. We are determined to conquer and we will conquer. No Duvalierist force can resist our firepower. To the Haitian people we ask: "Join us!" In the sacred name of our country, for the glory of our heroes, all rise in the Union which makes strength. Down with the regime of Duvalier. Down with the dictatorship.

*   *   *

Martin Xavier Casey, a onetime Marine, became involved in the planned invasion along with other soldiers of fortune, and related events to the author in the 1980s, after Casey had become a researcher for *Time* magazine's Miami bureau. (In later years he wrote articles for *Soldier of Fortune* magazine. Publisher Col. Robert K. Brown also was briefly involved in "Operation Istanbul"—until he returned to Vietnam for a second tour of duty.) In recalling the quixotic Haitian venture, Casey often let his Irish humor get the better of him.

Dubbing the operation "Looney Tunes," Casey still felt that it had been for a good cause and had been prepared to risk his life to get rid of Papa Doc Duvalier, whom Casey considered to be the most odious dictator in the Caribbean. Casey's account:

> We were followed [around Miami] by U.S. Customs, the CIA, FBI, and agents working for Papa Doc as well as Castro agents, the Jesuits, and the Miami police. Two Jesuit priests somehow became involved [possibly providing funds]—they were named Fathers Madrigal and Colmena. The Haitian revolutionaries were headquartered in a large two-story house at Southwest 33rd Avenue and 4th Street, an all-white neighborhood. They dressed in military fatigues, used to stroll down Calle Ocho, the main drag of Miami's little Havana section, for a cup of Cuban coffee.
>
> The Cuban members of the invasion force burned up roll after roll of film getting their pictures taken in uniform, each holding the one Thompson submachine gun the entire force possessed.
>
> Miami police led by a Sgt. McCracken raided the Haitian invasion headquarters house and were told that it was a meeting of the

senior Boy Scouts. Police saw a bed sheet fall from a 60-mm mortar and left. Robert Brown and I grabbed what weapons were in the house and hid them.

A CBS crew was staying at the University Inn in Coral Gables, and Andrew St. George, a former *Life* photographer, was their fixer. The Hungarian-born photographer had become well-known for his imaginative mind and inventive ideas. It was St. George who had enticed CBS's TV News into filming the invasion preparation. The CBS producer of the show named it "Project Nassau." St. George's daring had brought him worldwide recognition when he photographed Fidel Castro in the Sierra Maestra during the 1958 Cuban rebellion. He eventually turned against Castro and became involved in Cuban exile projects. CBS is said to have used 45,000 feet of film on "Project Nassau."

St. George eventually left the project after a series of mishaps. He had borrowed Masferrer's boat, a 26-foot steel hull open fisherman, and blew it up by overfilling the gas tanks. CBS had to replace the engine, electronics, and woodwork. St. George was fired.

Casey noted that arms dealer Werbell III liked to walk around with a rocket pistol [normally used to signal distress], pulling it out and firing it to demonstrate that there was no muzzle blast. He also liked to brag of his "company" [CIA] contacts. He procured some weapons and a sailboat, the *Poor Richard*, which was eventually seized by U.S. marshals for non-payment of shipyard bills.

There were a lot of fights between Masferrer and Napoleon Villaboa, who quit and was replaced by Adolfo Jiménez. CBS also packed up and left town. Another of the leaders was Julio Aton Constanso Palau, an ex-Castro rebel. Aton, as he was called, was slightly flaky. He loved to carry a silenced M-2 grease gun showing everyone how silently it functioned by firing a burst into the air. Aton did not like the olive drab color of the grease gun so he painted it black and hung it out to dry on the clothes line in front of his house. His mother, Maria, became one of Father Georges' *Santeras* and number-one adviser, telling him, "You must strike now; Papa Doc just had a heart attack."

The equipment assembled for the invasion was likewise unusual to say the least, explained Casey:

There was a number of one-of-a-kind in varying states of completeness. There were machine guns with no barrels, mortar tubes without firing pins. The strikers for the bombs to be carried and dropped by a still non-existent air force were defective. And there was a supply of grenades that were in reality nothing more than practice grenades originally painted blue and containing no explosives, that had been repainted olive drab to resemble the real thing. Believing they were real, Father Georges paid $30 each for the five dozen-plus military training relics to a Cuban from New York.

In late December 1966, the invasion was on again.

We, the American soldiers of fortune, had a meeting with Father Georges to state that we didn't think this operation was very well organized. We were told that Howard Davis, an ex-Army Ranger and at one time Raul Castro's personal pilot, had an air force ready for the invasion. We never saw any planes. There were many basic and simple things that were lacking. There were 40 to 50 Belgian rifles that were old, but in excellent shape. The rifles needed stripper clips in order to load them. I asked Father Georges for the money to buy stripper clips. He reached into his pocket, and pulled out three dollars and gave them to me. He was very conservative with money.

CBS TV news correspondent Bert Quint was ordered to Haiti from his Mexico City base, and on November 19, 1966, reported (as rumor) that an invasion force of 300 had landed on the north coast of Haiti. Quint went on national television with the story. ABC News, not to be outdone, reported the "invasion" as fact. Channel 7 in Miami, an ABC affiliate, carried the "invasion" as its lead story, stating that three boats carrying 500 men had left Miami the night before, even interviewing so-called eyewitnesses who said they had waved goodbye as the boats passed. Other news people got word of the invasion and headed to Port-au-Prince. Duvalier lost no time in declaring that Haiti had again been invaded from Castro's Cuba.

Duvalier's claim, according to Casey, prompted the CIA to offer aid to the group in Miami in the form of air transportation to the Dominican Republic, so that the Miami force could beat any Castro dispatched contingent to Port-au-Prince. "We were told we would be flown to the Dominican Republic, outfitted, and then transported to the Haitian border and that General Imbert Barrera had approved the operation. The next morning, though, the offer was withdrawn when the Agency realized there were only zombies roaming the hills of Haiti. Everyone went home."

Meanwhile, Casey explained:

Of the original 30 American soldiers of fortune, 16 had decided that this trip was not for them. Twenty-two Haitians, led by Col. René Léon, showed up at the house in the Florida Keys along with about 80 Cubans to wait for the boats. On New Year's Eve we were still waiting. There were more than 100 troops crammed into this limited space. There was little food and a lot of fights were breaking out. The Haitians and Americans were getting along well. The Haitians were not getting along with the Cubans. The Cubans were saying things like, "When I get to Haiti I'm going to screw the first woman I see." Late New Year's Eve, Father George showed up outfitted in a khaki uniform. He asked me, "Did you buy the stripper clips?" I replied, "No, we ate hamburgers." Bottles of rum were passed around and we celebrated, shouting *"Viva Haiti, Viva Cuba Libre, Viva los Estados Unidos!"*

On January 1, 1967, a boat arrived. It was a 30-foot lobster boat that Pepe had rented. There were to be two other boats. Neither got very far. One, which Pepe had purchased for $1,500, broke down in the Miami River. The other, I think was seized by the Coast Guard as being unsafe to sail any sea. The boat that did arrive had spent about five hours on a sandbar near the invasion embarkation house. With the boat tied up, Pepe removed the alternators from the vessel's engine, saying that he was going to get them fixed. He disappeared and was not seen again.

David Cabezas, an ex-CIA operative and the person responsible for setting up the proffered arrangement with the CIA and General Imbert Barrera in November (his brother, Fernando, was reportedly a high-level CIA employee), left Miami with two other Cubans on New Year's Day, driving to Coco Plum Key. When they reached Key Largo they had a flat tire. Customs agents tailing them called the Monroe Country sheriff to help the three Cubans change their tire, as Customs could see that their jack would not lift the heavy Ford van that was loaded with 2,000 pounds of explosives. The sheriff's deputies, disguised in paint-splattered overalls, pretended to stumble on the Cubans and helped them change the tire.

According to later accounts by the officers, the Customs agents following them wanted to net everyone involved in the invasion plot. But
Cabezas missed the turnoff to the invasion launching site and was
approaching the Seven-Mile-Bridge. The Customs agents were frantic. If
the Cubans should have an accident there were enough explosives in their
van to shorten the length of that famous bridge. So they stopped the van
and took the Cubans to the sheriff's sub-station. They quickly off-loaded
the explosives and, still bent on nabbing the lot, ordered the Cubans to
continue on their way, even giving them the correct directions to the invasion jumping-off site.

Casey continued:

> When Cabezas arrived at the house and told [the others] what had
> just happened, we, the Americans, decided it was time to bid this
> looney-tune caper adieu. Before we could even get our gear, the bull-
> horns were announcing, "U.S. Customs—come out of the house
> with your hands up."
>
> The rest was madness. Customs expected to find only 20 people
> in the house, but more than a hundred poured out, shouting, cursing,
> and screaming. Customs called for reinforcements. And soon FBI,
> Immigration and more sheriff's deputies started to show up. César
> Diosado, the Customs agent in charge, and I got into a shouting
> match and César had me handcuffed and thrown into a car. The
> Cubans started to make motions as if they were going to rush the car.
> The agents released me. Then César announced that everyone [else]
> should go home, that they were just going to arrest Rolando
> Masferrer, who was with the group. The Cubans said, "No! If you
> take Masferrer you take us all." They did.

It all ended on January 2, 1967, with subsequent arrests of the invasion
group's other leaders by U.S. Customs agents in Miami without a shot
being fired in anger. One shot was fired accidentally during a training
scene filmed by CBS at Kendall Park, Miami, and a Cuban trainee lost an
eye. He sued for a million dollars but settled the suit with CBS for
$15,000. The injured man stated he was entitled to workman's compen-
sation because he had played a bit part in filming by CBS of the group in
training. CBS's problems with Project Nassau were only beginning.

The media herd responding to reports of an impending Haiti invasion
was spectacular in itself.

On November 20, 1966, Henry Giniger, the *New York Times* correspondent based in Mexico City, arrived in Port-au-Prince to cover the "invasion." He was not alone. The Haitian capital was swarming with foreign newsmen drawn to the country by "tips" and rumors about an invasion. At the time Papa Doc's government was trying to launch a lucrative tourist season and was doing everything possible to prove that Haiti had not been invaded.

Giniger, fluent in French, reported in the *Times* on November 21:

> There is "nothing, nothing, nothing," Gerard de Catalogne, director of tourism, said in his strongly accented English. Apparently alarmed by an unusual concentration in Haiti of reporters from the United States radio and television networks and newspapers, Mr. de Catalogne called a news conference in his tourism office and for two-and-a-half hours attempted to allay suspicions. . . .
>
> The suspicions centered on reports that a group of men, consisting mainly of Cubans, had come from Miami and landed on the north coast of the adjoining Dominican Republic near Monte Cristi. From there, the reports said, they had crossed the Haitian frontier with the eventual aim of overthrowing the Government of President François Duvalier and using Haiti as a staging area for a new attack on Cuba.

De Catalogne, known as the "white bear" because of his beefy white skin, and a career sycophant who had served in most recent Haitian governments, did his best to prove that Haiti was not under assault. The government's fear was that word of an "invasion" might torpedo Haiti's tourist season. De Catalogne told newsmen that the struggle being waged against the regime was by the upper classes (of which he was a member), representing 5 percent of the population, who had been displaced by Duvalier's "social revolution."

During the press conference the telephone rang and, Giniger noted, the tourism director, taking the call, kept repeating, "Of course, Excellency. Naturally, Excellency. Exactly, Excellency." Col. Jean Tassy, head of palace security and a noted sadist, entered the press conference wearing his pearl-handled pistol and carrying copies of cables that newsmen had sent abroad, which Tassy had retrieved from the cable office. Some he read aloud, then, as Giniger reported, "reproached" their authors as "purveyors of misinformation."

"Asked why there was censorship if the situation was completely calm," Giniger continued in his dispatch, "Colonel Tassy said the government had to 'defend' itself against rumors. In a particular theatrical gesture when a newsman asked whether it was true that the Haitian Army had not been paid recently, Tassy dug into his pockets and showed off a wad of bills to prove that there were no salary problems in the ranks."

Father Georges never disclosed the names of his donors. British film director Peter Glenville had no such qualms. Glenville told me in an interview by telephone from his retirement home in San Miguel Allende, Mexico, that he had given Father Georges a generous contribution to his war chest, because he believed the Haitian people should be relieved of their loathsome "demonic Papa." (Glenville at the time was directing the movie version of Graham Greene's novel *The Comedians*, based on terror under Papa Doc's regime.)

Two months after the collapse of the invasion plot with the wholesale arrests, a federal grand jury indicted Rolando Masferrer Rojas, Father Georges, ex-OSS operative Werbell, ex-Haitian Army Colonel René Léon, Julio Aton Constanzo-Pelau and Martin Francis Xavier Casey. The indictment against Werbell was dropped. In dropping the charges against Werbell after consultations with then Attorney General Ramsey Clark, the U.S. Attorney in Miami said to inquiring newsmen: "No comment."

Recalls Marty Casey: "We were convicted of conspiracy to invade a friendly foreign power and conspiracy to export arms without a license. Masferrer received four years, I got nine months, and the rest got two months each."

The four-year prison term Federal Judge Ted Cabot imposed on 50-year-old Rolando Masferrer Rojas was assessed because the U.S. Attorney, during a ten-day trial in November 1967, depicted him as the leading man in the attempted invasion of Haiti. Father Georges was sentenced to 60 days in jail, but the judge permitted him to go free on a $1,000 signature bond, and also permitted him to return to New York, where he was a parish priest in the town of St. Albans on Long Island. Col. René Léon also received a 60-day jail term and was put on two years' probation.

It was all over but the writing, and St. George turned his hand at writing a remarkably imaginative piece for the April 1970 issue of *True* magazine entitled "The Mafia vs the CIA." If Haitians were not already confused about who was doing what to whom, St. George confused them further with his freestyle conspiracy theme. "For seven years," he wrote, "our two invisible governments (CIA and Mafia) have been fighting for control of the small impoverished Caribbean nation of Haiti. The outcome of the fight, between the CIA and Mafia, is still in doubt!" In describing how St. George managed to put his story together, *True* quoted him as saying he had hung out 50,000 words of notes on a cloth line to enable him to assemble the story. Critics of the writer who found his article more fiction than fact suggested he had dragged his notes out of a less sanitary zone.

On October 31, 1975, Rolando Masferrer was blown to pieces. A bomb had been planted in his car. The bomber was never caught. He was not without enemies. Ironically, only the day before he was killed, he had written an editorial in his newspaper *Libertad* in which he agreed with the work of a bomb maker who had been injured in preparing a bomb.

As for Father Georges and his relationship with the other Haitian exiles, the fact that he had made a pact with such a notorious Cuban exile as Masferrer didn't sit well. The priest was excluded from participation in the next projected invasion of Haiti, which had already been planned. It was Father Georges's "last hurrah" and he disappeared from the exile scene with a record of having tried more times than any other Haitian to unseat his onetime friend, François Duvalier.

*   *   *

CBS had its own troubles with the U.S. government. Inquiries and secret congressional hearings into whether the network financed the attempted invasion of Haiti dragged on into 1970, when public hearings were held. Syndicated columnist Jack Anderson called the invasion plot a "slapstick, Marx Brothers adventure, better suited for an episode of the spy spoof 'Get Smart' than a CBS documentary."

Former *New York Post* staff writer Gene Grove, in a long investigative piece in *Scanlan's Magazine* (March 1970), reported that CBS had begun filming a documentary in 1966 on the smuggling of arms into Haiti, and that during the summer and fall the filming progressed into a documentary on an invasion of Haiti to overthrow the Duvalier regime. Grove wrote:

"CBS was interested enough in a documentary on an invasion of Haiti to invest a large amount of money in the project. The network itself says the investment was $170,000, while other estimates ranged up to a quarter of a million."

William Chapman, writing in *The Washington Post* on April 16, 1970, said it "sounds at first like a comic–opera," the "assorted and bizarre details emerged from a House Commerce subcommittee's investigation of the CBS role in an alleged plot to invade Haiti." The *Post* writer reported that "congressmen accused network executives, among other things, of manufacturing news events, meddling in foreign affairs, and possibly urging others to commit criminal acts."

In response, CBS News Vice President William L. Leonard testified to the subcommittee, "We never staged anything." He noted that the project had been canceled and the film never broadcast. He had written a memo in late 1966 declaring that it all amounted merely to the "non-adventures of a rag-tag crew that would even make Duvalier looks good." CBS's invasion footage of "Project Nassau" eventually became such an embarrassment to the network that the film was dropped into the deep recesses of a CBS storage room and forgotten. The television network found it more difficult to bury its embarrassing involvement in the "secret" operation and had to answer to the U.S. Congress as to whether it did in fact fund a military expedition against a friendly country.

CHAPTER 16

Bahamas Disaster

On Monday morning, May 20, 1968, Port-au-Prince residents watched in amazement as a two-engine aircraft roared over the capital. Their skyward gaze quickly turned from fascination to fear when the plane began dropping silver cylinders. One of the cylinder-bombs exploded, jarring the populace back to reality. It landed on the sidewalk next to the National Palace, killing two women. The aircraft, identified as an American B-25 medium bomber of World War II vintage, then flew over the Haitian Air Force base at Bowen Field, dropping two more bombs—which failed to explode—before the plane disappeared to the north.

At the controls of the B-25 bomber was Jay Humphrey, an American pilot from Ft. Lauderdale, Florida. His co-pilot was Raymond Cassagnol, 48, an exiled former Haitian Air Force pilot. (Cassagnol had been one of six Haitian Air Force airmen who in 1942 won their wings at the legendary Tuskegee Institute in Alabama during World War II. He later flew anti-submarine patrols to keep Nazi submarines from using Haiti as a source of fresh food supplies during the war.)

The B-25 medium bomber, with a range of 1,200 miles, was the type of plane used by U.S. Gen. James C. Doolittle on his famous carrier-launched raid on Tokyo in 1942. A B-25 also crashed in a fog into New York's Empire State building in 1945.

Humphrey, a huge man, had acquired the aircraft from Hamilton Aircraft Co. in Tucson, Arizona, on April 11, 1968.

The B-25 that targeted Port-au-Prince that May morning in 1968 was not fitted with bomb racks, so a rookie bombardier had to roll the 200-pound bombs out of the hatch and into their descent with his feet. Lacking manufactured fuses, the bombs were fitted with homemade fuses: 12-

gauge shotgun shells that were supposed to ignite plastic charges on impact. Only one of the bombs exploded.

Nor was the government's reaction a case study in alacrity. There was no attempt to "scramble" the Haitian Air Force's single patched-up P-51 Mustang WW II fighter. Moreover, several T-28 trainer aircraft smuggled from the United States remained unarmed. At the National Palace an ancient anti-aircraft gun was wheeled out onto the shrubbery and pointed into the clear blue sky, too late to target the bomber.

Later in the day it was the turn of Cap-Haïtien. Capois, as the local citizens are known, watched two unscheduled aircraft fly in from the sea and circle nearby. The rustic airport was used exclusively by DC-3s operated by Haiti's domestic airline, Cohata, and flown by the Haitian Air Force. Flights were restricted to biweekly trips. Patrons at Cap-Haïtien's hilltop hotel, Mont Joli, with a partial view of the airport, marveled that the two planes were able to land, as the single runway was strewn with barrels to obstruct clandestine arrivals.

"Another man and I were told to jump from the low-flying plane to move the barrels," Gerard J. Pierre, a member of the airborne exile force recounted in his book, *The Last Captured*. "We had no parachutes, but we knew how to jump in a way to prevent injury. We would keep our legs relaxed so that when we hit the ground they did not buckle and break beneath us, but rather lead us into a roll." Pierre and other freedom fighters—their self-proclaimed title—said they cleared the airstrip of obstructions in a near-miraculous jump from an aircraft that must have been flying at a high speed.

The Duvalier government announced that the Haitian capital had been bombed by an aircraft from Cuba. The mention of Cuba brought foreign newsmen running, but on reaching Port-au-Prince, they were quickly stopped. No one could leave the Haitian capital without special permission from the military. The travel ban and a lack of credible sources heightened skepticism among newsmen and diplomats that an invasion had taken place. Because Duvalier had "cried wolf" so often, there was instant suspicion that this might be yet another vaudeville act staged by Papa Doc. It became the most confused story reported about any invasion against Duvalier.

However, for the 33 exile fighters in camouflage uniforms—whose labels bore the brand name "Big Game styled by Broadway"—who quickly secured the vacant Cap-Haîtien airport, the invasion was all too real, and terrifyingly so. It was the beginning of another week of bloodshed, death, and betrayal in Haiti, the black jewel of the Caribbean.

The invasion force was led by ex-Haitian army officers Raymond Montreuil and Fritz Alexandre, along with Bernard Sansaricq, a civilian and would-be anti-Duvalier revolutionary. They arrived in Cap-Haîtien airport in a hired Cessna "Sky-Bus" that carried 25 exile freedom fighters. Seven other invaders were aboard a smaller, twin-engine Beech craft. Both planes were flown by American pilots. An additional rebel soldier was aboard the B-25 bomber, which later landed at Cap-Haîtien. Each of the three aircraft carried an assortment of arms and munitions to be distributed to people who they believed would join the anti-Duvalier fight.

"We had not been long on the ground," wrote Gerard J. Pierre, "before people started running to greet us. The called us liberators. ... [They were] chanting and cheering. We threw guns off the planes and into their hands. . . . We were arming the people for the battle which was sure to come with the revolution." But as Pierre, who had fled Papa Doc's Macoutes for the Bahamas two and a half years earlier, conceded in his book, "a lot of those people lost their lives as a result of our failed revolution. . . . It was amazing how quickly things changed from being very good to very bad."

The invaders reached the airfield's perimeter road, which fronted on the sea coast, and commandeered the first car that approached. It was carrying two Roman Catholic priests and a nun. The startled priests and nun declared to Cap-Haîtien authorities later that the "rebels" claimed they intended to drive through Cap-Haîtien and take the city of 40,000 without firing a shot. The priests later said that they had advised against such a rash and dangerous act.

The invaders were surprised when shells began to whistle overhead. The Haitian Coast Guard cutter *Jean-Jacques Dessalines*, anchored in Cap-Haîtien since the previous Saturday, either by coincidence or design, received the order from Duvalier to open fire on the airport. Disconcerting as the dozen shells lobbed by the ship were, they did little damage and caused no casualties. By 5 p.m. the shelling ceased as the gunboat's crew battened down for the night.

The rebel mood at the airport changed from exuberance to dismay with the arrival of the B-25 bomber. Word soon spread among the ranks of the small rebel force that the attack on Port-au-Prince had failed to blow Papa Doc out of the palace. Nevertheless, in his book *Memoires d'un revolutionnaive*, Cassagnol says, "I had to convince Jay [Humphrey] to fly and drop one or two bombs on the Cap-Haîtien Casernes. One bomb was dropped and had the same effect as the other dropped on Port-au-Prince." He adds that "if these bombs had exploded, the situation would have been different."

With their planned key to success gone, Pierre recalls, they were informed their leaders were going for reinforcement, and the leaders flew off. Cassagnol states in his version of events, "After three hours, I saw Sansaricq and Montreuil arrive. They asked me to get in the Cessna with them. I thought they were going to make a reconnaissance flight. I took an AR-15 that Jay had brought along just in case we had to face the enemy. When I realized that they were heading north, I understood that they were abandoning the fight," Cassagnol wrote. He was furious. Before he left his colleagues, Cassagnol says, "Sansaricq had the guts to tell me not to mention we had abandoned the fight and say that the fight continued."

Raymond Montreuil, a nephew of ex-President Magloire, even in 2004 declined to discuss the subject of his and his fellow officers' leaving their troops on May 20, 1968, saying the topic was still too painful to discuss. Pilot Humphrey obviously had departed from his aircraft in such a hurry in Cap-Haîtien that he left the bomber's log and papers pertaining to his purchase of the plane, along with 28 bombs.

When Army Maj. Prosper Maura, commander of the Northern Department, arrived at the airport at 3:00 p.m., the rebels opened fire on his army Jeep. Wounded in the Jeep along with Maura were his soldier-driver and houseboy. Maura had been a 1959 Haitian Military Academy classmate of Roland Magloire and Felix Alexandre, two exile officers involved in preparing the invasion. There was speculation as to whose side Maura was on at the time. It had been rumored that he was with the plotters, but this was known only to the absent leaders who had fled the scene.

Another unlucky victim who happened to be visiting Cap-Haîtien and drove by the airport was Jean Theard, Duvalier's vice-consul in Miami.

The circumstances surrounding his death have never been explained. The Haitian government later produced a photo of Theard in the Port-au-Prince morgue with what appears to be part of a handcuff on his right wrist.

Four of the invaders, according to Dave Graffenberg, a member of the Christian Oriental Mission in Cap-Haïtien who arrived at the mission's radio transmitter close by the airport with orders to take over the missionary society's powerful radio station. The station, 4VEH, with seven transmitters ranging in power from 500 watts to 1000 watts on the broadcast band, had been broadcasting from Cap-Haïtien for ten years. Its daily programs from 5 to 9 a.m. and from noon to 10.30 p.m. offered audio classes in English, science, health, agriculture, and nursing. (At one time it had even broadcast anti-Communist lectures in Cantonese to Chinese left in Cuba.) Supported by American Protestant groups, the Oriental Mission was staffed by 20 Americans. It also operated a health clinic that treated from 150 to 200 patients daily five times a week.

The four rebels who arrived at the transmitter at 3:45 p.m. asked two young Haitians manning it for permission to broadcast to the United States. But the broadcast studios were eight miles away. Rebuffed, the four invaders departed without incident, warning that they were expecting a large contingent of reinforcements.

The reinforcements, according to Gerard Pierre's published account, were to arrive from a prison in the Bahamas. He reported the planes were to fly to Nassau to "pick up the ninety-four men who were in [the Bahamas'] Fox Hill prison. The plan was to break the men out by force. These prisoners were already well trained and would prove to be helpful in the revolution." However, the planes did not return, and as a result, Pierre said, "our hopes were dashed." The leaders had managed to sneak back safely to the Bahamas, their port of origin.

By early evening on May 20, confusion reigned at the Cap-Haïtien airport. No reinforcements had arrived. Gerard Beauville, a longtime Haitian exile in the Bahamas who had been an early recruit to the invasion force, encountered his friend Gerard Pierre. It was Beauville who encouraged his friend also to join the cause to liberate Haiti. When Pierre arrived in the Bahamas fleeing Haiti and the Tonton Macoutes two years earlier, it was Beauville who helped him. In his book, Pierre described their meeting at the airport. "Gerard [Beauville], the husband of a beautiful, loving wife [in Nassau] and father of four children, one of whom had just been born, wore a look of stunned disbelief.

"'Well, I'll be damned,' he told me. 'We're in trouble now.'"

And indeed they were in deep trouble. Without reinforcements, with the element of surprise gone, and knowing that Duvalier's troops would soon counterattack, the rebels, on the night of May 20, only a few hours after their arrival, fled their beachhead under cover of darkness.

As they moved out across an adjacent plain and into the hills away from Cap-Haîtien, Pierre Lacorps, who had been one of their principle instructors at the camp, assumed command. Lacorps decided to split the force into two groups, one of sixteen men and the other of ten. Gerard Pierre and Beauville were with the group of ten. (Pierre did not explain the fate of the remaining rebels.) They moved quickly and cautiously through the mountains in an effort to escape to the Dominican Republic.

Early Tuesday morning the Haitian Coast Guard cutter *Jean-Jacques Dessalines* opened up with another salvo at the now abandoned airport. Finally, under the command of Col. Franck Romain, the Dessalines Tactical Battalion, trained by the U.S. Marines, had arrived overland from Port-au-Prince with orders to retake the airport. The troops, according to reports from Cap-Haîtien at the time, went in firing in all directions only to discover that they had been fighting a phantom force. They encountered no return fire and found the airport deserted, except for the bodies of Major Maura, Jean Theard, two government soldiers, and the major's houseboy. There was also the corpse of an unknown peasant. How, when, and why they were killed remains a mystery.

*   *   *

Gerard Pierre and the nine companions of his contingent ran into a murderous militia-army ambush. Pierre credited his training for his quick move to take cover, while his friend, Beauville, fell along with others under withering machine gun fire. As Pierre watched from his hiding place, he recounts, "Three men grabbed one of my fellow revolutionaries and cut his head off with a machete." So traumatized was Pierre by this scene that he decided to end his life with a bullet from his own gun. He writes that he was not going to "let anybody put a knife on my neck to cut my head off." He describes how he placed his machine gun under his chin and pulled the trigger. There was only a click. The weapon was defective.

Having managed to escape, Pierre continued his cautious trek. When he was almost within sight of the Dominican border, army troopers seized him. They subjected him to such a beating, Pierre reports, that he lost consciousness. When he finally regained his senses, he found himself in the National Palace in Port-au-Prince. A leering Duvalier was asking him, "Did you come to see your Papa? Do you know who your Papa is?"

Members of the foreign media were invited to the palace to observe this strange scene and photograph Pierre along with two other rebel prisoners who sat next to him. "Duvalier offered me some coffee," Pierre recounts. A soldier poured the scalding hot liquid into his mouth, burning his tongue and throat.

It was pure Papa Doc Theater. The "president-for-life" turned the invasion into a public relations extravaganza. He invited prisoners from Ft. Dimanche to the National Palace, where he personally questioned them about those who were behind the invasion—conspirators in Haiti as well as in the Bahamas and New York. Most of the prisoners like Pierre were foot soldiers and knew little of the planning and leadership. One man who did, according to Pierre, was ceremoniously rewarded with fifty dollars from Papa Doc.

*   *   *

Within hours of the Cap-Haïtien landing, a fierce and furious battle of the airwaves began. The Haitian Coalition's early-morning short-wave Kreyól radio program, beamed from New York, broadcast battlefield "news" that had more to do with psychological warfare than reality. Papa Doc led the counterattack personally—with some result, as he declared the invasion was officially dead.

The Haitian Coalition's short-wave radio program over WRUL in New York on Tuesday, May 21, claimed that not only had Cap-Haïtien fallen to the invaders, but a radio that they had captured would soon broadcast. It said the town of Limbe, 20 kilometers south of Cap-Haïtien, had also been taken later in the week.

(Col. Jean Beauboeuf, the newly appointed commander of the department of the north, informed the American missionaries that on President Duvalier's orders their station was closed. Missionary Radio station 4VEH became another casualty of the invasion.)

Frustrated newsmen confined to Port-au-Prince were fed daily morsels of misinformation by Papa Doc's public relations chief, Gerard de Catalogne, an old hand at manipulating the news. De Catalogne clearly relished his job. His long pale face was all smiles as he belly-laughed his way through one press conference after another. Sometimes de Catalogne, whose official job at the time was editor-in-chief of the government's daily newspaper, *Le Nouveau Monde,* would check a question by telephone. There was no doubt about to whom he was speaking. De Catalogne's head would nod in servile assent as he repeated, *"Oui, excellence."* Papa Doc was on the line. *The New York Times'* Henry Giniger, fluent in French, was in the enviable position of understanding snatches of de Catalogne's end of these conversations.

However, in the absence of any eyewitness report, wildly erroneous accounts appeared in the foreign media. *The Miami Herald*, for example, stated categorically that exile fighters had taken Cap-Haïtien.

In an effort to prove that peace reigned in Cap-Haïtien, de Catalogne declaimed to the media about the wonders of tourism in the northern city. (It so happened that his family operated the Hotel Roi Christophe in Cap-Haïtien.) Spring carnival had attracted a record number of visitors, de Catalogne declared, displaying photographs of Norma Sherer, Miss Miami of 1968, who "lent her blonde beauty as an official emissary from Florida." A record—under Papa Doc—of 10,000 visitors had descended on the island in a three-month period, he added, predicting that tourists would continue to flock to Haiti. Photographs of visiting "jet-setter" and Greek shipping magnate Aristotle Onassis with Duvalier's son-in-law, tourism chief Luc Foucard, adorned government tourism publications while, at the National Palace, a feeble-looking, white-haired Papa Doc was seen hosting opera star Maria Callas.

*   *   *

Behind the "invasion" was a group of prominent Haitian politician-exiles who had founded the *Coalition Haitienne* in New York City in 1965.

They included former President Gen. Paul E. Magloire, who was from northern Haiti, and Luc Fouche, a native of Cap-Haîtien and former cabinet minister. The coalition also included ex-diplomat Joseph Dejean and Dr. Louis Roy, former head of the Haitian Red Cross. Placed at the helm of the *Coalition Haitienne,* as secretary-general, was a determined young man, 33-year-old Raymond Alcide Joseph. Son of a Baptist minister from Aux Cayes, Joseph became the backbone of the group, acting as spokesman, publisher-editor of the Coalition's weekly *Le Combattant Haitien,* and director of the exile radio program on WRUL.

The radio program, beamed from New York, became successful, and what the Coalition termed the "early-morning Mass" was listened to by those with powerful radio in Haiti. They, in turn, disseminated the daily reports by word of mouth. Joseph liked to refer to it as *Vonvon,* a "bug in Papa Doc's ear." The broadcasts were heard Monday thought Friday from 6 a.m. to 6:30 a.m. over WRUL, a short-wave outlet transmitting worldwide. Owned by the Church of Christ of Latter-Day Saints, the airtime was sold to the Coalition. The radio program managed to pierce Duvalier's extremely sensitive ear and his control of the news throughout Haiti. It became one of his major concerns. Papa Doc believed that the U.S. government, through the CIA, was financing the Kreyól broadcasts and made repeated official protests to Washington in an effort to close down the operation. Eventually the Kreyól broadcast became another casualty of the abortive invasion, and was forced by the U.S. State Department to close in July 1968.

It would be only a matter of time before the Haitian Coalition was drawn into the armed struggle against Duvalier. With funds reportedly provided by wealthy members of the business community in Haiti, a training camp was opened in the Bahamas in late 1967. The camp was run by ex-Haitian Army Officer Roland Magloire, involved in the 1963, plot. Bernard Sansaricq, living in South Florida at the time, was given the job of quartermaster, and set about purchasing everything from bread to a bomber with funds mostly provided by one of the most successful businessmen in Haiti, Jamaican-born O.J. Brandt. Several of the other ex-Haitian officers, including François Benoit, took time off from their jobs to offer assistance. Benoit made training films with his 8-mm camera.

The northeastern Bahamas islands offered an ideal secret training base, and among the 15,000 Haitian refugees living mostly illegally on the various islands in the Bahamas there was a reservoir of potential recruits, men like Gerard Beauville, who dreamed only of returning to a free Haiti. The islands were sparsely populated and their northeastern fringe frequented only by sport fishermen. It was a relatively short flight from South Florida, where the illegal arms and munitions trade still flourished.

The Bahamas, a chain of some 700 islands and cays, stretch 500 miles from Grand Bahamas Island in the north, where the secret camp was established, to Inagua in the south, just 60 miles from the coast of Haiti. While illegal Haitian refugees were routinely imprisoned and shipped back to Haiti, those who managed to escape the periodic roundups shared the hope that one day they would return to their native land liberated from dictatorship. Entwined with the Haitians' culture was a strong love of country. They were only too ready to listen to self-appointed "leaders" and return with rifles in hand to topple their country's dictatorship and live happily ever after on their farms and businesses without fear of the rapacious Macoutes. Ironically, they were often galvanized into action by the failure of fellow aspiring Haitian rebels.

*   *   *

In the tangled mangroves of Burroughs Cay off Grand Bahamas Island, scores of Haitians were soon in training. They became a formidable invasion force. However, one day toward the end of training, while dropping drinking water to the secret camp in the form of blocks of ice, a Cessna airplane from Melbourne, Florida, accidentally alerted islanders to the presence of the Haitians. They, in turn, informed the Bahamian police, who reported to headquarters in Nassau.

On March 26, 1968, the planned seaborne force was ready to embark for Haiti when a succession of calamities struck. As recounted by Gerard Pierre in his book, 78 Haitian recruits were boarding a ship when they learned too late it flew the Union Jack. (At the time, the Bahamas were still a British colony; independence didn't come until 1973.) The would-be liberators were detained en masse by the Bahamian police and diverted via a short sea voyage to the capital of Nassau, where they were jailed in the storied Fox Hill prison outside town. All were subsequently sentenced to a year in prison and, following completion of their jail term, were to be deported. (One of the camp leaders, exiled Pierre Legros, collapsed on shore and died of a heart attack when his men were apprehended.) After this episode recruits still in training, from the United States and Canada, believing the invasion was off, returned to their home. Others, mostly Haitians residing in the Bahamas, stayed in the camp. They numbered 35.

The vessel that was intended to carry the landing force to Haiti also was doomed. The expedition's leader, Raymond Montreuil, had called for volunteers to man the vessel. Eleven, mostly former army officers living in the United States, answered the call. Fritz Paret, then a young former Haitian Army officer in exile in Florida, put it this way in an interview with me in 2004: "We were impressionable and young with only one goal, to go home. We jumped at the opportunity to fight the dictatorship. We didn't know the details [but] at that time things were more relaxed. You could obtain weapons and leave the coast [of Florida] without being stopped."

Another ex-officer, François Benoit, took leave of his job and family in Michigan and joined his fellow officers on the *Yorel II*, a 60-foot cabin cruiser that Sansaricq had acquired. From the start it appeared that "Bill," the American captain of the *Yorel II*, knew little about marine navigation. They had hardly left Melbourne, Florida, when the captain somehow steered the vessel onto a coral reef, not once by twice. There was no reported damage to the boat. The first night out, running without lights, the boat and its exile passengers were stopped by the U.S. Coast Guard. Captain Bill was at least a convincing talker, and the Coast Guard vessel commander accepted Bill's story that they were out fishing.

However, the Haitians with their cargo of arms and munitions had barely gotten over that close call when one of the cruiser's two outboard motors gave out, followed by the second. For 48 hours they drifted northward in the Gulf Stream. During that time, Benoit recalled, since Sansaricq had not followed Benoit's advice to allow him to inspect the infantry weapons prior to purchasing them, he decided to open a few of the weapons cases. As an infantry officer and instructor at Haiti's military academy, Benoit was shocked with what he saw. "The armament consisted mostly of old World War II M-2 carbines, along with two BARs

(Browning automatic rifles). All the weapons were of poor quality, the steel was pitted, and they were still filled with hard grease," Benoit recalled in an interview with me. "Only 50% of the arms could function after I had cleaned them and changed defective parts."

"I asked Captain Bill," Benoit added, "'Which way are the Bahamas?' The Captain shrugged. He didn't seem to know. When one of the motors was fixed, we had Bill ask the first boat we sighted the way to the Bahamas. And we followed their directions, which proved to be accurate."

On the night of May 4, they finally spotted a light on land. It proved to be Grand Bahamas Island. It was decided that the *Yorel II* remain off the coast while Benoit and a colleague rowed ashore in the yacht's dinghy to make contact. Having hidden the dinghy in the mangroves, Benoit said, the pair walked along the roadway as if they belonged to the area. They were able to meet Sansaricq, Montreuil, and Felix Alexandre, and agreed on the final coordinated moves of their operation.

"At 4:00 a.m. that Sunday, May 5, Sansaricq and I went to rendezvous with the *Yorel*," Benoit recalled in his 2004 interview with me. "We were sipping coffee at a roadside eating place when we heard the wailing of police sirens. I remember making the remark, 'If we were on the road we could have thought that the police were after us.'"

He continued: "The police and ambulances were in fact on their way to pick up members of our expedition who had taken to life rafts when the boat took on water in a sudden storm on the way to our rendezvous and sank. A Pan-Am passenger jet flying overhead had witnessed the disaster and notified the Bahamian authorities. Eleven men were picked up and imprisoned at Fox Hill and charged with entering the country illegally."

In New York, the exile publication *Le Combattant Haitien* editorialized that the jailed men had not entered the Bahamas illegally because they were victims of a shipwreck and brought ashore by Bahamian authorities, not of their own free will. (Two weeks later they were released from Fox Hill, and those with U.S. residency flew to Miami on May 19.)

After the sinking of the *Yorel*, Montreuil, Sansaricq, and Alexandre met with Benoit at their still-secret camp to assess the situation. "It was decided," Benoit related, "that with the main force, a total of nearly 90 men, in jail at Fox Hill and having lost a boatload of arms and munitions, as well as the *Yorel* that was to transport us to Haiti, we could no longer carry out the invasion. It was also decided that I should go to New York and brief the heads of the National Coalition—Dr. Louis Roy, President Paul Magloire, Luc Fouche, Raymond Joseph, and so forth."

"While the New York meeting was taking place," Benoit continued, "the news came that an armed invasion had taken place in the North of Haiti. I had not been privy to their [northern invasion force] plan." Benoit reported that even the chain of command had not been established "when we left Melbourne, Florida, on the *Yorel*. I expected, in all logic, to go over these 'details' upon our arrival in the Bahamas."

Gerard Pierre recalls that the camp commandant, Pierre Lecorp, ordered the troops, all 35 of them, to fold up their camouflage tents and assemble for departure. The invasion was on. Pierre says that they were given a last minute pep-talk by Montreuil and Cassagnol.

Pierre describes an earlier plan to attack Papa Doc on May 18, 1968, Haiti's Flag Day, during the traditional ceremony at Arcahaie, where in 1803 the Haitian flag was born. Possessing the World War II B-25 bomber, the plotters believed it was possible to launch an aerial attack. Bombing Duvalier from the air had always been high on the exiles' wish list. Years earlier, in 1964, General Cantave had invaded Haiti from the Dominican Republic; he had made the mistake of paying for a bomb, pilot, and plane in advance. The pilot disappeared back to Miami with the funds for the bomb, pilot and plane.

Sansaricq had rented the larger aircraft with a capacity for 25 occupants and arms and the smaller, seven-passenger Beechcraft, both of which would make the initial airborne strike and be quickly reinforced.

The only hitch was that Papa Doc, it was learned virtually at the last minute on May 17, would not attend the Flag Day ceremony at Arcahaie. They reverted to their secondary target, Cap-Haïtien.

In the aftermath of the May 1968 invasion of Cap-Haïtien, Duvalierist Colonel Franck Romain and his troops, following their counterattack, had little mercy on local relatives of those said to be involved in the invasion. Moreover, in Port-au-Prince, the richest man in Haiti, O.J. Brandt, 78, was arrested on June 18 and accused of supplying funds for the invasion. (Brandt was said to have contributed most of the $350,000 cost of the invasion, making it the most expensive to date.) The multimillionaire industrialist of Jamaican origin had lived in Haiti for 55 years and built his fortune in his adopted country. Despite his arrest, he was never brought to trial, but instead given "provisional freedom" by Duvalier after two and a half months in prison. Brandt's 44-year-old son, Clifford, was also arrested, as was former Army officer Charles Plasimond, an industrialist who had been close to ex-President Magloire. Port-au-Prince lawyers Georges and Jean-Claude Leger were likewise arrested. Though their law firm represented large American companies in Haiti, they were both brothers-in-law of the exiled Dr. Louis Roy, a Coalition member.

In addition, Papa Doc had his military trophy—the B-25 bomber whose bombs had failed to hit the palace. The old craft was flown from Cap-Haîtien to the capital's new jet-accommodating Dr. François Duvalier Airport. The President-for-Life, dressed in Army uniform, went to the airport to survey his victory keepsake. His facial expression in photographs of the occasion reflected that of a stern commander-in-chief, rather than a smiling victor.

Other members of Papa Doc's inner circle were not that contained. Years later, when François Benoit was Haiti's foreign minister in the post-Duvalier military regime headed by Prime Minister Marc Bazin, he had a one-armed visitor who identified himself as one of the survivors of the May 1968 invasion. Pointing to his missing arm, the minister declared his arm had been personally chopped off by Dr. Roger Lafontant.

Launching a diplomatic counterattack, Duvalier startled the United Nations and Washington by lodging a formal complaint with the United Nations Security Council alleging that the May 20 air raid and landing in Cap-Haîtien was a threat to international peace. In addition to the note to the Security Council, Duvalier sent a parallel telegram to the U.N. Secretary General U Thant.

New York Times U.N. correspondent Juan de Onis filed a story on May 22 noting the unusual demand that the Security Council convene to declare the small airborne invasion of Haiti's north and the attempted bombing of the National Palace as threats to world peace. In his story, de Onis quoted U.S. sources as saying that the invasion group "appeared too small and poorly armed to represent a military threat to the Duvalier regime." Haiti's action also raised eyebrows because the government in

Port-au-Prince had already declared it had smashed the band of invaders.

While Haiti did not accuse any U.N. member state of abetting the invasion, de Onis reported that Duvalier had complained about the daily short-wave radio broadcast from New York which, as the reporter wrote:

> is sponsored by the Haitian Coalition. The note said that these broadcasts, against which Haiti has protested to the United States, have "done much to create the present threat against people involving Haiti, and continue to do so."
>
> Raymond Joseph, secretary-general of the Haitian Coalition, said by telephone from his New York office that his organization knew of the invasion plan. But he said the participants "were not acting on our orders."
>
> Mr. Joseph said the daily half-hour broadcasts were widely heard in Haiti despite jamming.

The *Times* story noted that Haiti's ex- President Paul E. Magloire and former Education Minister Luc Fouche were associated with the Coalition. Joseph ridiculed Duvalier's charge that Rev. Jean-Baptiste Georges was involved, as he was in New York, and Raymond Cassagnol, "a former Haitian air Force officer," was in Washington D.C. Joseph denounced the arrests of families of those named as involved in the invasion.

With the bizarre invasion, Haiti had captured world headlines during that tumultuous summer of 1968, along with student riots in Paris, the Vietnam war, and the assassinations in the U.S. of Martin Luther King and U.S. Senator Robert Kennedy.

*   *   *

Papa Doc ordered the army and militia not to kill all the invaders, commanding them to deliver prisoners to Port-au-Prince. Ten prisoners were brought from the north to be interrogated personally by Papa Doc at the National Palace. Each day of the two-month military trial, the prisoners were ordered to change from their skimpy Ft. Dimanche garb to suits and shoes issued by the government. Pierre noted how government officials made fun of the prisoners who "didn't know enough French to testify in the official language at their own trial," at which they were pictured as "mumbling in Kreyól and trying to comfort their feet in Government Issue dress shoes."

The military show trial ended August 5 with presiding judge Col. Franck Romain handing all defendants death sentences for treason. Romain listed other offenses, including an attempt on the life of the president and his family. The prisoners believed that they had little time to live.

One prisoner who cheated Papa Doc was Gerard Pierre, whose determination matched his belief in God—to whom Pierre prayed to help him break out of Ft. Dimanche. It took him and his cell mate, Lebrun Leblanc, more than a month working each night to carve out a hole with the small, sharp handle of their toilet bucket in a 30-inch concrete block in the back wall of their cell. They hid the growing incision in the wall by mixing the mortar they had scratched out during the night with their urine and pasting it over the hole. In the pre-dawn hours of August 6, the day after their sentencing, they escaped through the hole. Leblanc went his way and was later caught. Pierre, naked except for his prison trousers, managed to rush into the American embassy and was on the point of being thrown out when a Marine officer agreed to listen to his story. Finally, the American ambassador, Claude G. Ross, interceded, and gave the bare-chested Pierre a khaki shirt, hid him under a blanket in an embassy station wagon, and drove him to the Chilean embassy. There Pierre pushed his way in when an employee answered the door. One of the few prisoners to escape from Duvalier gulag, he was eventually granted political asylum. On October 18, 1968, he was given safe conduct to exile in Chile. Pierre had done the impossible—escape from Ft. Dimanche.

CHAPTER 17

The Gerard Baker Brigade

The Democratic Movement of Haitian Patriots (MDPH), seeking to put an end to the eleven years of bloody dictatorship of Papa Doc, has committed its forces on Haiti soil. After years and years of patient and tiring efforts—too often expended against our fellow citizens also opposed to Duvalier's regime—a force called the "Gerard Baker Brigade" (named after one of our gallant youths killed in the early process of building this operation) has been organized and dedicated to fighting injustice, crime, oppression, and poverty and to install in this unhappy and forgotten land of ours freedom, justice and democracy. May God help us.
—RENÉ J. LÉON, JUNE 4, 1969

The disastrous Cap-Haïtien invasion had hardly ended when, in December 1968, Haitians set up a new secret training camp in the Florida Everglades some 50 miles west of Miami. The leader of the new operation was René J. Léon, a former lieutenant colonel in the Haitian Army who had broken with Duvalier in 1962. He had participated in General Cantave's abortive invasions from the Dominican Republic as well as the so-called "CBS Invasion." Léon, a slim, handsome officer born in Pétionville in 1924, graduated from the Haitian Military Academy, class of 1945. Having furthered his military career with study at the U.S Army's Fort Benning in Georgia, as well as the U.S.-operated School of the Americas at Fort Gulick in the Panama Canal Zone, Léon was fluent in English.

Undaunted by the fact that he was also appealing a 1966 conviction for participation in the last Florida-based operation against Papa Doc, Léon had found sufficient funds from a mysterious "Robert" in New York to launch the new enterprise with the aid of a group of American soldiers of fortune. Léon's original plan called for Haitian recruits to be trained in guerrilla warfare, then infiltrated into Haiti to hide caches of weapons, munitions, medicine, and food around the country. (The supplies were to be dropped by air.) Meanwhile, the camp in the Florida Everglades would continue to train and send more recruits, and when sufficient numbers were on the ground in Haiti a guerrilla war against Papa Doc would be launched. There was one stipulation: No Cuban exiles were to be involved this time.

By mid-January 1969, 18 Haitian recruits were in training under the command of a Canadian volunteer who, in spite of a withered arm that prevented him from serving in the Canadian military, was able to outperform most of his recruits on the obstacle course. He was assisted by a former U.S. Navy veteran. Another training instructor, an American from Kentucky, had spent several years in the U.S. National Guard. A Haitian-born, self-described U.S. Marine deserter and Vietnam veteran was also an instructor. Adding to the international flavor was a Finnish-born former U.S. Army Ranger and Special Forces trooper, the group's explosives expert.

Ex-U.S. Marine Martin Casey, a close friend of Léon, explained to the author that "the reasons these unpaid volunteers [soldiers of fortune] chose to live in the swamps, eat poorly, sometimes freeze their butts off at night, and get eaten up by mosquitoes were a mixture of idealism, adventure, and a way to atone for past transgressions."

The Haitians, on the other hand, explained Casey, had plenty of personal reasons to fight Papa Doc. "Most had lost family to the Macoutes. Some had suffered beatings and one fellow had scarred buttocks where he had been beaten until the flesh rotted off."

The predictable cultural divide between trainers and trainees was illustrated when one recruit, who professed to be a *Voudou* devotee, awoke one morning upset because he had dreamed of a snake, the *Voudou* deity Damballa. Later the same morning, the recruit almost stepped on a very large rattlesnake, jumped back, and collapsed in a trance. When he came out of the trance, he packed his bag, quit camp, and walked out, all the way to Miami.

Prior to the opening of the camp, one of Léon's soldiers of fortune contacted a freelance journalist reported to have connections with the CIA.

He confidentially informed the journalist of the group's plans and asked him to learn whether Washington would oppose their operation. As no reply was forthcoming, Léon and his men concluded that the U.S. government would turn a blind eye because it favored removal of Papa Doc but was leery of any involvement.

A 65-foot boat was hired in Key West for $2,500 for a two-week charter to sneak men and weapons into Haiti. It was during the boat hiring that an Israeli businessman offered help that led to a series of meetings with the Israeli military attaché in Washington. The Israeli proposal, according to Léon, was to move the Haitian recruits to Israel for further training, equip them with Israeli weaponry, and then transport them back to the Caribbean. Two weeks after the initial contact, the Israeli military attaché in Washington telephoned Colonel Léon, the latter recalled, and informed him that the unusual proposal—which would have ensured a pro-Israel government in Port-au-Prince—had been turned down.

By March, the recruits were toughened up and there was an optimistic atmosphere in the camp. Two dozen new single-shot 22-caliber rifles were used for target practice. Several airdrops to re-supply the camp went without a hitch.

Then disaster struck. Gerard Baker, 22, the most popular Haitian trooper in the camp, was killed during training by a stray .22 bullet. The death of Baker led Monroe County sheriff's deputies to the secret training camp, resulting in the arrest of the Haitian recruits. (Léon and his soldiers of fortune were not at the camp at the time of the tragedy.) They were transported to holding cells on nearby Plantation Key. The deputies promised that the men would be held only as long as necessary for a coroner's inquest. The inquest cleared everyone, ruling Baker's death an accident caused by person or persons unknown. Once again, the Haitians had provided U.S. headlines: "Haitian Invasion Camp Raided in Everglades" (*The Miami Herald*, March 12, 1969.)

It was the end of the camp. Released from jail, the Haitian recruits returned to their respective homes in Florida and New York, mourning the loss of their friend. The withered-armed yet dexterous Canadian instructor was deported back to Canada. The enigmatic "Robert" in New York informed operation leader Léon that there would be no more funds.

Léon and his remaining soldiers of fortune spent weeks discussing their next move. When they heard that Papa Doc had suffered a second heart attack on May 8,' 1969, they plotted how to knock him out of his palace sick bed and into a body bag.

A collection was taken in New York to purchase an old four-engine Lockheed Constellation passenger plane in Canada. A pilot and co-pilot were hired to fly the aircraft to Grand Turk Island and told they were to haul a cargo of dresses from Puerto Rico to Miami.

On June 3, 1969, the "Connie" (as that workhorse plane was popularly known) landed on the island to load up large oil drums and weapons that they had cached near the airstrip. The police sergeant in charge on the island had to be coaxed off the airstrip by a ruse while the weapons were loaded aboard. When one of the boxes broke open next to the flight engineer and some hand grenades fell out, the pilot looked down, turned to Casey, and said, "Well, I don't like hauling dresses anyway."

An hour later the Connie landed at Georgetown, Exuma Island. The thirty-gallon oil drums aboard the Connie were filled with JP-4, a large box of hand-operated "pull" flares, incendiary devices made of white phosphorous, grenades, anti-tank rockets, AR-15 rifles, and various handguns. A customs agent asked the pilot why they had landed on Exuma and he truthfully explained they needed fuel for the aircraft. Told they would have to wait until morning for the fuel, the group had a restful night on the Bahamas island off Haiti's north coast.

In typical colorful fashion, Casey told the author of the strangest bombing raid ever attempted in the Caribbean. "The next morning we topped off the fuel tanks and taxied to the end of the runway. We stopped there. Several of us jumped out and placed a ladder by the side of the Connie and taped over the aircraft's identification numbers. Down the runway we could see a truck with the local customs agents aboard hurrying toward us. We quickly finished and re-boarded the plane. Once we were aboard, the pilot gunned the Connie and the truck wisely left the runway to us."

As they flew south toward Haiti, Léon was introduced to the on-board mechanic and flight engineer as the next president of Haiti. "In the rear of the old Connie we readied the drums for the drop," Casey explained. "We taped two pull flares to the sides of each drum, connecting them with cord so that both would ignite as the cord was pulled." Casey continued:

As we approached Port-au-Prince my knees started to knock. It was about 10:00 a.m. and everything looked quiet. We first buzzed the military field to be assured that there were no interceptors on the runway. It was clear. We flew out over the bay, trimmed our altitude to 500 feet, our airspeed to 100 knots, and lined up on the National Palace which was sitting like a big white wedding cake in the middle of the city.

The pilot was doing the calculations in his head. When we were about 300 yards from the palace he started shouting over the intercom, "Ready, ready, ready," and then he shouted, "Go, go, go!" Two of us had tethering lines on before the open door. We pulled the fuses and dumped the drums out the door. Léon and another soldier of fortune were behind us feeding us the drums, while two others were rolling the drums toward the door.

One of the fellows was wearing heavy gloves and was having trouble handling the pull-flare cords. Another bumped him out of the way and we finished off the first load of drums.

As we passed over the palace I could see people on the ground running in all directions. I remember one man driving a horse and carriage. It was as if time had slowed to one-fourth speed. The driver threw his whip into the air and jumped off the carriage. I watched a drum tumble and hit the apex of a shack. At first there was JP-4 flying everywhere, and then the shack disintegrated, followed by a ball of fire. The co-pilot yelled, "No, no, no!" I thought he was shouting above the roar of the wind and engines "Go, go, and go!" So I dropped two more drums in amongst some fancy homes. . . .

We were now over the hills above the city and there was still no ground fire. The pilot banked and lined up the palace again, this time dropping our airspeed to 95 knots and the altitude to 400 feet. . . . On the second pass we dropped ten drums of JP-4 in and around the palace. We could see smoke and flames coming from the barracks behind the palace [the Casernes Dessalines], where Léon had once been the commander. One drum had gone through a window on the east wing of the palace.

We were out over the bay when the co-pilot came back and asked if we wanted to make one more run. We all shouted, "Yes, yes, yes!" The pilot lined up on the palace again, dropping our altitude to 330 feet and the airspeed to an almost stall speed of 90 knots. The third pass was going well. We had a drum out the door heading for the palace. By the time we pushed the seventh drum out it was met by a barrage of ground fire. Stupidly, I looked out the door and saw soldiers firing every type of weapon, from .50-caliber machine guns to a soldier firing his pistol at us.

The plane was rocked by explosions and rounds were coming through the fuselage. Smoke was pouring out of the cockpit and I could hear the co-pilot screaming, "Jim, Jim, are you okay?" He repeated it even louder. The pilot replied in a matter-of-fact manner. "I'm trying to fly this fucking plane—please put the fire out."

The flight engineer was unconscious for a few seconds after getting hit in the back of the head by a piece of shrapnel. Luckily, the shrapnel first passed through a heavy leather flight case and some flight manuals before it hit him.

The co-pilot screamed, "Bring me the fire extinguisher—quick!" I remember grabbing the extinguisher and trying to carry it forward, but being able to make no progress as I was still tethered. I remember untying the line, but do not remember giving the co-pilot the apparatus. Later in the day he thanked me. I replied, "I did?" I truly did not remember.

Even though there was considerable damage to the avionics and we had holes in the plane which prevented us from maintaining air pressure, we headed north, dumping the rest of the drums on the mountains. Fuel was leaking from the wing tanks, but the pilot told us we were okay. The plan was to land on the north coast of Haiti at Port de Paix, where Léon and four of us [soldiers of fortune] would go into the hills to launch guerrilla warfare against the regime. Over Port de Paix the pilot announced that the runway was too short. We headed for Cap-Haïtien, which had a longer runway, but also a large garrison. God was with us that day. The Haitians were so scared by the bombing run over the capital that they put dozens of trucks on the Cap-Haïtien airstrip. Luckily, we could not land.

By 4:00 p.m. we were in the Bahamas still looking for a place to set down. All the islands with runways were socked in by thunderstorms. Even our contingency airstrip at Spanish Cay was out of the question. The pilot came back and gave us the news; we have to destroy any evidence and the only way to do that is to put this baby into water deep enough to sink it out of sight, and at the same time close enough to shore. We pulled out the rubber survival rafts and prepared to crash-land. The pilot gave an S.O.S. and was getting ready to land off the east side of Grand Bahamas Island when a voice over the radio: "I've got you in sight taking this heading." We landed at a U.S. guided missile tracking station where we were turned over to the Bahamian authorities, who sent us to Miami, except for the Canadian, who once again was sent back to his homeland, where he faced no charges.

*   *   *

Two members of the airborne expedition were released as soon as they landed in Miami. The rest of the group (Léon and the remaining soldiers of fortune) were arrested. They were charged, tried, and sentenced for violating U.S. neutrality laws and for exporting arms without a license. Léon and Casey were given two years in prison, and the others received terms ranging from nine to eighteen months.

The Haitian government announced that three people, including a six-month-old baby, were killed in the bombing. Papa Doc, speaking from his bedroom office while recovering from his heart attack, called it an "act of piracy" and told radio listeners to "trust in my star as well as my strong right arm."

René Léon returned to Haiti after the collapse of the Duvalier dynasty in 1986, following the flight of Jean-Claude (Baby Doc) Duvalier, and worked for the presidential candidacy of Louis Déjoie Jr. in Haiti's first post-Duvalier attempt at an election a year later, which was aborted by the military. Léon eventually left Haiti for Florida, where he died of natural causes in 1990. The Canadian became a landscape painter in Canada. Another of the soldiers of fortune became part owner of a computer store in the greater Miami community of Coral Gables, while yet another found employment in the U.S. Department of Agriculture. The Haitian-born former U.S. Marine disappeared. Marty Casey became an investigative reporter for various publications, including *Soldier of Fortune Magazine*, published by his friend Col. Robert Brown.

Their firebombing of the National Palace proved to be the last attempt to attack Papa Doc from Florida and the Bahamas, but more plots were to follow.

CHAPTER 18

Against All Odds:
The Time of the Left

In writing the chapter entitled "Communism Comes of Age" in a previous book, Papa Doc, *I was particularly careful in 1968 not to reveal the identities of the Marxist cadre fighting against Papa Doc. No writer wants to be responsible for the torture or death of anyone, no matter what their ideology. Now, nearly four decades later, I have decided to give in the chapter that follows faces to some of those young men and women who fought under the Marxist-Leninist label and were only to die like the other anti-Duvalierists in the war against tyranny.*

Papa Doc was aided in his counterattack against the Communist insurgency by his spies among the Haitian students abroad who had benefited from government scholarships, and some of whom were sons of Macoutes. The Communists were also under watchful eyes—those of the U.S. Central Intelligence Agency and its collaborators in countries such as the Dominican Republic and Mexico. It was remarkable that Haiti's latter-day, self-proclaimed Marxist revolutionaries managed to get as far as they did.

They did not reprise the role of fist-shaking Bolsheviks, waving hammer-and-sickle flags and manning street barricades, bent on destroying the bourgeoisie, as Stalinist Communists were often portrayed. Neither were they prototypical Marxist-Leninists, in spite of the proletarian political dogma that filled their clandestine publications. Among Haitian students during the 1960s and the 1970s the idea of an inevitable uprising and revolution by the oppressed was centered on their homeland, Haiti. Jacques Roumain, Jacques Stephen Alexis, René Depestre—Haitians all—were their favorite authors, and, though Marx Lenin, Engel, and

Mao were read too, the examples of Fidel Castro and Che Guevara were true to life and close to home. Exiled members of the two Haitian Communist parties were moving from one European city to another and feasted on the stories of Chinese, Vietnamese, and Cuban revolutions. The triumph of Castro and Guevara in the neighboring island inspired the Haitian youth.

Very quickly, as it is often the case among disenchanted petit-bourgeois, ideological choices moved from the left to the extreme left. "After admiring the Bolshevik revolution we learned to despise the revisionists and admired Castro and Che and Mao," one survivor recalled. The time had come for action, and even the conformist Parti Unifié des Communistes Haitiens (PEP) was unable to keep Haiti's radicalized youth in check and to persuade them to wait a bit longer for the development of "objective conditions" propitious for launching the revolution. The Marxist students saw the country they loved sinking deeper and deeper into the madness of tyranny. Thus, they decided to take fate into their own hands and join the war to free their people and replace Haiti's essentially feudal system with socialism. The PEP had modified its strategy, moving from non-violence to armed struggle and publishing its decision based on "Les voies tactiques vers la nouvelle independence" ("Tactical route to the new independence").

These were Haiti's anti-Duvalier Marxist rebels, and this chapter is about their war. Their clandestine struggle of the 1960s remains in the shadows even today. No known diary was left by the principal fighters, all of whom eventually were killed.

Much of the information that did become available on the war by Haitian Marxists against Dr. François Duvalier appeared in their own publications. However, those publications tell only part of their story. So too did the U.S. Foreign Broadcast Information Service (FBIS) bulletins. The FBIS provided regular translations in English of monitored radio broadcasts throughout the world, as part of the U.S. Cold War efforts to prevent Communist penetration. Nonetheless, neither the Marxists' clandestine exhortations nor the FBIS radio transcripts gave the slightest hint of the drama and tragedy of this last war against Papa Doc, who died of natural causes in the palace in 1971, but whose dynasty endured under his son, Jean-Claude (Baby Doc).

There tends to be a distinctly different perspective between those who write about Haiti from inside the country and those who write about Haiti from the outside. (This was once again illustrated in March 2004, when Haiti's neighbors in the other predominantly black countries of the Caribbean failed to understand why Haitians had ousted President Jean-Bertrand Aristide.)

Papa Doc's tyranny also hit painfully close to home for me, having launched my journalistic career as a resident newspaper publisher in Haiti. To cite but two examples: Pierre Sansaricq, who was brutally butchered to death in Jérémie in 1964 with his entire family, including women and infants, on Papa Doc's orders, had purchased his store in Jérémie from Jean Desquiron, my brother-in-law. And coincidentally, unbeknownst to its owner (who had been expelled from Haiti by Papa Doc), my house at rural Freres was rented for a period by the PEP central committee as a rebel "safe house." And it also happened that Joël Liautaud, one of the young revolutionaries who lived for a while in that same house, was a cousin of my wife's, who was not aware of who had rented the house.

As I conclude these chapters, I feel a need to cry out and exhort one and all: "No more! Give the Haitian people a chance to live in dignity, justice, and peace! Let there be an end to false preaching by false prophets!"

*   *   *

In the fall of 1967, a hunched-over, pale, and sickly looking man drove up to the rural home of chicken farmer Jean Desquiron and his wife at Freres, down the valley from Pétionville. The man, who appeared in his early 30s, introduced himself as Mario Théodore. "My wife," he said, looking back in the direction of his car where a woman appeared to be sleeping, "is not well. We have just returned from abroad and she needs peace and quiet. I have heard that there is a house on a neighboring hill for rent."

Having accepted 1,500 gourdes (U.S. $300) for three month's rent in advance, Desquiron turned to his wife and, shaking his head, said, "I can't place that Théodore." In Haiti during that time, members of the bourgeoisie not only knew each other but also their family histories dating back to the 1804 revolution.

The house on the neighboring hill was set back from the rutted Freres dirt road, two miles down the valley from Pétionville, the affluent redoubt overlooking Port-au-Prince. There was little traffic; even less since Papa Doc had closed the Military Academy located a mile further down the road. Interior Minister Lucien Chauvet, when he was not involved in chasing down Papa Doc's suspected enemies, would occasionally drive by in his French wife's small automobile to check on his dairy farm nearby. The American missionaries of the Church of the Nazarene on a hill across the valley had learned to mind their own business.

The couple who had rented the house was neither sick nor seeking peace and quiet. "Mario Théodore" was in fact Gérald Brisson, who despite his contrived appearance was actually a rugged former Haitian athlete who had only recently returned clandestinely from Moscow, France, Cuba, and the Dominican Republic. (Not long thereafter, Brisson really became sick. Found to be suffering from peritonitis, he was rushed to Hopital Canapé-Vert and hospitalized under a false name. Dr. Adrien Westerband operated, despite the risk.) During his stay in Cuba, Brisson had joined other Haitians, along with Central American rebels, in guerrilla training. The woman in the car was a Communist Party member.

Not long after the house was rented, Mrs. Jean Desquiron, driving on the normally deserted Freres road, passed a blue Volkswagen. Later she told her husband, "If I didn't know that Joël Liautaud was studying in Germany I would have believed it was he I passed on the road today." Much later Jean Desquiron found Jacques Stephen Alexis's former driver cleaning the floors of the house when Desquiron went to pick up the rent money.

Returning Communists from Europe and Mexico were breathing new life into the Marxist-Leninist *Parti d'Entente Populaire* (PEP) which had been founded by the late Dr. Jacques Stephen Alexis in 1959. It was a daunting task of not only moving the party into the new and dangerous phase of armed struggle against Duvalier but also keeping Haiti's two major Marxist parties united.

Both the PEP (*Parti d'Entente Populaire*) and the older PPLN (*Parti Populaire de Liberation Nationale*) had suffered serious setbacks during the 1959-1966 period. The 1959-1961 student strike to secure the freedom of the members of the PEP's central committee, headed by Joseph Roney, who had been secretly arrested and imprisoned, won their release, but Duvalier destroyed the university and left the party in disarray. Then, in 1961, Alexis' capture at the tip of the Mole St. Nicolas peninsula in Northwest Haiti and secret execution was an even greater blow. (This episode is described more fully in chapter 13 of *The Price of Blood*, the first part of this two-part account.)

A bullet, fired accidentally, wounding a PPLN member during a clandestine arms-training session in a Pétionville house led to the arrest on July 27, 1965, of the PPLN co-founder, Professor Jean-Jacques Dessalines Ambroise, and his pregnant wife. Details of their horrendous torture death at Police Headquarters came to light during the trial of one of the torturers, the renowned Luc Desyr, in 1987 after the collapse of the Duvalier dictatorship. Architect Albert Mangonès had acquired for the PPLN the vacant house at the end of a quiet Pétionville street from one of his brothers.

Quickly alerted to the accidental shooting by his comrades, he warned them to "disappear," as the police would be drawn to the scene. Anticipating his arrest, Mangonès told the author in 1987, he had given his comrades time to flee before going to Port-au-Prince Police Headquarters voluntarily and telling police that he had no knowledge of who had been in the house, as it had been vacant for some time. Mangonès knew his position was even more precarious because his brother-in-law, Auguste Denizé—one of the country's top surgeons, an earlier partisan of François Duvalier and Papa Doc's first Minister of Health—had been jailed along with his wife, Monique Mangonès, for months. After months in prison, both Denizé and his wife had been released and allowed to depart for exile in New York. Duvalier ordered that the "artist son of my friend Edmond Mangonès" be released. The architect subsequently learned that Duvalier had in his student days consulted Mangonès' father's vast collection of historical data on Haiti. But that single bullet led to the physical decapitation of the PPLN and the eventual death of leader Professor Amboise.

The following year, in October 1966, almost by accident, a roundup of Jumellists in St. Marc who were plotting an uprising led to the arrests of members of the PPLN cadre in the Artibonite Valley. Some were tortured to death while others were to spend years in Ft. Dimanche. (Claude A. Rosier, in *Le Triangle de la Mort: Journal d'un Prisonnier Politique Haitien 1966-1977*, recounts the story of the PPLN roundup and his years in the feared Ft. Dimanche.) In charge of the interrogation of Rosier and other PPLN members in St. Marc in 1966 was army Col. Breton Claude, a soldier whom Papa Doc had promoted to officer rank and whose loyalty, like that of Gracia Jacques, another reassigned soldier, was not to any Military Academy class but to Duvalier. In the years to follow Breton Claude became the scourge of the Communists.

After four years of division, the PEP and PPLN had begun unity talks that started in Port-au-Prince on July 4, 1963, attended by delegates from throughout Haiti. The result was an agreement between the PEP and the PPLN to form a united front, the FDULN (*Front Democratique Unified de Liberation d'Haiti*). The unification pact was finalized the following year at a secret meeting in Prague.

The PEP was well known in leftist circles abroad, in part because the books by its founder, Dr. Jacques Stephen Alexis, had won recognition in intellectual circles, especially in France. Alexis also impressed Communist China's Mao as well as the Soviet leaders and those he met at important Communist Congresses in the Soviet Bloc.

On the other hand, the PPLN, founded in 1954, had a low international profile, with its leaders preferring to devote all the party's energies to building its clandestine network in Haiti. Jean-Jacques Dessalines Amboise, a co-founder, was a studious, self-effacing Marxist who cleverly shunned the spotlight. Many of the PPLN cadre were unknown to each other and used simple noms de guerre. Also confusing was the PPLN's change of names. It ultimately became known as PUDA, *Parti de l'Union des Democrates Haïtiens*, although it was also identified as PPLN-PUDA.

The final official acronym of the Communists in Haiti was to be the PUCH—*Parti Unifié des Communistes Haitiens*. The PUCH was announced formally on January 18, 1969, but the new name had been in common usage earlier.

Youthful Raymond Jean-François (pseudonym "Levantin"), who had replaced Jacques Stephen Alexis as secretary of the Central Committee of the PEP, returned clandestinely to Haiti in 1964. He came from a humble Port-au-Prince family—his mother was a street *marchand*. In 1961 he had been arrested for his involvement in the strike by the *Union Nationale des Etudiants Haitiens,* which had finally forced Duvalier to release Joseph Roney and 12 comrades from prison. Jean-François was himself released after three months in prison by the threat of a strike by fellow students at L'Ecole Normale Supérieure. He had been tortured upon his arrest, and interrogators had broken his arm and denied him medical treatment, but he had steadfastly refused to talk. He had collaborated with Brisson to produce *Les Fondements de L'Entente Populaire en Haiti.*

Gerald Brisson, son of a respected and well-known notary public, was a talented Port-au-Prince youth who played the saxophone at his school, St. Louis de Gonzague, and served as maestro of a small band known as Groupe Tchouboum. The musical group of young petit bourgeois of Groupe Tchouboum played dance music in the capital's nightclubs and private clubs. In 1958 Brisson had won a bronze medal for Haiti in the high jump at the Pan American Games in Chicago.

A graduate of Haiti's law school, Brisson had worked at his father's notary office and taken on one criminal case as an *avocet-stagiaire* (a type of legal apprentice), but by 1959 he had through his friend Ernest (Nino) Caprio become interested in the personalism of Emmanuel Mounier and Marxism. That same year he became one of the founding members of the PEP and was thrown into prison for no apparent reason. The story of Brisson's arrest that later circulated in the capital was that the powerful secret police chief, Clement Barbot, had arrested him, and just before he was to be executed beside the grave he had been forced to dig at Mais Gate (the land on which the jet airport was later built), Barbot had been asked to intercede and received a generous payment for saving his life.

The true story is different. J.J. Craan, working with her mother, shopkeeper Mrs. Maglio, on Port-au-Prince's Grand Rue near the Cafeteria police post, witnessed Brisson being forced into the building by detectives. The Italian shopkeeper alerted a friend of the Brisson family and Notary Emmanuel Brisson quickly sought help. He later recounted to his family how he had first approached Col. Paul Laraque, who told him he could do nothing because he also was implicated. Next, Police Chief Pierre Merceron, Laraque's brother-in-law, reportedly said, "Tell Maitre Brisson I am not here." Finally, in desperation, Maitre Brisson approached Barbot. "This is a John Beauvoir coup," Barbot told him and agreed to talk to the president. (Beauvoir was a tough research criminal police officer and had a personal grudge against Gérald Brisson.) Lt. François Benoit, on returning from the FAd'H Rifle Contest in Panama and hearing that his close friend Gérald Brisson had been arrested, asked Col. Daniel Beauvoir to intercede. Meanwhile, Brisson had been transferred to Ft. Dimanche. Finally after ten days he was released. Duvalier's condition was that he immediately leave Haiti for a country in which there were no Haitians. On the day of his departure, Lt. Benoit drove Gérald Brisson to the airport. En route they encountered Lt. John Beauvoir driving in the opposite direction. Brisson kept out of sight as Benoit exchange salutations with his fellow officer.

Brisson departed from Haiti and began his exile in Colombia. In fact there was a Haitian in Colombia, Gérald's half-brother Emmanuel Brisson, who lived in a small town near the Venezuelan border.

Gérald's fiancée, Jacqueline Volel, joined him in Colombia in 1960, and they began their long trek to Moscow. Jacqueline originated from Jacmel and grew up in a large family of five boys and two girls. They were all imbued with the spirit of rebellion against injustice. One of the brothers had joined with the Baptiste brothers and spent months in Duvalier's prison for the foiled attack on the Jacmel airport. He also had written a student pamphlet criticizing Duvalier's ideology. Jacqueline's elder brother had to flee Haiti for exile.

From Baranquilla, Colombia, Gérald and Jacqueline flew to Jamaica, where they decided to get married. The newlyweds then flew to Paris, where they received a scholarship from the Soviet embassy to study in the Soviet Union. At USSR's Patrice Lumumba People's Friendship University they both attended social science classes with Latin American and African students. The Brissons each received a monthly stipend of 90 rubles and an allotment for clothes, as well as food and board. In Russia, Jacqueline gave birth to a son and then a daughter. Gérald named their son Vladlen (a combination of Vladimir Lenin). Their daughter was named Françoise after Gerald's friend François Benoit. (Later, when the children's grandmother, Mrs. Emanuel Renée Brisson, flew to Paris to bring the two children back to Haiti, it was decided to change Vladlen's name. He was named René after his grandmother.)

Gérald had become preoccupied with the need for land reform in Haiti, where, although much of the land was held by peasants, there was still land in the hands of the government that was leased out by the authorities to favorites and big "Don" landowners, who in turn had poor farmers work it for the Don's benefit. During his time in Moscow and Cuba, Gérald worked on the study *Les Relations Agraires dans l'Haiti Contemporaine.*

Upon completing their studies in the Soviet Union, the couple moved to Cuba, where Jacqueline Brisson Volel was employed as a hydraulic engineer.

*   *   *

As a "safe-house," the Freres home was ideal. It sat alone on a hill, and was insulated by a high wall in front and ravines at the back, ensuring both privacy and a quick exit if necessary. The peasant neighbors, Mercius Cesar, Boss Fifi, and Boss Marc—the local farmer, *houngan*, and upholsterer—were neither Macoutes nor informers and were good friends of the owner. And the view was of Lake Saumatre and the Dominican border in the distance, from where some party members trekked to the house. Ti-Freres, the houseboy and guardian who lived with his family on the property, was told by Brisson that his services were not required. He remained but minded his own business. Apart from their clandestine agenda, to the Brissons and other party members, after five years of frigid European winters and spartan living at Lumumba University in Moscow and in France and German, Freres was heaven.

At night those using the house tuned in to Radio Havana and Radio Moscow, the latter having started to beam a nightly Kreyól program to Haiti in 1968. The occupants sometimes communicated with each other in Russian out of habit, or in Spanish, besides their native French and Kreyól. It was not long before the mimeograph machine was churning out copies of *Voix du Peuple*, the PEP party organ. Later they published mimeograph copies of *Avant Garde*, the PEP's inter-cadre publication dealing with ideology, ideas, concerns, and self-criticism. (Few copies of *Avant Garde* appear to have survived.) Communications with overseas contacts were established by simple code or by means of ingeniously developed invisible ink, and dispatched by mail or courier. The simple Haitian invisible ink was nothing but lime juice.

Coming in waves to Haiti from their studies in Europe, the young Marxists had their travel and documents carefully arranged and controlled by the Party. Some arrived via the Dominican Republic, others by air from Jamaica, Canada, and Martinique. Those who came in through Port-au-Prince's Dr. François Duvalier Airport used false passports and other counterfeited documents prepared by the Party. Brisson, alias Tilandeng, got through the airport controls wearing large glasses and thread balls on each side of his mouth, changing his appearance from slim to chubby. A group sneaked across the border from the Dominican Republic. Some had undergone guerrilla training in Cuba and China. They were among Haiti's brightest young students. And, unexpectedly, many originated from middle-class or wealthy families and attended one of the two top-level Haitian Catholic schools.

By the summer of 1967, those from abroad had assumed a clandestine life in Haiti, often passing their parents' homes or relatives in the street without being detected. Gérald was known to stand quietly across Avenue John Brown to glimpse his parents as they sat on the verandah of their house in the cool of the early evening. Some parents believed their children were continuing their studies abroad.

One returnee who emerged from covert disguise long enough to speak to his shocked father was Gerard Wadestrandt. He needed his father's help in acquiring another safe-house. His father, according to what the young man's family later recounted to the author, pleaded with Gerard to give up the fight, reminding him that the family had already lost one son, Jacques, who had died fighting with the 13 who landed from the United States in 1964 only to be exterminated after battling the regime for three months. When his father realized that there was no way he could convince Gerard to quit, he aided him by talking a neighbor on Chemin des Dalles, Emmanuel (Mano) Pierre-Louis, who operated the established Paret-Pierre-Louis funeral parlor, into renting the Pierre-Louis two-story house in the Boutillier mountains, high above the capital, to some "friends." It was a new safe-house for Gerard and his friends, but engineer Leon Wadestrandt knew the penalty of aiding anti-Duvalier rebels. He sent his wife, Odette Bouillon, into exile in New York, where she found a job in a factory, and he himself went into hiding in Haiti, which he refused to leave, ultimately dying of a broken heart, having lost two sons in the fight against Papa Doc.

From Cuba, where she quit her job as a hydraulic engineer, Jacqueline Volel Brisson had made a long air odyssey back to the Soviet Union then to France, and finally to Port-au-Prince. After clearing immigration and customs with false documents, she was about to step into a taxi at the Dr. François Duvalier Airport when she saw a blue Volkswagen signaling her. The driver was "Fritz Levy" (Joël Liautaud), who had entered Haiti in July 1967, dressed as a priest. Liautaud drove Jacqueline to the Freres safe-house, where she was reunited with her husband and put to work preparing and mimeographing the PEP's *Voix du Peuple*.

One day two women friends of Jacqueline recognized her driving a small Renault, despite the wig she wore. She ignored their salutation, and, intrigued, they followed her and saw her enter another safe-house in Montagne Noire.

Joël Liautaud was not atypical of the young men who had made the decision to fight and, if necessary, die for their country. He was born on December 26, 1943, in Port-au-Prince, the eldest boy in a large closely-knit family which he himself termed "petit bourgeois." His father was the business manager of Behrmann Motors, an auto dealership, while his mother worked in the Tabou flower shop in Port-au-Prince. In such a poor country, Joël was lucky to live among the few privileged people and attend one of the best schools in Port-au-Prince. He was very active in sports and trained in jujitsu, judo, and boxing at Bico Villedrouin's Port-au-Prince boxing establishment. Among the top athletes of his school, where Gerald Brisson also excelled in sports, Joël was to become a member of Brisson's urban guerilla commando.

Joel was notably bright. He developed skills in electronics while still at secondary school, but he was also attracted by foreign languages, learning English, Spanish, and German, and he was a passionate member of the German Institute in Haiti. As a very attractive young man, he had amassed a number of adolescent love trysts.

In 1960, Papa Doc, having developed all of the worst features of a Third World tyrant, set his repressive sights on professors and students of the University of Haiti and state high schools. It was then that Joël Liautaud took part in his open battle against the dictator, leading a strike at his Catholic school in support of jailed students despite his parents' anxiety and fear. This first effort was only partially successful, as the outcome was that Duvalier created a new entity, the State University of Haiti, where his Macoutes dictated the rules.

But for many privileged Haitian students it was time to open their eyes to the overall distress of the Haitian people and the unacceptable disparities between the country's privileged and its poor. With several classmates who had participated in the strike, Joel decided to leave the Catholic school and spend his last year at the private Centre d'Etudes Secondaires.

The atmosphere in the Centre was openly nationalist, with an underground promoting revolutionary ideas and encouraging the spirit of revolt against the dictatorship. One central player was Max Chancy, a leader of PUDA. As Duvalier singled out particular professors as dangerous to his regime, some were forced into hiding while other fled the country, accepting teaching positions in Africa and North America.

Joël Liautaud had left for West Germany to study electronical engineering in Aachen. His parents were relieved, since Haiti's dissident youth were in grave danger. Following his second year at the West German university, Joël learned that one of his uncles, a former Haitian army officer, had been executed along with 34 other former officers by Papa Doc. Joël also learned that his uncle's son, Charlie Forbin, a very close cousin, had left the U.S. Army to take part in the Jeune Haiti 13-commando team, which had landed at Dame Marie and fought to the death during a remarkable three-months campaign. All were eventually killed, overwhelmed by thousands of Duvalier's militia and army troops. Word of this epic fight of the Thirteen had a motivating effect on other Haitian youth, as well as members of the Haitian Federation of Students in Europe (FEHE), in which Joël was an active member. They decided to put an end to a wait-and-see attitude. Radicalized Haitian students were enrolled in Communist-country military training programs, sometimes in Red China but more frequently in Cuba. Then they received the call. The

PEP was preparing the armed struggle along with the PPLN-PUDA.

There was young Jean-Robert "Ti-Bob" Desir, who had been studying economics in Strasbourg, was along with a fellow Haitian student, Eddy Petit. There was also Gerard Wadestrandt, who had completed his architecture studies in Mexico and gone to Cuba and then the Dominican Republic. Eden Germain (alias Edouard Emmanuel Calixte) and Bernard Pierre-Louis left universities in Berlin for Haiti. Michel Corvington had not left Haiti and was waiting for them in Port-au-Prince, as were other Party members. Not all of them agreed on the PEP line, being closer to Foquism or Maoism than to the conventional alignment with Moscow. But they thought that they had to utilize the PEP-PPLN-PUDA infrastructures as a first step.

A propos of this approach, Eddy Petit, on the eve of his clandestine travel to Haiti, told a friend: "I do not agree with the party leaders but we cannot miss the opportunity to fight for the Haitian people; even if we die, at least they will know that we tried to end the fascist-Macoute regime. They will understand our ideals and rejoin the revolution camp."

Joël Liautaud, for his part, eventually made contact with two of his brothers in Port-au-Prince. He told his brother Bernard: "Only violence can remove violent dictators such as Duvalier and I could hardly make a choice of living with a charming wife in Europe while our people are martyrized daily. Only the Communists have a strong network in the country, and we will use this channel and fight for a new line from the interior of the organization."

The atmosphere among Haitian students abroad, especially in France, had been infectious. Gérald Brisson's sister Monique was involved with the clandestine progressive Catholics. They had sprung from the scouts, a student youth group formed in 1960 at College Saint Martial by young Haitian priests at La Bibliotheque des Jeunes. They defined themselves as anti-Duvalier, non-confessionnelle and anti-system, and they called themselves "Haiti Progres." Among the group's founders were Monique Brisson, Lionel Loubeau (a youth who also belonged to the Jeuness du PPLN and became an early victim of Duvalier repression), and Father Paul Jean-Claude. There was also Renauld Bernadin, who had been the president of the Catholic University Youth (JUC) from 1959-60, and was forced to flee into exile in 1961. Others in the movement included Fathers

Max Dominique and Lucien Smarth, sociologist Laennec Hurbon, and Prof. Guy Alexandre. While the underground mimeographed opposition broadsheet *Haiti Progres*, which had been founded by the young Catholics, continued to circulate, it lost its vigor after the failed student strike and the resulting crackdown on liberal Catholic priests.

It was in Paris in 1966 that Monique Brisson, who had arrived in France a year earlier, again met Alix Lamaute, who was eventually to become part of the Communist struggle against Papa Doc. He was born on July 25, 1941, into a poor yet middle-class family (unlike in some countries, the Haitian middle class was often very poor) in the capital. From his days at Petit Seminaire College Saint-Martial, he displayed a quick intelligence that got him hired after graduation by an American-owned electric company. He became an active member of L'Union Intersyndicale d'Haiti (UIH) and began writing in *Le Travailleur*, the union's publication. While attending the faculty of law at the University of Haiti, he joined the L'Union Nationale des Etudiants Haitiens (UNEH) and wrote for *Tribune des Etudiants (FEHE)*. Later, under the pseudonym Lionel Camaz, he wrote articles on Marxist theory for *Avant Garde*, the newsletter for PEP cadres. One day in November 1961, a period when the Duvalier dictatorship viewed all students as the potential enemy, Lamaute was interviewed by Monique Brisson. She was then a student of social science at L'Ecole Normale Supérieure, and working on her thesis on labor unions in Haiti. The labor union expert's answers impressed her, and her questions impressed him. Two very intelligent young people became good friends.

In his second year at law school Alix received a scholarship from the West German Federal Republic, where he completed his law studies in two years and went on to study economic science at the University of Freiburg. In 1966 he began his trek back to Haiti clandestinely. He met up with Monique Brisson in Paris, and one day they went to Maspero Publishers with his essay *La Bourgeosie Nationale une entité controversée* to have it published as a book. Shortly afterward, PEP's Gerard Pierre-Charles in Mexico asked them not to publish it. (It was not published until after the collapse the Duvalier dictatorship. In 1999, the 30th anniversary of Cazale, it was published with a foreword by his daughter, Nathalie Brisson Lamaute.)

*   *   *

Adrien Sansaricq, like his brother Daniel, carried the terrible burden of having lost his entire family to Papa Doc. The two brothers were the last members of a large, well-known family in Jérémie. Duvalier had ordered the family executed in 1964 when the Thirteen invaders had come ashore. Thirteen members of the Sansaricq family, including a six-year-old boy, a four-year-old boy, and a two-year-old girl, were brutally butchered like beasts on the ends of bayonets and machetes. The macabre killings took place next to Jérémie's small airport, where a mass gave had been dug and the bodies of the prominent townspeople, 27 in total, cast into the hole by their gloating executioners. The soldiers and Macoutes didn't even bother to make sure their victims were dead as they threw their bloodied bodies into the pit.

While the nightmare memory of their family's liquidation was forever with them, they both considered themselves more revolutionaries than avengers, with the moral duty to liberate Haitians from the jaws of the Duvalier dictatorship. Born in Jérémie in 1937, Adrien, upon graduating from college in Haiti, received a scholarship to study medicine in Mexico City. He was followed there by his younger brother, Daniel. By 1961 both had joined the PEP, and the following year Adrien represented Haiti at the World Youth Festival in Helsinki.

Adrien decided to complete his medical studies in Cuba and after graduation came to the notice of Cuban authorities for his outstanding post-hurricane relief work in Oriente Province, where he had chosen to do his social service. When a group of black Cubans were recruited in 1965 to fly to Africa to join Che Guevara's expedition to support rebel leader Kabila in the Congo rebellion, Dr. Adrien Sansaricq was among those chosen. He was the only foreigner in the group. Piero Gleijeses notes in his book *Conflicting Missions: Havana, Washington, and Africa*: "In Zaire he, Sansaricq, worked more as a doctor than as a guerrilla; he would have preferred it the other way around but Che did not allow it." Back in Cuba, Dr. Sansaricq fell in love and married an Argentine musician. They named their son Ernesto, after Che. Ernesto was to become the last male Sansaricq of the Jérémie branch of the family.

The May 1965 edition of the Switzerland-published *Ralliement* carried a long letter from Daniel Sansaricq addressed to "La Presse Combattive d'Haiti." In it, the tall and handsome Sansaricq, who had been studying architecture in Mexico City, announced his entry onto his country's political scene, "at a painful time for me, but it is also painful for 4 million of my compatriots" caught in the vice of dictatorship. His letter cited the litany of crimes of the Duvalier dictatorship and condemned U.S. President Lyndon B. Johnson's intervention that year in the Dominican Republic. Daniel Sansaricq declared the Haitian left's solidarity with the Dominicans fighting against the intervention forces.

Ralliement, purported to reflect the views of the PEP (Parti Entente Populaire) and the PPLN (Parti Populaire de Liberation Nationale), had stated in its September 1964 issue that the comrades would see the end the Duvalier dictatorship. They were stronger than ever, united, and believed no force was capable of halting a "popular revolution" in Haiti.

Ralliement branded the non-Marxist guerrillas as "cowboys and adventurers, and toys of the imperialists." The publication also rejected the classical coup d'état as a solution, calling it a device offered by the U.S. State Department to prevent a "popular revolution." The United States was accused of endeavoring to use traditional Haitian politicians and "renegade Duvalierists" to replace Duvalier, in order to maintain Haiti's feudal 19th-century economic and political system.

The Communists' publications acknowledged that during most of his murderous rule, Duvalier had used the Communist threat to blackmail the United States. However, as the history of the period makes clear, the Communists in turn had taken full advantage of the climate provided by the bloody dictatorship to boost their proselytizing.

In a letter in *Ralliement*, Daniel Sansaricq described the Haitian student population in Mexico City as a microcosm of Papa Doc's Haiti, with what Sansaricq called "scholarship-Macoutes"—sons of Macoutes and Duvalier functionaries who benefited from government-paid scholarships—on one side and anti-Duvalierist on the other. According to Sansaricq these "Macoute-students" had the task of spying on other Haitian students for Papa Doc, and took their task seriously.

He recounts that in April 1964 a fight had erupted in which a scholarship-Macoute had received a bloody jaw and in retaliation his companions had wrecked a restaurant. During the brawl, Sansaricq had received a painful kick in the head. As a consequence, he states, back in Jérémie his father was called in to the local Casernes—the Macoute-students, whom he names in *Ralliement*, had declared that he would pay for his actions. His father advised him to leave Mexico, and Daniel recalls that unfortunately his departure from Mexico coincided with the landing of the Thirteen rebels in Haiti. Moreover, the student spies had reported to Port-au-Prince that Daniel Sansaricq had left Mexico City at about the same time. Also, many of the rebels were from Jérémie and had been his childhood friends.

Sansaricq noted a particularly macabre illustration of Duvalier's brutality in his October 26, 1964, decree declaring "Civil Death" for the families and friends of the Jeune Haiti fighters, who themselves had already been executed.

Daniel Sansaricq ended his long letter in *Ralliement* with an unusual call for a united front against the dictatorship. Daniel himself went off to train in Cuba for his war against Papa Doc.

*   *   *

Mexico City had long been considered by successive Haitian governments as a dangerous leftist center. The fact that the Soviet Union and other Communist countries, including Castro's Cuba after 1959, maintained large embassies in the Mexican capital made the Western Hemisphere's rightist dictators nervous, and so they kept their own groups of spies there to report on activities of their exiles. Mail between Mexico, the Dominican Republic, Haiti, and other countries was often read by their respective security forces.

Gerard Pierre-Charles, who was to become the most visible Haitian Marxist-in-residence in Mexico City, had arrived there in 1960. His destination choice of exile had been determined by the fact his fiancée, Suzy Castor, had been studying there for her doctorate in social science. Born into a large Jacmelian family—Gerard's father had passed away when he was an infant and his mother died when he was ten, leaving ten children—Gerard learned only years later that his father had sometimes written articles denouncing the U.S. occupation of Haiti that were published in the Port-au-Prince newspaper, *Les Temps*.

Pierre-Charles and Gérald Brisson had been neighbors in the Port-au-Prince residential district of Bois Verna. One day Brisson invited Pierre-Charles to meet Dr. Jacques Stephen Alexis. On the day of the introduction, Alexis, the founder of the PEP, was busy working in the garden of his Canapé Vert home. Pierre-Charles found Alexis to be indeed a man of many talents, among them gardening and furniture-making, as well as being a physician and writer.

When Brisson left Haiti on December 18, 1959, Pierre-Charles followed in February 1960, when he found it expedient to depart after fomenting a strike at the French-owned cement plant 15 miles north of the capital, where he was employed as an accountant. In Mexico City, Pierre-Charles, who had earned a college diploma in social sciences and administration in Haiti, began post-graduate studies at the Autonomous University of Mexico City (UNAM) and married his sweetheart.

Originally from the town of Aquin in South Haiti, Suzy Castor had been a boarder at St. Rose de Lima Catholic girls' school in Port-au-Prince. After graduating from the L'Ecole Normale Supérieure in Port-au-Prince, she traveled to Mexico City in 1959 to study for her doctorate in social science.

Tragically, shortly after their second son, Gary, was born in 1962, Pierre-Charles was stricken with polio and placed in an iron lung. Doctors said he would never walk again. He refused to give up and was transported to Canada for further treatment. Ultimately Gérald Brisson heard of Pierre-Charles' plight and arranged for him to be treated in the Soviet Union. Though Pierre-Charles had not been able to walk for two years, by degrees, with the help of braces and crutches, he again managed to stand tall. Resuming his post-graduate education at UNAM, he won a degree in economics as also continued his studies of Marx and Lenin. After returning to Mexico City, he eventually joined the UNAM faculty. Suzy, with her doctorate degree, also joined the faculty at the same institute.

Despite Pierre-Charles's physical handicap, he pursued his work for the PEP as a member of the central committee in charge of international relations. As part of the party's strategy Pierre-Charles became skillful at practicing deception and traveled to meetings in Chile, Cuba, and Europe. During the mid-1960s his family foyer in Mexico City also served as a Marxist study and discussion circle for expatriate Haitian leftist students.

Most who attended the meetings were inspired to join the PEP.

The respected husband-and-wife professors were also of interest to the CIA and to Mexico's powerful chief of the Federal Security Directorate (secret police agency), Fernando Gutierrez Barrios, who was known to work in liaison with the Mexico City bureau of the CIA, sharing information and providing services. Early one summer evening, on a visit to the Pierre-Charles home in Mexico City's Colonia Napoli neighborhood, my wife and I witnessed what was clearly a brazen bugging operation by Mexican agents. In terms of covertness it was a ridiculous sight. Two men sat in a parked, unmarked automobile before the Gérard-Pierre Charles apartment with the car's windows rolled down, permitting a clear view of their radio receptor and recording devices for a microphone bug undoubtedly planted somewhere in the Pierre-Charles apartment. Conversation in the apartment that night was markedly guarded, as they also knew of the presence of the agents in the car. Suzy often joked that another man, who lounged around the neighborhood, obviously keeping them under surveillance, was so well known to her that she waved hello when he appeared. He never returned the salutation. The surveillance came each time there was political trouble in Haiti.

Yet while the Mexican secret police agency and the CIA may have had difficulty penetrating the PEP and PPLN/PUDA movements in Mexico, Papa Doc's spies—the "scholarship-Macoutes"—stayed extremely busy reporting any movements of their suspected fellow students. Often lacking solid information, the Macoute-students were known to brag that they sometimes lacquered their reports with fiction and fantasy to keep their bonuses coming from Port-au-Prince.

*   *   *

Despite being geographically contiguous, Haiti and the Dominican Republic have always been culturally and politically distant neighbors, and even frequent enemies. Yet in 1965, not a few Haitians fought on the side of Constitutionalist forces in Santo Domingo against United States troops. One of the Haitians involved was leftist poet Jacques Viau, a longtime exile in the Dominican Republic who died as a result of wounds received on June 15, 1965, while battling in the front lines against the

U.S. 82nd Airborne troops. Fred Baptiste and his "Kamokin" guerrillas also fought as a commando unit in the forces under Col. Francisco Caamano Deno.

In 1966, the first such group of Haitian Communists arrived in Santo Domingo. As early as 1961, Juan Ducoudray, representing the *Partido Socialista Popular Dominicano* (PSP, later the *Partido Communista Dominican*, or PCD) had met with PEP leader Jacques Stephen Alexis in Moscow, where the two Hispaniola Marxists had fashioned a historical first "declaration of intent" for their respective parties to support each other's struggle.

Following the capture and execution in Haiti of Alexis that same year, the Dominican and Haitian Communist leaders continued their talks in successive meetings at congresses abroad in the U.S.S.R, Chile, and Cuba. In Havana in December 1965, according to Dominican participant José Israel Cuello, he and countryman Narciso Isa Conde met with Prof. Gérard Pierre Charles of the PEP and sealed an agreement of reciprocal support for their respective struggles with absolute independence in defining their own methods of struggle. Cuello notes that this agreement was accomplished without any Cuban participation whatsoever.

In an interview I conducted with him in Santo Domingo in April 2004, the short and stocky Cuello recounted, with obvious admiration for his Haitian comrades, how the latter had used the Dominican Republic to prepare for their war against Papa Doc.

The first contingent arrived after the Revolution of April 1965 and included Gérald Brisson, Gérard Wadestrandt, and Daniel Sansaricq. The next group included Guy Pierre, who did not enter Haiti. A distinguished intellectual who had been living in Paris, Pierre had married Sabine Manigat, herself an accomplished sociologist and daughter of Marie-Lucy Chancy and Leslie Manigat. Another Haitian was known simply as "André."

The last group of Haitian infiltrators to arrive succeeded in winning over the migrant Haitian sugarcane-cutter population in the bateys, which became a principal source of recruitment for the Haitian Marxists and was important in organizing their lines of communication with Haiti.

Within a short time, Cuello noted, the Haitian Communists developed a network of connections with their organization inside Haiti also with help of the Dominican Communist Party. The Haitians established contacts in Barahona and San Juan de Maguana for their routes into Haiti, which were fluid and were organized to be quickly changed.

The clandestine activities of members of the PEP in the Dominican Republic were all the more remarkable because, in the aftermath of the Dominican civil war and the U.S. intervention (April 1965-September 1966), the Dominican Republic was anything but safe terrain for political leftists. In fact, it was an extremely dangerous place even though rightist President Joaquín Balaguer, who had returned to power in 1966, paid lip service to democracy and declared his commitment to peace and goodwill towards former leftist fighters. Hired enforcers known as "La Banda" were beginning to target leftists of any stripe.

The career of the tireless and versatile Jose Cuello—a printer and publisher—included anchoring an hour-long morning television talk show in Santo Domingo. He recalled in his interview with the author that Gérald Brisson had lived in a boarding house on Calle Salcedo in Santo Domingo's San Carlos district. Architect Gérard Wadestrandt likewise lived in a rooming house, at the corner of Avenida Bolivar and Jules Verne Street. Wadestrandt is remembered for having introduced karate to his fellow boarders and then to Santo Domingo itself. Daniel Sansaricq did not marry in Santo Domingo but, according to Jose Cuello, "he left us a daughter and a quasi-widow who kept his memory alive for many years and perhaps until now."

The Haitian Communist leadership operated in the Dominican Republic with absolute political and administrative autonomy, Cuello said, and even developed its own lines of financial credit. The Communists were also very strict with their budget, living expenses, and transportation.

During their stay in Santo Domingo and after they returned to Haiti, the Dominican Communists selected one of their members to handle the administrative relations between two parties. Another PCD member was in charge of "special matters" between the two parties. There was never a meeting between the Haitians and Dominicans to discuss their political lines.

At first the PCD loaned the Haitians vehicles, but the visitors soon returned them, having obtained their own. The Haitians also managed to collect a limited number of weapons that were smuggled into Haiti in a black Chevrolet driven by Dominicans. But the Haitians admitted they were still in need of arms and munitions.

When Gérald Brisson was finally prepared to return by the regular Pan American Airways flight to Haiti, Cuello recalled, "The last place he visited in Santo Domingo was my apartment at the corner of 19th of March and Archbishop Nouvel streets. In saying goodbye we discussed the possibilities of success and Gérald frankly admitted their chances of success and survival were indeed slim, but he was determined to take on the Duvalier dictatorship." Cuello added, with a sigh exuding nostalgia, "I still have Brisson's notes on 'agrarian-related questions in contemporary Haiti.' We were going to publish them but we never did."

When, in September 1966, Daniel Sansaricq was stopped at the airport, arrested, and jailed, the ensuing "Daniel Sansaricq affair" illustrated the bond of sympathy that had been established between liberal Dominicans and the Haitians.

Sansaricq and Camille Montero, accused of being in Dominican Republic illegally, joined a group of Haitian cadres who had already spent months in La Victoria prison.

In mid-February 1967, there was a most unusual happening. Thirty Haitians, including activists Roger Bardot, Louis Jean François, Le Gouaze Coquillon, Robert Moise, and Sauveur Guerrier, had been handed over by the Balaguer Government to Duvalier at the Dominican border post of Elias Penas. Remarkably, protests were raised to such a pitch among the Dominican public, the media, and ex-President Juan Bosch's congressmen that Balaguer was forced to request the return of those exiles to the Dominican Republic. The fact that among the 30, 5 Parti d'Entente Populaire activists were returned produced a declaration from the PEP publication *Voix du Peuple* that it was "*incroyable*—unbelievable, that they had been saved from the mouth of the wolf."

Nevertheless there were reports of a sinister pact between Balaguer and Duvalier that allowed the imprisonment of Haitians in the Dominican Republic without recourse to the law, judicial proceedings, or even knowledge of the specific charges against them.

Finally, in desperation, the Haitian prisoners in La Victoria launched a hunger strike in Feburary 1967. After five weeks, surviving only on water, seven of them were transferred to the Moscoso Cuello hospital and most of the others to the Padre Billini and Luis E. Aybar clinics in Santo Domingo. Because of the gravity of the health of the hunger strikers, they had to be given life-saving serum. (Three prisoners, Daniel Sansaricq, Montero, and Robert Moyse, refused for security reasons to leave the prison clinic for even a private hospital.)

In late March, one of them, Fernando Graham, still had enough strength to declare "we prefer to die now than return to the prison. The hunger strike will end with our death or our freedom."

The heroic attitude of the Haitian prisoners swayed Dominican public opinion in their favor. Again Juan Bosch's congressmen interceded directly with Balaguer, and various Dominican media outlets and student associations came out in support of freedom for the Haitians. Dominican sympathizers had picketed the National Palace and had to be dispersed by police using tear gas.

Finally Balaguer could no longer ignore the protests, and the prisoners were released. On March 30, Daniel Sansaricq was freed and placed on a plane to Chile. The freeing of Sansariq constituted a victory for the Haitian cause. *Lambi* reported, "The Dominican police and the United States CIA exercised all kinds of pressure . . . every effort not to liberate him."

On the day of his departure, the Dominican media paid homage to the man who had lost his family in the Jérémie massacre perpetrated by Papa Doc. Daniel Sansaricq quickly left Chile with the aid of the Chilean Communist Party and managed to infiltrate Haiti through the airport, disguised and with new papers to join the fight on national soil.

Whether it was the "Daniel Sansaricq Affair" that had alerted the Central Intelligence Agency to the fact that Haitian Communists were on the move is not known. By the summer of 1967, the American spy agency had, according to released secret documents, more than a passing interest in the activities of the Haitian Communists. A CIA "Information Cable" dated August 21, 1967, and released on November 13, 1997, titled "Preparations of Haitians in Cuba for infiltrating Haiti," appeared well informed on the PEP's activities. With sources blacked out, the document revealed:

Haitian Communists, as well as the Cubans with whom they are in contact, have concluded that the Communist forces should infiltrate into Haiti immediately in order to take advantage of the present conditions existing there. A first team of 12 members of the Party of Popular Accord (PEP) already had arrived in Haiti and a second team was preparing to leave Cuba for Haiti within four to six months. Training was taking place in three camps located in Cuba and was being conducted in three stages, the most significant of which was the second stage—guerrilla training. . . .

The second group of Haitians now in training in Cuba in preparation for infiltrating into Haiti—(the following four lines are blacked out)—eventually will join the first contingent which already had arrived in Haiti and once there, they will recruit and train other groups. These probably are the only Haitians now in training in Cuba. Of the other Haitians who have been living in Cuba, none are suitable for training, and the more recent arrivals have either left Cuba, have been expelled or are considered politically unreliable. Candidates for training are drawn only from University circles in Europe and Canada.

Only Haitians are participating in the insurgency plan because few French speakers are available. Latins would be unacceptable because they would be mistaken for mulattoes by the peasants, whose assistance is essential; since the peasants are too ignorant to distinguish Latins from Haitians and believe all Haitian mulattos have connections with the hated Duvalier regime, they certainly would not be willing to cooperate.

It is estimated that 90 percent of the Communists in Haiti will support the insurgency plan, but only a few will join the armed struggle; mostly the very young. No date has been set to begin armed struggle; it depends on the success of the first contingent in recruiting supporters who are willing to go to the mountains. The entire second contingent is planning to infiltrate into Haiti with false documents provided by the USSR, but no landings are envisaged.

Whoever the CIA informants, they were obviously not knowledgeable about the actual identity of the infiltrators, as many were mulattos, and overlooked the fact that all Haitians spoke Kreyòl.

In Paris, when Monique Brisson applied for a visa to visit with her sister in New York en route back to Haiti, she was questioned by the United States consul about the activities of her brother, Gérald. In Puerto Rico, Prof. Jean-Claude Bajeux was visited by the FBI, who demanded to know if Jeune Haiti had reconstituted their group in Haiti. Around the same time, a former CIA station chief in Port-au-Prince appeared in Mexico City asking questions about the "Haitian Communists."

*   *   *

"*Radio Ava-a, Kiba, Kap pote iou pwogram nen leng kreyol pou pep ayisyin.*" This Kreyól radio call to Haitians from neighboring Cuba, launched in 1963, became popular with Haiti's limited radio audience. By 1967, small secret radio listening clubs had been formed to listen to *Radio Havana's* twice-daily, hour-long Kreyól program.

The daily broadcasts from Castro's Cuba, beamed on the 49-meter band at 6,400 kilocycles, cut clearly through Papa Doc's news blackout. The soft, reassuring voice on the program was that of Haitian poet René Depestre. Ironically, while Depestre's anonymous voice became well known, few knew his name.

On one typical day in 1964, he had explained, in an editorial, the aims of the FDULN (Front Democratique Unifié de Liberation National), which had been formed by Haiti's leading leftist parties at home and in exile with the aim of launching a "democratic and popular revolution" against Duvalier. Besides lifting the morale of the Haitian left, Radio Havana painted a rosy picture, recounting progress in Cuba and Communist successes in Vietnam. American "imperialists" were held responsible for "arming and building up the 'Duvalier monster.'" Depestre, who avoided being identified with either Haitian Communist party but appeared to lean toward the PPLN, drew particular interest by reading items from the clandestine Haitian press. *Voix du Peuple's* pages, like other mimeographed Marxist broadsheets of the period, eventually become unreadable because of the fading ink. The radio broadcasts from Havana proved to be an important arm of Communist proselytizing in Haiti. Out of Duvalier's reach, the programs enhanced Communist prestige and the readership of their clandestine publications.

It was the time of "*El Foco*"—a Communist strategic concept inspired by Fidel Castro, urging guerilla methods of warfare. From Havana, Depestre read chapters of French writer Régis Debray's book *Revolution within the Revolution*, published in 1967. On January 28, 1967, Depestre told his Haitian listeners, "Let us begin with the chapter in which Régis Debray speaks of self-defense. He goes on to say 'self-defense is only one of the great many tactics. This is why revolutionary guerrillas, who want a complete war, employ all kinds of tactics and have as their task of operation the entire country in which they struggle.'"

Depestre read out an interview with Debray from the Cuban daily *Granma*, in which the Frenchman said he was reminded of what Jean-Paul Sartre had written about the militant man being "like a cog in the party's machinery, a mechanical piece in a party that has the mission of transforming history and society." Debray also referred to meeting Latin American revolutionaries who were both militant party members and men of action, "true men who are neither politicians nor opportunists."

(It was not until the spring of 1968 that Radio Moscow joined the Radio Havana airwaves offensive, with daily 30-minute broadcast to Haiti in Kreyól. It was after Radio Moscow began broadcasting in Kreyól that the U.S. government was reported to have taken note of a rising interest in Haiti on the part of the Communist world.)

In January 1969, my wife and I received an invitation to cover the tenth anniversary of the Cuban revolution for *Life en Espanol*. It was later suggested by an official at the Cuban embassy in Mexico City that the invitation came about because Fidel Castro had been impressed with the Spanish-language *LIFE* magazine's coverage of the 1968 student protests in Mexico City. The protests were ended prior to the Olympic Games by Mexican President Gustavo Díaz Ordaz, using extreme force. In fact, there may have been another reason for the invitation. At the mammoth anniversary rally in Havana's Jose Marti Square, Fidel Castro mounted the podium with a copy of *Life en Espanol* in hand. Cuban spy master Manuel (Barba Roja) Pineiro, standing nearby, joked to me, "Now you are in for it!" I had met Pineiro in January 1959, when he seized the Santiago de Cuba airport. He was wrong. Castro, although he identified *Life en Espanol* as a Yankee magazine, then read an article in which Cuba was singled out as among the few countries in Latin America that had then reached the goals of Kennedy's Alliance for Progress.

During our tenth-anniversary visit to Cuba, we met up with René Depestre, whom I had known in Haiti before he departed during the Duvalier regime. Depestre was another well-known Haitian writer. He had been a close friend of Jacques Stephen Alexis but had disagreed and aired their disagreement in a public polemic. He was somewhat reticent about meeting up with us at Havana's Hotel Nacional. It was much later that I realized why. He was deeply involved with his broadcasts and it was a crucial time, the decisive year for the PUCH's war against Papa Doc.

"Marronnage," they called it—a modernized version of the guerrilla warfare initiated by their escaped slave ancestors known as the Maroons, who fought the French colonial masters and helped win Haiti's war of independence in 1803.

The first such action for the PEP, however, in its sophisticated planning and implementation was hardly reminiscent of the group's ancestors, who were restricted to more primitive means such as the musket and machete. Brisson had recovered from his operation to remove his burst appendix, and on the morning of November 8, 1967, the military wing of the PEP launched its first armed action.

The militants had learned that a transfer of U.S. dollars from the Banque Royale du Canada building to the Banque National de la Republique d'Haiti [Central Bank] across the street was to be done in a very Haitian manner. The dollars were in a safe to be transferred on a dolley pushed by a bank employee, assisted by another employee armed with a revolver.

At 7:45 a.m., "Comrade" Ti Boute, at the wheel of a French-made blue Dauphine sedan, was the first to arrive and parked before the Royal Bank of Canada. A few minutes later, a Ford Falcon station wagon scraped another car as it took another parking spot on the street. Before a crowd could gather, the driver of the station wagon admitted his fault, apologized to the irate sideswipe victim, and paid him generously to repair the damage.

Two comrades (Adrien Sansaricq was identified as one of them) got out of the station wagon and stood waiting before the bank. Eden Germain waited before the Banque Nationale across the street. Gérald Brisson drove up in the same black Chevrolet that had been used to smuggle arms from the Dominican Republic. Joël Liautaud, in a blue Volkswagen, cruised around the block, then took up a lookout position. On cue, a Royal Bank of Canada employee, escorted by a guard, appeared pushing the steel box on a dolly. Halfway across the street the PEP comrades swung into action. They blocked the adjacent intersection with the station wagon and black Chevy. Men waving weapons seemed to witnesses to be everywhere. Not a shot was fired; when the bank guard was slow in handing over his revolver he received a silent whack on the head with the barrel of a submachine gun. At his office window that looked out onto the street, the Royal Bank of Canada manager, Bernard Lanthier, couldn't believe his eyes. He later conceded that he just stood their too flabbergasted to move. "Three men," he later told a press conference, who carried out the actual holdup and had trouble hoisting the steel safe into the station wagon "did not even care to mask or disguise themselves." With blaring horns, thus giving the holdup an official-sounding touch, the first bank robbers in Haiti's history made their escape.

The comrades, however, had trouble breaking the lock, so they broke open the bottom of the safe with a steel cutter, rather like a can of sardines, and then stashed the money in bags. The comrades abandoned the station wagon which they had stolen the night before from the "Turian Kindergarten" along with the empty bank safe on Ruelle Nazon, which had been renamed Martin Luther King Boulevard.

The morning crowd had watched in amazement. There was a general consensus among the astounded onlookers, reflected by winks and shakes of the head, that the palace obviously needed dollars or the Macoutes hadn't been paid.

The "great holdup," *Le Matin* called it. On the morning of November 8, 1967, the French-language morning daily reported, "Four armed gangsters made off with $77,800 dollars." It was a "big operation, carried out with such perplexing boldness and speed."

No one, it seemed, knew who the bank robbers were, not even the National Palace. And the Communists didn't publicize their actions.

The Dominican Communist Party, for its part, was startled when they learned the truth about the bank hoist. Following the incident, the PEP even sent funds to pay small debts its members had incurred in Santo Domingo during their stay. However, José Israel Cuello told the author that he believed the holdup was a serious tactical error on the part of the Haitian comrades.

"Once the leadership had settled in Port-au-Prince, they decided on an action which we deemed daring but unnecessary, as its consequences were to jeopardize years of work," Cuello said. "We felt it showed a capacity for action, and a presence in the country of military resources, which were far and above the true resources of the organization at the time. They didn't need to compromise years of work. The operation in principle was precise and successful [but] they didn't [even] have a plan to hide the money and they sent most of it to the Dominican Republic to pay outstanding debts. The lady on Calle Salcedo where Gérard Brisson slept and ate and did his intellectual chores, meeting with people who spoke a strange language she didn't understand, never expected he would send the last two month's rent he owed. From the day Brisson disappeared without saying goodbye, the lady had lit a candle and prayed for him every day."

In spite of their Dominican counterparts' skepticism about the operation, the PEP was indeed in dire need of funds, not only to pay debts but also for travel expenses, to rent safe-houses, to purchase arms, and for a myriad of other necessities. In a fundraising drive in Mexico City, the PEP had even republished an old Haitian classic by Justin Lhérisson (1873-1907), entitled *La Famille des Pitite-Caille.*

*   *   *

Each cadre arriving at Port-au-Prince's Dr. François Duvalier International Airport was carefully controlled by the party. It was imperative that their arrival be coordinated to avoid a party member being forced to take a taxi, which was highly risky. However, it didn't always work. When Alix Lamaute arrived from Europe in August 1967, there was no one to meet him. Forced to take a taxi, he was fortunate that the taxi driver was not a Macoute. Even so, arriving at the home of the mother of his friend Yves Medard (aka Rassoul Labuchin) at l'Avenue Christophe, the founding member of the PEP had to wonder about his party's organization—or lack thereof.

A major obstacle for party members arriving by air was Elois Maitre, chief of the Service Depistage (SD). The secret police chief controlled arrivals at Dr. François Duvalier Airport and arrested any suspected subversives trying to slip into the country. On Dec. 7, 1967, when Maitre left

Dr. François Duvalier Airport, a team of Marxists headed by Gerard Wadestrand was waiting. They opened fire as he drove off. The gunfire caused panic in the airport and left Maitre seriously wounded. In the following days he had to undergo three operations to save his life. Six months later, on June 12, 1968, Maitre was dismissed as chief of the SD (now Service Duvalier, a new title for Papa Doc's secret service), no longer able to carry out his duties. Maitre's car, punctured with bullet holes that gave testimony to the attack on his life, was transported to Ft. Dimanche, where it joined other junked wrecks in a macabre automobile graveyard.

In keeping with their initial policy and unlike former anti-Duvalier groups, the Communists likewise observed strict silence about their attempted assassination of Elois Maitre. Published reports in the usually well-informed New York–based *Le Combattant Haitien* suggested it was all a palace plot. There were whispers that the shooting was engineered by Papa Doc himself because Macoutes were suspected of having carried out the robbery of the bank of Canada. After all, the robbers had worn Macoute-type reflector dark glasses. Everyone except the Communists was suspected of the Maitre incident. Interestingly, that same month the commander of Ft. Dimanche had died under mysterious circumstances.

Meanwhile, the young Marxist activists continued their efforts to strengthen party cells in the towns as well as in the countryside, and to establish the *foco*. They also sought to stockpile weapons. Joël Liautaud, in charge of maintaining the weapons, found that he and his comrades had managed to collect a strangely varied assortment of guns, ranging from shotguns to Dominican-made San Cristobal and U.S. Springfield rifles. While Cuba had provided training for some of the Haitians, the Castro regime had provided no weapons, and they desperately needed more arms.

It was an attempt to purchase an Israeli-made Uzi submachine gun from a Duvalier militiaman that landed Ti Bob Désir in prison. Ti Bob was a nephew of Jacques Innocent, a renowned Haitian doctor who later married Jacques Alexis's widow. The militiaman had purportedly agreed to meet in Pétionville's Place Boyer, where the transfer would take place. No sooner had Désir arrived with the money than the militiaman sprang the trap.

Eddy Petit, a student in economics in Strasbourg, had been a leader of the Haitian student movement in Europe. He was considered an advanced Marxist ideologue, and his addiction was books. Without incident, he returned home legally, but for the safety of his parents he left home and joined his comrades in the clandestine struggle. While working in the mountains of the Chaîne des Cahos he was forced to kill a suspicious militiaman who had attempted to apprehend him. The killing led to a widespread search, and he was finally captured by the Macoutes, who administered a severe beating and in the process sliced off one of his ears. Forced to walk painful kilometers with his hands tied with rough sisal rope to Petite Rivière de l'Artibonite, he was eventually transferred to the St. Marc prison and then the National Penitentiary in Port-au-Prince.

The captured comrades were locked up together in a cell, and Petit sculptured a chess set from dried orange peel. During his nine months in the National Penitentiary before he was taken out and executed along with the other jailed Marxists, Petit played chess with Joël Liautaud, but for him the hardest part was to be deprived of his beloved books.

As a security measure, and to avoid involving their parents, returning PEP members were warned against any contact with family or friends. There were, however, exceptions as they sought arms and logistical help.

Joël Liautaud sent his younger brother Gilbert into shock when he suddenly appeared as if from nowhere. He was easily recognized even with a mustache and beard. It was difficult for Gilbert and later his brother Bernard to keep their secret from their parents, who were overcome with anxiety when they realized that Joël had disappeared from school in Aachen, Germany. His father, Ernest Liautaud, and mother became so concerned that Joël's father flew to Europe to search for him. They had been very close. After a futile search, Mr. Liautaud returned heartbroken to tell his distraught wife that there was no trace of their eldest son.

In the autumn of 1968, Bernard Liautaud, who later became a well-known French-educated dermatologist, met with his brother Joël, Gérald Brisson, Bernard Pierre-Louis, and Eddy Petit. He described them as "enthusiastic and confident they would win their fight." Party member Franck Eyssallenne was the one who generally coordinated the meetings between Bernard Liautaud and the clandestine fighters.

For years afterwards, however, Dr. Bernard Liautaud had found the subject of his brother was far too painful to talk about, and it was only in 2004 that he felt able to revisit one of the most difficult periods in his life in an interview with the author. Bernard Liautaud said he had marveled at the time at how the PEP comrades had managed to keep moving in a city filled with Macoutes, knowing the government was actively searching for them. "Their *sang-froid*," he said, "was incredible. I even went with Gerald to get an ice cream. He parked his car in the center of the town in front of Le Bec Fin bar. He knew he was at the top of Papa Doc's most-wanted list. Yet he knew no fear."

Dr. Liautaud continued: "Joël told me that only one of my young brothers, a close cousin, and an uncle knew he was living in Haiti and had tried to help by providing funds and old pistols. It was extremely painful for Joël to pass nearby his mother's business or his father's office. Joël once had to leave a bar in a hurry as he recognized his godfather about to sit behind him."

Joël had returned to Haiti in July 1967 with a cover name: "Monsieur Fritz Levy." It was an odd choice, as his grandfather, Emmanuel Dreyfuss, was Jewish. With a fishing boat based along the coast south of the capital, "Levy" began fishing, which was a dangerous choice of trade since Macoutes were particularly active in watching boats along the coast. Ashore Joël Liautaud lived for a while in the Frères safe-house.

*   *   *

There were selective bombings. Even an anti-Duvalier poster near Ft. Dimanche was booby-trapped and caused severe wounds to the soldiers instructed to remove it. The main Marxist action came in July 1968, when a PUCH commando team carried out a devastating hit-and-run attack on a military post in the small Artibonite Valley town of La Chapelle, located between Deschapelle and Mirebalais. Casualties were all on the government side, said to number eight dead. On Saturday night, August 3, 1968, another PUCH commando unit attacked Duvalier's country estate at Carrefour St. Medard, a short distance from the town of Archaie. Two guards were killed and arms were seized.

Just over a week later, on Monday night, August 12, the same commando team that had operated in the Artibonite Valley overran the military post of Terre-Rouge, located alone high on the summit of Morne-a-Cabrit Mountain on the road leading from Mirebalais and the Plateau Central to Port-au-Prince. The Communists captured weapons and munitions. A sergeant and two soldiers were killed in the combat. There were no guerrilla casualties in any of these surprise attacks.

A Communist cadre in Cap-Haïtien was having some success in early 1968. On March 4, a student activist killed a Macoute in circumstances that were not revealed. The Macoute's gun had disappeared. The following day, all the high school students at the city's Lycee Philippe Guerrier declared the school in a state of rebellion, protesting the arbitrary expulsion of fellow students, disciplinary beatings in school, and being forced to contribute $10 to the state. They managed to hold their own until March 7, repelling Macoutes and soldiers with rocks.

But the price was to be paid by another young Marxist. One day in mid-October 1968, when Joël Liautaud returned from fishing, two Macoutes were waiting and tried to seize him. He fought them off, but as he was making his escape, a contingent of soldiers and Macoute reinforcements arrived. They beat him senseless, and when he arrived at the police criminal research station for interrogation he was severely beaten again.

In spite of the hermetic secrecy surrounding PUCH prisoners, Bernard Liautaud says, contact was established with them through a soldier at the Penitencier National who would:

> [deliver] a brief note on a slip of paper to my mother at the Tabou flower shop which only ended with: "I love you." My family was able to send vitamins for a while without being sure if he received them because of the prison surveillance system. We learned later from a surviving detainee named Ti Hall (Jean Claude Hall, now living in Florida) that he was for a while in the same cell as Joël, who, fluent in German, offered classes in the language to other prisoners. They knew they faced their own mortality and it was only a matter of time before they were executed or transferred to Ft. Dimanche to die a slow death by disease. As prisoners, legally they were nonexistent. My father met once with "The Terrible" Luc Désyr, who used to enter my father's office when he [Désyr] bought cars or parts. One day my father courageously asked the head of secret services if he could confirm that his son had been arrested. Désyr cyni-

cally pretended not to hear the question. My father knew it would be foolish to repeat the question.

More activists were ending up in prison. Bob Désir was among the first to be arrested and tortured. The pain and humiliation of these torture sessions was nothing compared with the deep regret the young Marxists felt for their mistakes that led to their being captured.

On the morning of November 4, 1968, criminal research officer Lt. Edouard Guilliod spotted a suspicious late-model Renault traveling on Rue des Miracles in the center of Port-au-Prince. When he tried to intercept it, the occupants sped off, and Guilliod enlisted the help of a well-known motorcyclist Macoute, Antoine Khouri, who was armed and willing. Khouri, who enjoyed serving as a volunteer motorcycle escort for Duvalier, pursed the suspicious Renault. When the Renault turned into Rue Pétion, it was halted by a charcoal merchant with her donkey in the middle of the street. Gun drawn, Khouri approached the right back door of the vehicle, aiming at the driver (Brisson). As Khouri fired his first shot, Théodore, inside the car, managed to hit Khouri's hand and deflect the bullet, which grazed Brisson's hand on the steering wheel. Then Théodore fired a single shot from his small Beretta pistol, striking Khouri in the lower abdomen. A Coast Guard officer happened upon the scene, drew his gun and began firing at Brisson. Both Théodore and Brisson made their escape. Meanwhile, Lt. Edouard Guilliod had run for cover and dived into an open sewer hole. A young woman who claimed she had been given a ride was found sitting innocently in the Renault. Identified as a vacationer, she was expelled from the country the same day. (Some suggested the woman was Garry Hector's wife.)

Later that month, on Brisson's suggestion, René Théodore, alias "Lesly," was dispatched abroad to represent the PEP-PUDA at that year's World Youth meeting in Budapest, Hungary (November 18-21). There, 67 parties pledged solidarity with the Haitian Communists. From Budapest, Théodore went on to attend the World Congress of Communist Parties in the Soviet Union. Another reason he was in Moscow was to arrange for student reinforcements for the PEP-PUDA to infiltrate Haiti. Théodore also spoke over Moscow's Radio Paix et Progrès program beamed to Haiti.

Théodore was born in the Haitian northeast border town of Ouanaminthe, across the Massacre River from the Dominican Republic, on June 23, 1940, the son of Hebert Théodore, whose father was Haitian President Davilmar Théodore (1914-1915). René had attended the Normal teaching college in Port-au-Prince, graduating with a decree in mathematics and physics. In 1957, at age 17, he had joined the Ligue des Jeunesses Socialistes, and later was the league's representative at the birth of the PEP, led by Jacques-Stephen Alexis.

In 1966 Théodore had been one of the first of the Moscow group to return clandestinely to Haiti to prepare for the armed struggle as a member of PEP's military wing.

*   *   *

If there is one locality that embodies the two and a half years of the Communist armed struggle against Papa Doc, it is Cazale. The pleasant mountain village in the Chaine des Matheux, a dozen kilometers off Route Nationale near Cabaret (Duvalierville), had been special since 1804. In that historic year, some of the 400 Polish legionnaires who had survived Haiti's war of independence, having quit Napoleon's army to fight with Dessalines, were awarded Haitian citizenship—and had settled in Cazale. As the population in that area was lighter-skinned than in other parts of Haiti, it was supposedly a better place for the light-skinned militants to assimilate.

Nonetheless, René Théodore told the author in an interview in 1987 that at Cazale the Marxist anti-Duvalier campaign plan went abysmally wrong. There had been no decision to launch an attack on March 27, 1969—it came about purely through circumstance. The comrades had established what Théodore called "El Che Triangle," which encompassed Cazale and the towns of Arcahaie and Cabaret, as three points of contact for proselytizing. In addition, the Communists were moving arms to Chaine des Cahos, sometimes called the Montagnes Noires, on the upper rim of the Artibonite valley, separating Haiti's northern and southern regions. The area had a historical significance as well, since it was home to the Crete-a-Pierrot, the fort from which Dessalines inflicted enormous casualties on the French during the war of independence..

René Théodore recalled that in 1968-1969 there were lots of questions among the Communist cadre as to whether to launch rural guerrilla action, continue the urban fight, or quit and regroup, especially after some militants were captured. The military structure in "El Che Cazale," he said, was confrontational.

When, in 1967, Alix Lamaute returned home from Europe, he was assigned by the party to Cazale to work with Roger Mehu and other comrades to establish a "political-military *foco*." The Cazale area was fertile ground for revolt, the comrades soon discovered, as the peasantry was the victim of all kinds of abuses with absolutely no recourse to the law. The local Macoutes and the chef-de-section (rural police chief), with a group of *chouket la Rouze* ("aides"), were particularly arrogant and aggressive in collecting taxes and mistreating the peasants. Lamaute and Mehu were in charge of seven rebels, who included rural schoolteacher Nefort Victome, brothers Thomas and Theophile Victome, Jérémie Eliazer (a former soldier and member of the Casernes Dessalines tactical battalion), Max Belneau, Willy Joseph and Lamarre St. Germain. These activists worked side by side with the peasants, tilling the soil and otherwise participating in their daily life. It was perhaps the Haitian cadre's most impressive attempt to win over the peasant farmers by living with them and suffering their abuses at the hands of the Macoutes.

Working together with, and witnessing the daily abuses of, the peasantry was one thing. But the Communist activists could not, for any extended period, accept the peasants' subhuman canine-like passivity toward their tormentors who took delight in harassing them.

It was not long before Alix Lamaute began to voice his misgivings about their work in Cazale, on rare trips to clandestine meetings in Port-au-Prince with Monique Brisson, who had returned to Haiti in June 1968..Theory was one thing; with the group in the field far from academia, he had discovered a far different story.

But it was the time of *"el foco,"* the revolutionary strategic doctrine of Fidel Castro and Che Guevara as described by Frenchman Régis Debray in his book *Revolution within the Revolution,* published in France in 1967. This was a guerrilla technique designed to seize total power through arms, beginning with a focal point that would spark the larger movement—and roll back a dictatorship. The model was Castro's triumph in Cuba, which had begun in the Sierra Maestra with a dozen men left from Castro's disastrous landing from Mexico in 1956, and had seen the Castro take over his country two and a half years later. Castro's victory was a sign to young revolutionaries throughout the Western Hemisphere that a dozen dedicated men could ignite an unstoppable revolutionary uprising against a corrupt dictator and his army.

But as Alix and his comrades were finding out, Haiti was not Cuba and Duvalier was not Fulgencio Batista. Cubans from all walks of life were fed up with Batista and openly or surreptitiously supported young rebels attempting to overthrow him. Other revolutionary movements sprouted, and the corrupt over-fed Cuban army collapsed. Haitian peasants were far too poor and intimidated to aid the guerrillas, and those who did paid a heavy price. In addition to the Army and Macoutes, they had to fear Papa Doc's huge uniformed militia force, the Volunteers of National Security (VSN). The hapless Haitian peasant could only survive by obeying the dictates of *L'Etat*—the State, coming after only God.

At Cazale, the setting up of a guerrilla "focus" (or "foyers" in French, although the Haitian rebels retained the Spanish word, *foco*, for it) should have been a meticulous and lengthy process. But in any corner of Haiti a strange face is reported to the Chef de Section, the rural police chief. Alix knew that he and his comrades were playing with fire, and that if that fire was accidentally ignited they would have no alternative but to fight to the bitter end.

*   *   *

Revolutions cannot dampen love. In the words of Pablo Neruda, *"es tan corto al amor, y es tan largo el olvido"* ("Love is so short, remembering is so long"), and so it was for Monique and Alix. Despite being separated first by an ocean, then by clandestine war, they saw their romance survive. When Monique had returned home in 1968, one eventful result of their relationship was his wish to have a child. However, by then, because of their political commitment, their chances at domesticity were just about nil.

Monique had gone to live at the home of activist and friend Rassoul Labuchin, and on March 7, 1969, she had checked into the Hopital Saint Francois de Sales under the name "Madame Serge Victor." The following day, Monique and Alix's daughter Nathalie was born. "It was one of the happiest days," Monique recalled to the author in an interview in 2004 at her bookstore in Port-au-Prince. Holding his newborn daughter, Alix was ecstatic with joy.

Two weeks later he was dead. His head had been severed and transported to the National Palace as another trophy for Papa Doc. The dam Alix had feared had burst. The immediate cause was not the abusive taxes the peasants had to pay at the Cazale market (12 gourdes, for instance, for a small pig). Adding to the local tension had been the peasants' restrictions in the use of water from the river that crossed the valley. Only two days a week were they allowed to take water from the river. On the prohibited days, the water was used by Duvalierville, Papa Doc's supposedly model town located where the pretty village of Cabaret had once stood. Anyone caught taking water from the river during the restricted time was arrested, beaten, and ordered to pay a 50-gourdes fine, which was prohibitive, being far beyond the means of the local farmer.

This was the eventual cause of the explosion of anger when an order had been received in Cazale for the arrest of an unfortunate peasant accused of using the water during the restricted time. On March 26, 1969, the government command at Duvalierville, already concerned about reports of armed men in the region, ordered Lt. Adage from the Duvalierville Caserne up the mountain to Cazale to investigate and arrest the accused water thief, Jérémie Eliazar. The officer and his men arrived, only to face angry peasants and armed comrades of the PUCH. The uprising had begun. Local Macoutes joined the officer and his men in a fast retreat down the mountain.

Oddly it was an almost peaceful affair. The comrades took over the police and VSN militia posts. During the six hours that the PUCH held Cazale, its members raised the pre-Duvalier red-and-blue Haitian national flag, spoke to the citizenry, and informed the people of their struggle against the Duvalier tyranny.

Notwithstanding the Cazale revolt's short-lived tenure, the PUCH headquarters made the most of it, propaganda-wise. The party's official publication, read over Radio Havana, called it a "classic action in the beginning of a revolutionary struggle . . . an act which has historical significance. It is, in fact, the first time that true revolutionaries sought the support of peasants in the mountains and, at the same time, explained to them the PUCH struggle for all the people, and that the time has come for the people to join the action." The publication went on to stress that "the time has come for all Haitians to rise up and help the revolutionaries, and continue the operation that has begun in Cazale, and which might very well make the starting point of a glorious struggle of national Liberation."

In spite of all the propaganda potential of the uprising, on a practical level the PUCH was in no condition to send substantial reinforcements to the comrades in Cazale. The best aid the party could manage was, on Saturday, March 29, to lob two grenades into the downtown Port-au-Prince Petit Bar de l'amis Eugene, a gathering place for Macoutes that belonged to Macoute Ti Cabiche, brother of Elois Maitre. Only one of the grenades exploded, wounding ten patrons.

Duvalier dispatched not only his U.S. Marine-trained Dessalines Tactical Battalion, under the command of Officer Pierre Toussaint, but in what was said to be the largest deployment of force against the rebels, sent troops and Macoutes from Gonaives, Mirebalais, Saut d'Eau, Arcahaie, and Duvalierville on a search and destroy mission. From March 27 to April 11, the rebels held out in the inhospitable Matheux mountain range.

Finally, Alix Lamaute and Lamarre St. Germain fought their last battle on a rocky pinnacle known as Morne Tiso, where, surrounded by soldiers and Macoutes, the two died fighting. On Duvalier's orders, their heads were cut off and transport in *bokit* ("iron buckets") to the National Palace, where Duvalier could confirm that they were dead. The grisly well-paid task (Duvalier's rewards were generous for the capture or killing of his enemies) had become a ritual designed to offer a gory trophy-present to the President-for-Life. Bloody, merciless, and savage retribution was taken against anyone suspected of being contaminated by Communism or having assisted the Communists. Prisoners were tied to the old village *quenepier* (canapé) fruit tree and executed by rifle, pistol, or machete. In all, 23 were put to death in Cazale. Even the village barber, accused of cutting the rebels' hair, was ceremoniously shot. The spectacle harked back to acts committed by the Nazi SS in occupied Europe.

Alas, Cazale proved a turning point in Papa Doc's favor. Instead of sparking a revolution it triggered wholesale repression.

At the end of March, after Rassoul Labuchin had been arrested, Monique Brisson and her three-week-old daughter were placed under house arrest. Monique was then subjected to three days of interrogation by Caserne Dessalines commander Col. Breton Claude and Papa Doc's powerful aide, Luckner Cambronne, at the Casernes Dessalines. "They wanted to know about my brother Gérald and what contact I had with him but I told them the truth, that I had not seen Gérald since 1966 in Paris," Ms. Brisson told the author.

*   *   *

The Mano Pierre-Louis's Boutillier mountaintop was one safe-house that proved anything but safe. They had long since vacated the Freres safe-house. The all-male house was beginning to attract attention. Winchel Mitchell, who at the time was developing an extensive housing project across the valley from the Freres safe-house, had told Jean Desquiron, "I hear a bunch of *masis* [homosexuals] are using Bernard's house. You see only young men there coming and going, no women."

As dawn broke on April 14, 1969, Jacqueline Volel Brisson and Adrien Sansaricq realized that the house was surrounded by heavily armed men and armored vehicles. Raymond Jean-Francois and Gérald Brisson, who had gone out the previous evening, had not returned as expected, possibly because they had found the house surrounded by Macoutes and soldiers. As the force moved toward the house, Adrien and Jacqueline opened fire with their old semi-automatic Dominican San Cristobal rifles and managed to escape from the house. An officer, Lt. Hervé Magloire, was fatally wounded in the first exchange of fire. Retreating down the mountainside to the main road leading from Kenscoff to Pétionville, Sansaricq stopped an automobile. In the automobile was government Finance Minister Clovis Desinor, en route to his office from his residence in Kenscoff. Sansaricq's rifle jammed. Either his driver or Desinor himself drew a gun and shot him. Jacqueline Volel, out of ammunition, hid in a hole in the nearby sand quarry but was soon found by a group of militiamen. They beat her on the hands and feet with thorny branches, demanding to know who else was in the house. When she told them to go and see for themselves, they struck her on the head.

The next door neighbor, who watched from the safety of his home, said he saw Macoutes come out in droves from their hiding places when the shooting died down. Transported to the Pétionville police station, Dr. Sansaricq lay there. No attempt was made to get him medical help. There was a report at the time that an individual named Raymond Moise had administered a coup de grace to the prisoner. Jacqueline Volel Brisson, wife of the man they considered "enemy number one," contrary to rumors never met with Duvalier. Later that same day Army troops returned to the now-abandoned Pierre-Louis house, set up a 57-mm cannon, and, at point-blank range, fired 13 shells into the house, with predictably devastating results.

Another safe-house in Pétionville was surrounded by Macoutes and soldiers the same day. There was no shoot-out, and the Macoutes arrested Paul Neptune, a former taxi driver known as Papa, and Bernard Pierre Louis and his wife Gertrude (Gertha) Levesque. Gertrude was imprisoned at the Casernes Dessalines with Jacqueline Brisson.

Taken alive, Jacqueline Brisson wished she had died. But her hell was waiting for her. The death of Adrien Sansaricq was a terrible blow to the PEP, but there was no thought of giving up the fight. In fact, Gérald Brisson and the other members of the Central Committee decided that they now had to advance their plans for active battle.

René Depestre wrote a tribute to his friend Dr. Adrien Sansaricq, in Paris' *Le Monde* and in the October 1969 issued of *Lambi*. More than ever, he wrote in *Lambi*, Haiti was the "blood-soaked sponge" ("*Haiti una esponja de sangre*") that Nicolas Guillen mentioned in his famous elegy to Jacques Roumain. Describing the insatiable bloody sponge, he pointed out that Adrien Sansaricq had "fought like a lion" and quoted him as saying before leaving Cuba to fight in Haiti:

> *Une vengeance personnelle n'aurait*
> *aucun sens. Le peuple Haitien les*
> *vengera, eux et tous les autres.*
> *Non une vendetta, mais la révolution.*

*   *   *

Papa Doc ordered that the PUCH women were not to be killed. He said nothing about torture. On May 8, 1969, he suffered another heart attack. Only two months later, in July, Nelson Rockefeller was due to visit Haiti as part of his hemisphere fact-finding tour for the newly installed U.S. President Richard Nixon. Physically feeble, Papa Doc had already decided this would be an appropriate time to clean house and end what he termed the "Communist menace."

Duvalier's Orwellian press had carried a small note on May 3, 1969, announcing the killing of what it described as "35 Communist terrorists." The note was signed "Claude." (Col. Breton Claude was in full charge of the anti-Communist campaign.)

PUCH survivors said they were having a hard time finding safe-houses, and they noted that every time they found a new place, they came under surveillance. As they constantly moved around, trying to limit the number of people in a safe-house, they began to realize they had a traitor in their ranks, tipping off Breton Claude and his goons.

"At Savane Salee [at the rear of the Caribe Hotel at Martissant], 35 communist terrorists have been killed and buried where they fell," the official note stated. There were no details, nor were those purportedly executed identified.

In fact, only four comrades, not 35, had fought off the Army at Savane Salee until their ammunition was exhausted. Among the wounded fighters was Arnold Devilme, a longtime PPLN leader who in January 1969 had become adjunct secretary-general of the newly formed PUCH. Taken prisoner, he quickly "disappeared." Beautiful Yanick Rigaud, a onetime member of the Catholic youth organization and later Haiti Progres, had given up her medical studies to devote herself full-time to the cause of the PUCH. She was executed in the safe-house's bathtub in a grisly manner. Arrested once more was Joseph Roney, former secretary-general of the PEP. At the time the PUCH members said that they had been denounced by a certain Joseph Jean-Pierre but gave no details.

On May 3, 1969, the same day of the Savane Salee attack, the then-prison commander Maj. Jean-Baptiste Hilaire told members of the bereaved families years later, "They came to the National Penitentiary and took away the young Marxists prisoners." Among those taken from the Penitencier on the capital's Rue du Centre were Joël Liautaud, Eddy

Petit, and Ti Bob Désir. Some unconfirmed reports had them executed at Ft. Dimanche or Ti Tayen; another report says that on the night of April 14 they were driven to Mano Pierre-Louis' house in Boutillier, where Macoutes considered it payback time for the friends they had lost in the morning confrontation with Jacqueline Volel Brisson and Adrien Sansaricq. Two survivors (Patrick Lemoine and Claude Rosier, in their books) separately mentioned April 14, 1969, as the day prisoners were removed from their cells and never came back. No matter where they were executed, they left no trace.

The end of the Marxist rebels as an organized force came early one Monday morning, June 2, 1969. "The Central Committee of the Haitian P.C. liquidated," was the lead story in *Le Nouvelliste*. It quoted the commander of the Casernes Dessalines, who declared in five numbered paragraphs to President Duvalier:

> . . . 2. This morning at 6 o'clock a contingent from Casernes Dessalines surrounded a house on Avenue Dr. Martin Luther King in which had taken refuge a certain number of Communists and launched an attack. The occupants of the house numbered twenty-two. After an armed resistance during which they used hand grenades, bombs, automatic rifles and pistols they were killed by the forces of order, except two women, Rosalia Roseus and Bernadette Louis (Gertrude). One of them had an eight-month-old baby, and they tried to flee but they were taken prisoner.
>
> 3. . . . Among the bodies, those of the following have been identified: Gérald Brisson, Daniel Sansaricq, Gerald Wadestrandt, Jacques Jeannot, former abbe of the l'Ecole Apostolique, Niclert Casseus, all members of the Central Committee of the party and who have for some time been actively searching for. The other bodies were identified as, Jean-Pierre Salomon, Surpris Laventure, Francois Darius, Gaston Savain, Desirma Laurent, Racine Codio, Andre Dumont, Rodrigue Barreau. Gaveau Destrosiers, Kernel Jean, Prosper Estiverne, Paul Max Belneau, Willy Joseph, Augustin Elien, Andre Raymond.
>
> 4. A large stock of arms and munitions, explosives and hand grenades were seized along with G-s HK automatic rifle, MI-Rifles, pistols and revolvers. A quantity of subversive propaganda material was also seized.
>
> 5. Four soldiers were severely wounded.
>
> (S) Claude.

Duvalier was pleased: 22 was his magic number. That same Monday morning, a group of Party members was shot to death on Pilbourra Mountain en route to Cap-Haîtien. But the secretary of the Central Committee of the PEP was not among the dead. Raymond Jean-Francois had been in Cap-Haîtien. Finally, a month later, on July 2, 1969, Duvalier's hunters caught up with him on a street in Cap-Haîtien. Refusing to be taken alive, his drew his revolver and was shot to death by Papa Doc's agents. He had already lost one brother and one sister to fighting on the side of PUCH comrades.

*   *   *

It had been without a doubt the best-organized clandestine force, and possibly the best-prepared, disciplined and dedicated of all those battling Papa Doc. The Marxists had fought for more than two years and inflicted casualties on the regime, but it was a regime undeterred by casualties. The PUCH put its own total casualties at 400 killed.

Strangely, the Marxists' war—though widely reported by the Communist media—was all but ignored by the U.S. press, perhaps because it was for the most part secretive. A belated exception was Robert Berrellez of the Associated Press. The usually well-informed roving Caribbean correspondent wrote a story which, ironically, was published in the *Miami Herald* on June 1, 1969, the day before the government assaulted the "22" in the capital.

Under the headline "Papa Doc Scours Haiti for 'Phantom,'" Berrellez's story suggested that Gérald (erroneously called Gerard in the story) Brisson "has become a one-man guerrilla operative known as The Phantom." The correspondent, who had good embassy and CIA sources, added: "The hit-and-run exploits, still unconfirmed, have brought a colorful dab of reality to an anti-Communist campaign the government has been pushing the last six months." The day after the article was published around the world, Brisson was dead.

*   *   *

Nor would it seem that Haiti's young Marxists aroused much concern in Washington. An eleven-page CIA secret report, declassified in 1997 and entitled "Haiti: Duvalier's Primitive Totalitarian State," was mostly concerned with Papa Doc's health and who might replace him. Under the subtitle "Subversion," and with several passages blacked out, the CIA report, dated November 1, 1968, at the end of the Lyndon B. Johnson presidency, stated: "Inside the country, only the Communists seem to have any potential for subversion. So far, however, their two largest parties, the United Haitian Democratic Party (PUDA) and the Party of Popular Accord (PEP), together have only approximately 600 members. They are weak and disorganized, and maintain a generally passive role designed to avoid a government crackdown."

While noting that Communism was outlawed in Haiti, the CIA analysis reported that "Communists have not been singled out for control or repression provided they do not engage in overt opposition activities."

Nonetheless, the report added: "Recently, however, following reports of small-scale terrorist incidents instigated by the PEP, Duvalier ordered his Military commanders to arrest Communists in areas where terrorist attacks occurred. This is the first time in the past few years that militant Communist activity has been reported. Although further incidents may occur, neither Communist party appears to have the capability to be a serious threat to Duvalier."

The CIA went on to advise that "Radio Havana continues to broadcast in Kreyól 14 hours a week, but there is no evidence that this program—which condemns Duvalier and the support he is alleged to receive from the United States—is having any significant effect on the Haitian people."

President Johnson was ending his presidency mired in Vietnam, and the island of Hispaniola was for him only a minor distraction. The CIA report appears designed to dismiss any Communist threat in Haiti. And in 1969, under newly elected President Richard Nixon, the agency's assessment proved close to the truth.

Both the CIA and the Duvalier appeared well informed on the Communists. The regime's instant identification of the 22 bodies listed in Col. Breton Claude's communiqué to Papa Doc as well as its naming of the two captured women, in the immediate wake of the assault on the Avenue Martin Luther King house on June 2, 1969, seemed clear enough proof that a Communist Party member who knew each comrade by his or her real name as well as their noms-de-guerre had switch sides.

For the surviving cadres, no further proof was needed when, for the rest of the Duvalier dictatorship, PEP central committee member Franck Eyssallenne (known as Charley and No. 2 in command of the armed group) had the job at Casernes Dessalines of helping Col. Breton Claude identify Communists among his prisoners. Another bit of damning evidence was the fact that although Eyssallenne had been reported arrested in May 1969, just when Breton Claude launched the last offensive against the Communists, an activist reportedly sighted Eyssallenne free as a sewer rat in the Capital. The question that has never been answered by the PUCH survivors: Who was this man? Paradoxically, some PEP members at the beginning had considered him their best military strategist.

In September 1969, with the blood of his comrades reportedly on his hands still not dry, Franck Eyssallenne exchanged wedding vows, in a ceremony in Pétionville, with a cousin of regime strongman Luckner Cambronne. Duvalier saw to it that his spy had a big wedding as a reward for his services to the dictatorship.

Upon Eyssallenne's word in the years that followed hung the lives of scores of innocent Haitians. Besides his job at the Casernes Dessalines picking out Communists, he also worked at the airport checking on Dominicans. Still another day job to which he was assigned by Papa Doc was as engineer assistant to the mayor of Pétionville, Max Penette (1977-1983). Mayor Penette recalls that Eyssallenne was a competent enough engineer, but when asked where he had learned engineering, Eyssallenne told the mayor he'd learned by means of correspondence school.

Eyssallenne's job ended when Jean-Claude (Baby Doc) Duvalier fled the country on February 7, 1986. He reportedly fled with his family to the Dominican Republic, where his mother was born. (His father, a respected businessman, had disappeared years earlier when he heard that his son had betrayed his comrades.) Franck's sister Hilda had married agronomist Jean L. Dominique, who later was to make his mark as a radio journalist, only to be assassinated. Some believe Franck had begun as an early member of the Roger Mercier cell of the Haitian Communist Party (PCH), a small group believed to have kept ties with Duvalier's government, as Mercier was said to have been a friend of Duvalier since 1946. Other members of the PCH who collaborated with Papa Doc, becoming his *poto-mitan*, included brothers Jules and Paul Blanchet and agronomist Eduardo Berrout. During the author's search, Dominican officials found no record of his having crossed the border legally. It has been speculated that Eyssallenne may have later moved to the United States, where his former patron and cousin-in-law Luckner Cambronne quietly settled to live out his life in Miami, Florida, with only memories of his days of power.

Also a member of the PEP's military wing in 1968, Théodore told the author that several of their failures could have been caused by a traitor in their midst. For instance, he recalled, they had meticulously planned the kidnapping of the visiting secretary-general of the Organization of American States who was scheduled to stay at the Montana Hotel. The kidnapping was designed to free comrades who had been arrested. All was in place, Théodore reported, but at the last minute the OAS secretary-general switched lodgings, and didn't stay at the Montana that night. He recalled another incident in which Eyssallenne failed to fuse a land mine and another operation was jeopardized.

Only Franck Eyssallenne knew whether he was indeed a traitor to his comrades, whom he may have betrayed and when, and how many pieces of silver he may have received from Papa Doc—in addition to the gift of being allowed to survive and prosper..

*   *   *

Recovering from his May 8, 1969, heart attack, Duvalier invited the foreign press to see the five imprisoned Communist women being held at the National Penitentiary. Reporters stated that they found the jailed women "in good health and good spirits." (A man of about 34 who was also with the women said he had been beaten in prison "for fighting back at the officers who arrested me." He was not identified in the 5/25/69 Associated Press dispatch, only that he said he had been educated in Florida and returned to Haiti in 1967.)

On October 4, 1969, the government's mouthpiece, *Le Nouveau Monde*, announced on its front page that women prisoners whom the President-for-Life had released from confinement had written letters of thanks (on command) to Duvalier. These women were Mme. Jacqueline

Volel Brisson, Mrs. Bernard (Gertha) Pierre-Louis, Ms. Suze Domingue, and Ms. Claudette A. Mirville.

The letters of "*merci*" were dated September 22 and were uniformly full of praise for Duvalier. They were the price of clemency.

Jacqueline Volel Brisson declared in her missive that she would never deceive the confidence placed in her by Duvalier. (The newspaper noted that Jacqueline's mother, Lyliane Craan Volel, was thrilled to see her freed daughter.) Gertha Pierre-Louis said she had read Duvalier's "Essential Works" and hoped "the star of Duvalierism would continue to shine" with "its particular brilliance in the constellation of doctrines in our universe." Suze Domingue renounced her beliefs in Communist doctrine and pledged untiring devotion and indefectible fidelity to the cause of Duvalierism. Claudette Mirville stated that she had not stopped reading and re-reading Duvalier's booklet, *Breviary of a Revolution,* and had discovered that Duvalier was devoted to the defense of the weak and oppressed and the sacred cause of liberty.

The letters contained such transparently exaggerated sycophantic Duvalier prose that they were laughable to all except Papa Doc. They were a ticket to freedom, little else. In releasing the women, Papa Doc knew that they would never really be free, that they would be ostracized by society as Communists and always under suspicion for having survived.

As for Jacqueline Brisson, she remained as much a prisoner in freedom as she had been in jail. Released as a zombie without hair (her hair had fallen out because of pain inflicted upon her), she clung to her bed in a fetal position for days at a time, prostrate with the loss of the man she loved and her comrades. She had to live for her two children.

In a small corner room, with encouragement from her family and few friends, she began to work as an engineer again. Her Russian and Cuban credentials were not recognized, so she had to study and pass Haitian engineering exams—even though her knowledge of mathematics far exceeded that of her teachers. She had two children to support, and life had to continue.

Both *The Washington Post* and *The New York Times* happened to have correspondents in Haiti during the first week of June 1969, and their interest was, primarily at least, in answering the question, as the *Post* headlined: "Caribbean Mystery: Who is Running Haiti?" Correspondent Jim Hoagland reported that "an eerie calm has gripped this provincial capital of 300,000. . . . Green tarpaulins were draped over three tanks and two anti-aircraft guns that stand on the lawn of the shining white National Palace." Hoagland's long report was mostly speculation on Papa Doc's health, his heart attack the previous month, and the mystery as to who might be actually in charge of Haiti. There was not a word about the destruction of the PEP's Central Committee.

It appeared that Hoagland felt that Duvalier had cried wolf too many times to be taken seriously when his news outlets exultantly announced the end of the "Communist menace."

H. J. Maidenberg, reporting for *The New York Times* during the same week, did note that *Le Nouveau Monde* had reported that 22 Communist leaders had been killed in a suburban hideout. However, Maidenberg's dispatch was tinged with the implied skepticism: "Those who saw the bodies [exhibited at the prison] the next day said privately that 20 of them were badly decomposed and some were the remains of those who had vanished into Fort Dimanche."

In sum, these two major U.S. newspapers missed what was really the big story that week. This fact stands as an example of why the quixotic rebellion against Papa Doc by young Haitian Communists has long remained one of Haiti's best-kept secrets. That secret is being revealed, for the first time, in these pages.

Excursus: Thirteen Years After Papa Doc's Death

The last act at the airport upon the arrival of Pope Jean-Paul II on March 9, 1983, was: Le Chef du Protocole presente au Saint-Père quelques descendents des Polonais qui ont participé aux cotes des Haitiens à la Guerre de L'Independence Nationale.
—THE GOVERNMENT PROGRAM FOR THE VISIT OF POPE JEAN-PAUL II

More than a decade after Papa Doc's death and the accession to power of his son, Jean-Claude, Pope Jean Paul II paid a visit to Haiti. As part of the ceremonial greeting for the pontiff, the Baby Doc government chose a very special group from Cazale and transported them to Port-au-Prince to be presented to the Pope at the end of the airport ceremony, during which President-for-Life Jean-Claude Duvalier and his divorcée wife, Michele Bennett, welcomed His Holiness. As the palace band played the Polonaise no. 2 of Frédéric Chopin, the curiously historic encounter took place between the Polish-born Pope and the special invitees from Cazale—descendents of Polish Legionnaires who had married into Haitian families.

In 1982, Monique Brisson, daughter of Nathalie and Mireille Lamaute and a sister of Alix Lamaute, had tried to visit Cazale, only to be prevented by the famous river flood. Finally, in 1986, with the end of the Duvalier dynasty, mother and daughter managed to journey to Cazale. They found that the people of Cazale, with the financial help of relatives who had migrated to the U.S., had built a monument to those killed by the tyranny. The list of names proved to be incomplete, and the missing names were eventually added to the monument, which was set next to the canapé tree where some of the Cazale people had been executed. It was only during that 1986 visit that Nathalie learned the gruesome details of how her father had been beheaded, as had St. Germain. Their heads, they were told, were dispatched to Duvalier at the National Palace.

The following year, in 1987, a memorial service, one of a few to take place in post-Duvalier Haiti, was held at Cazale. René Théodore, the last secretary-general of the PUCH, spoke of the heavy price paid by his comrades. Human Rights activist Prof. Jean-Claude Bajeux spoke of all the victims of the Duvalierist tyranny. Lilianne Pierre-Paul, one of the courageous radio reporters, gave a vivid account of the Cazale memorial service over Radio Haiti-Inter. The Salesian Father Jean-Bertrand Aristide celebrated Mass in the open air.

For a time there was continuing special interest in Cazale. The French introduced solar power to the town that had not known electricity. Jean-Claude Bajeux, among other good Samaritans, brought *cochons noirs* from Leogane to help reestablish pigs in the community. Cazale and other areas of Haiti had suffered the devastating loss of their porcine population after Jean-Claude Duvalier agreed to the slaughter of the nation's pigs to help prevent swine fever from reaching the U.S. On top of the loss of pigs, many of the trees in the area had disappeared as charcoal farming became one of the country's last cash crops. In many ways Cazale was symbolic of countless such villages that had not only been brutalized by Papa Doc's Macoutes, but also devastated by the poverty inflicted by the years of tyranny.

Following the Ruelle Nazon extermination of the remaining members of the Central Committee of the PUCH in Haiti, Duvalier decided it was time to rid the country of liberal Catholic priests.

Foreign Minister René Chalmers called Archbishop Ligonde to the Foreign Ministry along with Father Antoine Adrien, superior of the Holy Ghost Order in Haiti, who was in charge of Petit Seminaire St. Martial College. Also summoned was the school's professor of literature, Father Max Dominique.

At the Foreign Ministry the trio of clerics was confronted by Chalmers, whose portfolio included the ministry of Cults. Present with Chalmers, who was a curiously large man, was Army Col. Claude Raymond, a Papa Doc favorite.

It was a strange scene, recalled Dominique. Minister Chalmer sat as though in judgment, and Dominique soon realized that he himself was on trial. Three witnesses in this kangaroo-court of sorts were brought into the room to testify for the state against Dominique. The government witnesses included former PEP members Franck Eyssallenne and two prisoners, Joseph Roney and Jacqueline Volel Brisson. Both Eyssallenne and Roney described Dominique's room at St. Martial in order to prove that they had been in contact with him. They identified the priest as a liaison between the Catholic anti-Duvalier movement, then known as Haiti Progres, and the PEP. The Catholic movement published the clandestine Progres.* Jacqueline Volel Brisson, he said, told of receiving from Joseph Roney stencils and a newspaper, Le progress, to be printed with the PUCH press. (Jacqueline Volel Brisson later denied this report, since she had not met Joseph Roney in prison and met him only once clandestinely after the Khouri attack on her husband and Théodore. She also said she had not met Eyssallenne while in custody or heard of Haiti Progres at the time.)

---

* The name Haiti Progres was taken many years later by a New York–based leftist weekly publication that was in no manner or form connected with the original Catholic group.

While steadfastly denying that he was a member of the Haiti Progres movement, Father Dominique was nonetheless shown the government's treason exhibit—mimeographed copies of the subversive Haiti Progres publication. Though the Haiti Progres movement was Catholic in origin, it used Marxism as an instrument to analyze Haitian society. The movement was directed against the dictatorship and sought an anti-Duvalier front.

Colonel Raymond then spoke up, stating that it was his duty to arrest Father Dominique. The colonel's sudden declaration was followed by a long period of silence. Chalmers finally stirred; picking up the telephone, he called the Palace. Speaking quietly into the phone, he obviously was speaking to Duvalier. The room was tense, and Father Adrien, who was not a member of Haiti Progres, appeared understandably upset and perplexed. When Minister Chalmers put down the phone he turned to Father Adrien, superior of the college, and said, "I'll place Dominique with you. He is your responsibility. He is a rebel and he could take to the hills."

Father Dominique was also ordered to immediately stop teaching the social doctrine of the church at the state's Lycee Toussaint Louverture. Father Adrien went even further and put Dominique in charge of sports, an area in which the professor of literature had no interest at all.

In 1957 Dominique had gone to France to study and had won a coveted literature prize for his works on Claudel. He went on to study in Rome for two years, returning to Paris in 1965 with a *Licence en Lettre*. In Paris, he met Monique Brisson, Guy Alexandre, and Leslie Manigat. Together with an article sent by Claude Moise, they had published an article entitled "Haiti Enchaînée" in the magazine *Frères du Monde*. Dominique used the pen name Alain Ramire.

During the summer of 1969, Duvalier chose to strike directly at the Seminaire St. Martial. Seals went up on the doors of the large institution, one of the best high schools in the country. Nine priests, along with Pierre Cauvin, head of the social Christian PNP (National Progressive Party), were to be expelled from the country. On the list were Father William Smarth and Father Paul Dejean, who were Archbishop Ligonde's secretaries and who at the time were responsible for publishing of the church review, *Eglise en Marche*.

On August 15, 1969, the decree of expulsion prepared by Chalmers and Duvalier was published in the official gazette *Le Moniteur,* which made it effective. The decree was a curious document stating that Haiti Progres was a rightist party with leftist tendencies. (The quote from the document illustrated this schizophrenic accusation.) As usual, the decree carried a potpourri of other accusations.

Father Adrien, at the top of the expulsion list, had left before the expulsion order to confer with the Holy Ghost order in France. Father Dominique, also among the nine, at first refused to leave. However, Father Verdieu informed Dominique that if he didn't depart the regime would surely kill him. Finally, without any personal belongings, not even an overnight bag, and without any of his precious books, Father Dominique left Haiti along with the other teacher-priests for exile in Brooklyn, New York.

Father Berthaud had left his passport behind at the school and was permitted to return to St. Martial to retrieve it. He reported that he was shocked and sickened when he return to the school to find Archbishop Ligonde with a group of Duvalierists in what Berthaud described as a celebratory mood. The school was now theirs.

Moreover, the cautious Catholic bishops in Haiti at the time made no public declaration protesting the expulsion.

Superior General and theologian Fr. Joseph Lecuyer traveled from France to Haiti on August 25 and spent five days conferring with the government, the five Diocesan bishops, and the remnants of his Holy Ghost order. He did not see President Duvalier, but met the Minister of Cults, René Chalmers, who repeated the government charges without furnishing any proof.

Three days after Father Lecuyer's departure, on September 3, the Duvalier government passed a law taking away the direction of the college St. Martial from the Holy Ghost Fathers (while leaving them the ownership of the property) and handing it over to the Archdiocese. Meanwhile, the government-controlled press kept up attacks on the other Holy Ghost Fathers in the country, accusing the Congregation of "intrigues of a clearly anti-clerical and anti-national character."

Regretfully, the Superior General and his council decided to withdraw the remaining 20 Holy Ghost Fathers from Haiti, "considering that the measures taken by the Haitian Government and the campaign in the government press makes it impossible for the *Spiritans* in Haiti to exercise their ministry in a normal way." The 20 Fathers were from France, Switzerland, Holland, and Canada, and the last of them left the country on September 23, putting an end, at least for the time being, to over a hundred years of work by the Congregation in Haiti. College St. Martial was one of the oldest high schools in Haiti, founded by the Congregation in 1862. Some of Haiti's most brilliant men had graduated from the college.

Looking back, Father Max Dominique said with bitterness that the young men of PUCH had made "the ultimate sacrifice for nothing." The PUCH members, he told the author in an interview in Port-au-Prince on February 19, 1991, used to visit the Petit Séminaire St. Martial College, where he taught, and some would seek him out, as he was known as a liberal priest. Among of those who came to see him were Franck Eyssallenne of the military branch of the PUCH and Joseph Roney, when the latter was secretary-general of PEP. While he was studying in Paris, Father Dominique had also met up with young Haitian activists, mostly associated with Haiti Progres. (Father Max Dominique died in 2005.)

CHAPTER 19

The Last Salvo

It proved to be the last salvo against Papa Doc, a salvo that even for Haiti, where the improbable has a way of happening, was astounding. At 11:45 a.m. on Friday, April 24, 1970, three cutters of the *Garde-Côtes d'Haiti* (Haitian Coast Guard) stood two miles off Port-au-Prince and began shelling the National Palace.

The three-vessel rebel flotilla was led by its venerable flagship, the 95-foot patrol boat *Jean-Jacques Dessalines* (GC 1O), on loan to the *Garde-Côtes d'Haiti* by the U.S. government—which initiated the attack with its 5-inch, 25-caliber deck gun.

Capt. T.K. Treadwell, U.S. Navy adviser to the *Garde-Côtes d'Haiti,* recounts in his unpublished memoir (which Col. Charles T. Williamson quotes in his book, *The U.S. Naval Mission to Haiti [1959-1963])* that when the vessel had been inducted into the Haitian Coast Guard in a ceremony at the Bizoton station,

> . . . the GC-10 wasn't much of a warship but did have a nice 5", 25-caliber deck gun, the type I'd worked with on submarines. The ceremony commissioning the ship was attended by a horde of government dignitaries headed by the president himself. I was proud of her and during the guided tour extolled her fighting capabilities, although whom she might actually fight was completely unclear. We wound up on the foc's'le looking at the cannon; Duvalier peered through his thick glasses at the shells stacked neatly on deck, walked over and stroked the gleaming barrel and addressed me in Kreyól.
>
> "Looks nice. What can it do?"
>
> "Once we get the crew trained it can fire a round every thirty seconds."
>
> "To what distance?"
>
> "Maximum of about five miles, but not too accurately out that far.

But at a couple of miles I can drop a shell in your . . . hat."

He gazed thoughtfully across the bay at the white domes of the presidential palace, hardly a mile away, nodded his thanks to me and departed down the gangway with his entourage.

The next morning when I arrived at the base I was met by a distraught Capt. Albert Poitevien* [Haitian Coast Guard Commander]. During the night a detachment from the Presidential Guard had boarded the ship, off-loaded all the ammunition into a truck and taken it to the palace. Duvalier wasn't about to have anyone dropping 5" shells in his hat.

A decade later, a former favorite of Papa Doc, Army Col. Octave Cayard, 48, who despite his Army status had been appointed commander of the *Garde-Côtes d'Haiti,* was trying to do just that—drop a shell into Papa Doc's hat.

Prior to launching his attack, Cayard—who was not known to be allied with any political group—radioed the Palace with a pro forma request that Duvalier surrender power, knowing full well he would not. There is no record of the exchange that took place but according to Cayard he then gave the order to fire. With shells whistling overhead that Friday, the streets of Port-au-Prince quickly emptied, with only soldiers and Macoutes in evidence. Duvalier ordered the Air Force's lone fighter aircraft, a World War II propeller-driven P-51, to attack the "rebels." The problem was that the P-51 had been disarmed on Duvalier's orders years earlier, and neither its guns nor ammunition could be found in the palace arms depot.

After several harmless passes over the vessels, the fighter returned to its base. The Army's artillery unit was ordered to fire on the ships from shore with a 105-mm. howitzer, but the gun crew's aim was completely off target. Neither was there any way of putting out to sea in the remaining Coast Guard cutters because, under Papa Doc's reign, the vessels had been allowed to become rusting hulks.

Cayard's flagship, the *Jean-Jacques Dessalines,* formerly the *USS Tonowanda,* had been loaned to Haiti in 1960, along with two ex-U.S.

---

*Poitevien was shot to death by Macoutes in April 1963, when Duvalier gave the order to shoot on sight any and all former military officers.

cutters, the *Independence* and *Capois la Mort*. Prior to being handed over to Haiti, the ships had been reconditioned and Haitian crews trained to man them. The cutter *Vertieres,* which had undergone a complete over- haul at the Norfolk, Virginia, U.S. Naval Base in 1959, was no longer seaworthy in 1970; neither was the smaller cutter *22 of September*. At the end of 1960, Haiti's Coast Guard for the first time had four warships, thanks to the assistance of the U.S. Naval Mission in Haiti and the U.S. Navy.

Duvalier's disregard for the country's Coast Guard, besides the fre- quent purging of its trained men, was evident in the subsequent use of the *Jean-Jacques Dessalines* as a cement barge. In December 1962, the proud vessel was being utilized by the regime to deliver 90 tons of cement to Jérémie for an unknown project. So overloaded was the craft that it ran aground in a storm and had to be rescued by a U.S. Navy tug dispatched from the Guantanamo Naval Base. An American naval officer found that Haiti's entire fleet had, in the space of two years, deteriorated into deplorable condition due to lack of maintenance. In 1970, only the three rebel ships of the fleet were operational. It was discovered that most of the ships hadn't put to sea in two years, remaining at their berths at the Bizoton naval yard to grow barnacles on their rusting hulls.

Interestingly, one of the Haitian Coast Guard vessels that might have put to sea on the April day in 1970 would have been no match for the rebels' guns. It was officially listed as an armed trawler, the *Mollie C*— whose un-Haitian-like name betrayed the boat's intriguing history. The *Mollie C* was formerly a Key West, Florida, fishing boat that, in July 1958, had been used by Capt. Alix Pasquet and his little band of invaders in an attempt to overthrow Duvalier. (This episode is discussed in detail in *The Price of Blood*, the first part of this account of Duvalier's brutal repression, covering the years 1957 to 1961.) It was also ironic that more than a dozen years after Pasquet seized the Casernes Dessalines barracks and his appeal for the Army to revolt was met with dead silence, Cayard received the same response. Both had hope of touching off a military uprising by attacking the palace.

When Papa Doc suddenly realized that he was under attack by Colonel Cayard, Duvalier personally took charge of the response, and ordered the airport closed to all traffic, telephone communications suspended except for official use, and a curfew imposed from 7 p.m. to 5 a.m. Troops were ordered to patrol the coast and prevent any force from invading. Widespread arrests prompted a run on Latin American embassies for asylum. Cayard's own family managed to obtain asylum in a Latin American embassy.

Haiti's ambassador to Washington, Arthur Bonhomme, told newsmen in Washington that he had relayed a request by Papa Doc to the U.S. State Department for help to put down the mutiny. Specifically, Haiti's "President-for-Life" had requested planes from the U.S. Naval Base at Guantanamo, Cuba, to neutralize the Haitian rebel ships. The administration of President Richard Nixon gave a quiet but firm "no," stating that it would not intervene in a matter of this kind, and suggested that Haiti go to the Organization of American States (OAS).

(With a touch of imagination, Bonhomme charged that the mutiny was part of "a Communist plot against the Caribbean" and noted that only days before, Trinidad's Defense Force regiment had mutinied during destructive Black Power riots in that island nation's capital, Port of Spain.)

The Haitian mutineers also made a radio appeal—as Cayard later recalled in Miami during interviews, "to the free world for assistance," specifically fuel. Cayard himself was an unlikely mutineer. Born in Port de Paix in the north of Haiti on Sept. 8, 1922, upon graduating from the military academy he was assigned to the nation's police department, where he served from 1947 to 1960. At the police department headquarters in Port-au-Prince he was known as a quiet, disciplined officer who, like his fellow police officers, became an early Duvalierist.

In 1963, as commander of the Casernes Dessalines, he was ordered to arrest his friend and classmate Col. Charles Turnier. After witnessing the bloody torture of Turnier, he went to the cell of the battered Turnier in the evening and secretly handed him a gun. The following morning, armed with the revolver, Turnier shot his way out of his cell, only to be killed on the Casernes's parade ground. So affected was Cayard by Turnier's treatment that he requested a transfer, and he was given the usually quiet post of commander of the Coast Guard. (Aside from his military duties, Cayard had become an enterprising farmer with a dairy and poultry business outside Port-au-Prince, which he prided as a well-run operation.)

As the shelling continued, Papa Doc worked the telephones, talking with U.S. Ambassador Clinton Knox, an African-American Massachusetts native who had entered the Foreign Service in 1945 as a researcher and had taken time out to get a Ph.D. in political science at Harvard University. Interestingly, he had been ambassador to the African nation of Dahomey when the movie version of Graham Greene's novel *The Comedians* was filmed there—a fact that had not endeared Knox to Papa Doc, but their relationship had warmed. Responding to Duvalier's appeal amid the incoming Coast Guard shells, the U.S. envoy also relayed to Washington Papa Doc's request for help.

That harrowing day is recalled with crystal clarity by Papa Doc's son, and later presidential successor, Jean-Claude Duvalier. In my interview with him in France in 1996 (a decade after being ousted from power himself), Jean-Claude recalled: "When 'ces messieurs' began to shell the palace, we moved to Lorsier's small inner office near the Salle des Bustes [away from the exposed presidential office at the front of the building], and I personally placed furniture against the door. My father spoke with Ambassador Knox a number of times about the ships." The ships were clearly visible from the U.S. embassy situated on the waterfront.

Gerard de Catalogne had rushed into the newsroom of the government daily, *Le Nouveau Monde,* shouting, "Everyone go home, hurry up, go home, we don't know what is happening, go home. The Coast Guard is shelling the palace, protect yourself." The editor and close aide to Papa Doc rushed outside, and his staff heard him order his driver, "Palais Nationale, vite! Vite!" The following Monday, de Catalogne shared his act of bravery with a hushed newsroom, remarking that he knew that at such times of danger, fidelity is important. What he didn't say was that his gamble was worth the risks. A soldier accompanying him had received a piece of shrapnel in the leg as they arrived at the palace, he said. "It is at a time like that you understood what a 'garçon' Duvalier is," he declared as he gave details of the Palace under attack. "The president", he said, "was in a small interior Palace office with Mrs. Duvalier, son Jean-Claude, and General Gracia Jacques. A large wooden armoire had been placed against one door, and when the shells hit the palace the building shook, the armoire began to sway. If that armoire had toppled over, it would have crashed down on our heads, but I watched the President, who kept reassuring us softly with 'it is nothing, it is nothing.'" Duvalier, he noted, had been on the phone to Ambassador Knox at the American Embassy a number of times, and it appeared Knox was being helpful as they mentioned several times the U.S. Naval Base at Guantanamo.

The attack went on intermittently, but with fuel running low and no sign of having triggered a revolt ashore, Cayard ordered a last shot fired on the next day, Saturday, and sailed his small flotilla off to the U.S. Naval Base in Guantanamo, Cuba.

The U.S. authorities, upon Cayard's arrival in Cuba, decided to process the crew's claim for political asylum in Puerto Rico, a U.S. territory. Escorted by a U.S. warship, they sailed for the Roosevelt Roads Naval Base in Puerto Rico, and had hardly come in sight of port when two of the Haitian cutters began taking on water. One suffered engine trouble and had to be towed into port. Not the most graceful end for a mini-armada bent on toppling the hemisphere's most resilient tyrant.

*   *   *

When an irate Duvalier spoke over national radio, he accused Cayard of seeking to establish a "popular democratic Marxist-Leninist regime," declaring that documents of a Communist nature had been uncovered among the colonel's papers. (Cayard later explained to newsmen that two-year old PEP propaganda tracts had been picked up by enlisted men and brought to his office. He said he had taken some of the Communist literature home while some had remained at his office at the Coast Guard base at Bizoton. He duly notified Duvalier at the time, Cayard said.)

The west wing of the National Palace, Duvalier declared, had been "severely damaged." (There were, indeed, four shell holes in the Palace's west wing.) He also listed, in his radio speech to the nation, damage from the shelling as including "the Court of Justice, the Jean-Jacques Dessalines barracks, Ft. Dimanche, the State University, the residential areas of the public markets, the ministries, and the national penitentiary," adding, "They inflicted numerous losses of human lives and caused important damage."

"The rebels were covering themselves with shame," he said "by committing acts of piracy on the open sea, by attacking merchant ships of allied powers, taking by force food supplies and fuel." The rebels denied Papa Doc's charges, contending that they only asked third parties for assistance.

Papa Doc had triggered the revolt, according to Cayard, through his murderous actions. Cayard said he had received a telephone call from Papa Doc on the preceding Thursday night asking him to bring two of Cayard's officers to the Casernes Dessalines. After consulting fellow officers, Cayard recounted to newsmen upon his arrival in Miami with 119 fellow rebels seeking political asylum, it was plain that the two officers, to whom he felt devoted, were not being called to the barracks to be decorated or for any other appropriate purpose.

The 1970 Coast Guard revolt, Cayard told *Miami Herald's* Don Bohning in an interview after arriving in Miami, was "a spontaneous" action touched off by Duvalier's ordering him to bring two of his officers to the barracks. There was, Cayard insisted, "no conspiracy."

In his May 6, 1970, interview with Bohning, Cayard made these additional points: Under his country's then-existing dictatorship he faced a Hobson's choice: Either deliver to certain death officers devoted to him, or take advantage of what Cayard termed the "psychological atmosphere of the army and the population" and attempt a military action.

- After consulting his key officers, he and they decided on the second action, sailed, and began shelling.
- As a military man, not a cruel man, he did not intend that anyone should be hurt in the shelling. In shelling the presidential palace, his intention was not to kill Duvalier or anyone else but to provide the spark for a general uprising.
- He never considered shelling the oil storage tanks [next to the Coast Guard station] or electrical plant on the Port-au-Prince waterfront because it would cause misery to innocent people.
- He knew that in the Army there were still people at all echelons thinking the way he was.
- At no time prior to the rebellion had he been involved in, or linked to, any plot against the government. (Earlier the same month there had been a number of arrests related to an alleged conspiracy against the Duvalier regime. Among the purported conspirators was a Col. Kesner Blain, a classmate of Cayard, promotion 1945, who was eventually to die in Ft. Dimanche. Cayard said that although he was a friend of Blain he had not been contacted or

told anything about the purported plot.)
- Cayard's brother, Volvik Cayard, vice president of the legislative assembly, though completely innocent, had been arrested and imprisoned.
- If the rebellious Coast Guard had had enough fuel for another two days, the odds were that their action would have been successful.
- The death toll from the off-shore revolt was put at two persons killed and 34 wounded.

Though Cayard and his officers and men survived, they paid a high price in other ways. After declaring a state of siege on April 25, the day after the uprising, Duvalier's obedient legislature announced that "Col. Octavo Cayard, the officers and sailors and their accomplices who participated in the 24 of April 1970 mutiny, are declared to have forfeited their rights of Haitian citizenship under law."

The parliamentary pronouncement added: "The personal and real properties of any kind of these former Haitian citizens are confiscated in behalf of the state."

"We must deprive all traitors of their Haitian nationality," declared Deputy Michel C. Auguste.

And so the last attempt against Papa Doc ended with a chorus of Pavlovian support from his rubber-stamp congress.

The Haitian Coast Guardsmen received political asylum in the United States and started life over again. One officer, engineer Lt. Fritz Tippenhauer, who contended that he had not participated in the revolt, returned to Haiti immediately. In Port-au-Prince, Duvalier greeted him as a hero.

Following the end of the Duvalier dynasty in 1986, Cayard quit his teaching job at South Shore High School in Jamaica, New York, and returned with his family and had his properties restored.

At the beginning of 1970, Papa Doc knew his time was short, and for months had carefully planned his succession, aiming to effectively establish his family dynasty through his son Jean-Claude. Doc also knew that members of his own cabal, including key cabinet ministers, were not happy about the prospect of being ruled by a 19-year-old "President-for-Life."

Thus, when Papa Doc, in the wake of the Coast Guard mutiny, ordered the arrest and imprisonment of his justice minister, Rameau Estime, most saw it as an effort to remove any obstacle to his plan to have his teenage son succeed him. Making good on his old motto that gratitude is political cowardice, the older Duvalier had no qualms about throwing into prison a close relative of former President Dumarsais Estime. Papa Doc had campaigned in 1957 as the political heir to President Estime.

A year later, on April 21, 1971, Duvalier was dead at 64. When French doctors arrived from Paris to treat Papa Doc's diseased heart, advanced diabetes, and prostate problems, they found, they said, a wizened, bedridden, emaciated old man whom everyone appeared too fearful to even touch. The chief French physician said that because the patient was too weak to stand, he had to place Duvalier on his knees and hold him like a child in order to take an X-ray.

Emotion and fear hung over the city like a Damocles sword. Some Haitians refused to believe that Papa Doc, the self-proclaimed "immaterial being," was gone. To others in a country where the cult of the dead is very much alive, fear and foreboding were at their peak.

For thirteen years he had outwitted conspirators, thwarted plots, repulsed invasions, and outlived obituaries. For thirteen years Haitians had done little else but consume the thoughts and deeds of Papa Doc. His legend of invincibility had assumed a deified aura. But Papa Doc proved he was mortal.

As the 13th year of Duvalier rule ended, Papa Doc knew that despite all the sloganeering on mortality there was a limit to even his lifetime reign. He was more suspicious than ever of those still around him. He believed that his most trusted aides were plotting against him, and some of them were. Paranoia increased with his physical deterioration. For most of his reign he had acted like a lion in the jungle of Haiti's politics. Now he was a tired and sick old lion. Self-preservation takes precedence over everything else in Haiti, and Duvalier had been skillful at preserving himself and his power. Now he had to worry about how to retain that power to the very end and then pass it on to his son and heir.

The circle of those he could trust had become very small indeed by 1971. The great majority of Haitians were but witnesses and suffered their misery in silence, passive and fearful. Duvalier's purges had extended to his own family, and Duvalierism was hardly a solid unified block.

The Duvalierist revolution had an abnormal appetite for devouring its own sons.

What had 13½ years of Duvalierism wrought? It had been a diseased political system that he had taken a step further to total sickness, explained the kindest critics, and Duvalier was both a product of that system and an instrument of it. Different people assess the Duvalier years in different ways. Some credit him with giving power and dignity to the poor rural people by making them Macoutes, instruments of his terror; others find it hard to give him any credit at all, saying those years simply retarded progress. Duvalier was not always coherent, but his determination to remain in power, no matter what, was perfectly clear.

The jet airport and the Peligre dam, which gave Haiti its first hydro-electric power, were material accomplishments. On the negative side of the balance sheet, every institution had deteriorated, and some had been destroyed. Even the country's national sport, soccer, had declined. Education suffered as hundreds of teachers and other technicians, including jurists, chose to go to Africa to escape Duvalier. Doctors went to Canada. The brains drain was considerable. Voudou suffered his Machavellian touch, and the country's prestige suffered internationally. Morals declined and values changed. Fear became a daily companion to many Haitians. Haitians lived behind masks, suffering indignations, and survival was all that mattered. Duvalier set a precedent of ruling in the harshest manner. He was different from other rulers in that he was more corrupt and more violent. As a role model, he showed that a man with total disregard for human life could retain power and even insult the great neighbor to the North. He destroyed the traditional sense of values and work ethics and, in exchange, forced Haitians to make deceit a prime art for survival. The age-old greeting of the peasant, "honor and respect," lost its meaning when people broke into his home, dragged him off, and stole his coffee and his land. Any accomplishments must be weighed against the high costs in human life.

The old rage was apparent as Duvalier began his last year in office, 1971, with his customary January 2 Independence Day message. Plotters had cheated him of his great moment, the moment he had awaited for so long, to be able to stand above the Peligre Dam, throw the switch, and turn on the lights generated by Haiti's first hydroelectric power plant.

*   *   *

To prove that Papa Doc was indeed dead, his body lay in state in the palace, open to the public for the first time in 13½ years. It laid under glass and fluorescent lighting, dressed in his habitual black suit and formal white bow tie, a gold cross on one side of his pillow, a red leather-bound copy of his *Memoirs of a Third World Leader* on the other. The honor guard consisted of twenty-two Army soldiers.

The new chief of state's handlers wanted to turn Papa Doc's funeral into a new beginning, giving foreign newsmen the run of the palace. It was not a very good idea, as news photographers turned the solemn occasion into a free-for-all photo opportunity. During the religious service the following day, they clambered around the gleaming coffin of bronze into which his body had been transferred. (Jean-Claude Duvalier told me that before the coffin was closed he had placed his father's magnum pistol in the coffin.) Any sense of decorum was lost as photographers popped up on the altar during the liturgy conducted by Duvalier's Archbishop Francois Wolff Ligonde. They posed Jean-Claude next to his father's coffin. They could have propped up Papa Doc for a last portrait and no one would have objected! Madame Simone Ovide Duvalier and her three daughters were escorted around by Gen. Gracia Jacques, holding a submachine gun with a finger on the trigger.

When Papa Doc's remains finally emerged from his citadel of power and the hearse passed through the tall iron gates, a sudden strong gust of wind raised a column of dust on the Champ de Mars. To the relatively small crowd of poor mourners it was Papa Doc's *Lwa* ("spirit") refusing to leave the palace. A tailor from Belair recalled the scene for me, saying it was a supernatural moment, with Papa Doc's *Lwa* transferring the reigns to Jean-Claude Duvalier.

As the mourners followed the funeral cortege along rue de L'Enterrment to the Port-au-Prince cemetery, the tension suddenly snapped like a taut wire, and the mourners stampeded for their lives, leaving a street covered with abandoned shoes. It was later determined that the first stampede of frightened mourners was caused by a crowded balcony that had collapse onto the street.

"The city lay silent in the midday heat except for the dolorous music of the bands and the distant sullen banging of the 'cannons of condolence,'" Homer Bigart wrote in *The New York Times*. Then "suddenly the street was churning in a wild melee of Haitians who ran madly about in search of escape. They were slammed against the metal shutters of closed stores. Two men fell out of sight down a sewer manhole. Members of a marching band dropped their instruments and ran for cover. Militiamen with rifles and pistols at the ready ran about in circles shouting orders at the crowd.

"It took several minutes to restore order. Then the slow march resumed only to be interrupted a half-hour later by the same inexplicable wave of fear that sent the crowds careening into the side streets. Again the march was delayed for a few minutes."

Even in death, Duvalier had the ability to cause blood to flow, but none of the mourners' injuries were fatal. Blood had become a symbol of his regime. The power of blood was Papa Doc's power, and the price of blood paid by Haitians during 13½ years of barbaric and bestial rule cannot be measured in human terms.

9 781558 765429